THE BIOLOGY OF GOD

ALISTER HARDY

Fellow of the Royal Society
Emeritus Professor of Zoology, University of Oxford

THE BIOLOGY
OF GOD

A scientist's study
of man
the religious animal

JONATHAN CAPE
THIRTY BEDFORD SQUARE LONDON

FIRST PUBLISHED 1975
© 1975 BY ALISTER HARDY

JONATHAN CAPE LTD, 30 BEDFORD SQUARE, LONDON WCI

ISBN 0 224 01129 4

SET IN 12 PT BEMBO 1 PT LEADED

PRINTED IN GREAT BRITAIN BY
BUTLER & TANNER LTD, FROME AND LONDON

'Man is by his constitution a religious animal'
Edmund Burke in
Reflections on the Revolution in France

To
Sylvia

Contents

A*

Preface

This book, which is so much concerned with relating religion to biological evolution, has had an evolution of its own. The ideas giving rise to it were first put forward in my two volumes of Gifford Lectures, *The Living Stream* and *The Divine Flame*, published some ten years ago (London, Collins, 1965 and 1966); since then, they have undergone a considerable development.

In 1969 the Hibbert Trustees invited me to give a series of Hibbert Lectures, kindly saying they would like to see my ideas more widely known. I was then on the point of launching a research unit at Manchester College, Oxford, to undertake a systematic study of records of religious experience, and so was only too anxious to elicit either criticism or support. Normally, a course of Hibbert Lectures had consisted of a series of three or four, given at perhaps two universities and then published as a book. I suggested to the Trustees that if they particularly wished these ideas to be as widely known as possible, they might better achieve their object if I were to give more or less the same single lecture in ten different universities, and then later on expand the theme of such a lecture into a full-length book. I was indeed gratified when they readily agreed to such a proposal. I had already lectured on this subject at Oxford and Cambridge; the ten other universities at which the lecture was given, under the auspices of the Hibbert Trust, were Birmingham, Bristol, Cardiff, Edinburgh, Glasgow, Hull, Leicester, London, Manchester and Nottingham. I wish to thank the Hibbert Trustees for the trouble they took in making the arrangements, and the various university departments for their kind hospitality.

That was five years ago. Since then there has been a further evolution. As I was heavily engaged in the work of starting our new research unit, the conversion of a single lecture into twelve chapters has been much delayed; this, however, has I believe been an advantage, for many new developments in the field have taken place which I have been able to discuss. The present book, then, is a Hibbert Lecture which has undergone much expansion; I am most grateful to the Trustees for being so patient in waiting for its growth. I only hope they will not find that the creature that has come from the egg they incubated in 1969 is too strange a bird.

I wish here to express my thanks to my colleagues at our research unit for kindly reading different parts of the manuscript, making valuable comments and criticisms, and taking part in a general discussion of the book as it has developed. And I wish to make special mention of my gratitude to Mrs Philippa Fraser Harrison and Mrs Judy Carver for the valuable suggestions they made for rearrangements and improvements of parts of the book, to make a better presentation of the material for the general reader; these I gladly adopted.

All quotations are acknowledged with references where they occur in the course of the book.

1. The approach

Whatever may be thought about religion—whether it be regarded as based upon reality or illusion—few, if any, will deny that it has been one of the major forces moulding the course of history. The wars of religion or ideologies have been, and still are, more bitter than those fought for economic ends. We are only too well aware of the clashes between rival religious communities in the world today: between Hindus and Moslems in India and Pakistan, between Moslems and Jews in the Near East and, alas, between Catholics and Protestants in parts of our own country.

Religion, primitive or sophisticated, whatever the psychologists may say about its cause, is as much a part of human natural history as is sex, but much less understood. And like sex, it can arouse deep, passionate emotions. By religion, I do not here mean institutional religion or the theological dogmas of any particular faith; I am concerned with it as a basic preoccupation of man.

A true biology, covering the whole of life, should not ignore this element of our make-up. If we acknowledge that, in the past, religion has been a vital influence in building up our civilization, should we not, in thinking of our future, regard it as a subject for careful systematic study, however doubtful we may be as to its real nature? Is it just based upon primitive man's fear of the unknown: his attempted explanation of natural phenomena such as thunder, lightning or earthquakes, or his concern with the problem of death? Or has it some more profound significance? Can we be sure that it does not have some deep biological foundation? If it should be shown to be an element in our make-up which is more real than many suppose, may not our civilization stand in peril if it be neglected? How much may the dissatisfaction and unrest of the younger generation be attributed to the disturbing effect of being persuaded that science has dismissed the spiritual side of the universe as a superstition to be grown out of, when they have an intuition, perhaps ill-defined, that tells them otherwise? As long ago as the 'twenties, Aldous Huxley, in his *Proper Studies* (1927), was saying, 'Much of the restlessness and uncertainty so characteristic of our time is probably due to the chronic sense of unappeased desires from which men naturally religious, but condemned by circumstances to have no religion, are bound to suffer.'

Am I justified in calling my book *The Biology of God* instead of, perhaps, 'Biology and God'? I hope as we proceed that I shall vindicate the choice. I may here say that I prefer the word 'God' rather than 'religion', because the latter has so many different meanings. I must make it clear at the outset that by God I do not mean a deity in actual human form, although I readily grant that those who are conscious of this element may have a feeling towards it of a *personal* relationship – indeed a devotional love-relationship; this, however, may be for good biological or psychological reasons linked with the emotions of an early child-parent affection, but none the worse for that – and no less real.

I hope that my speaking of the biology of God will not be thought by the devout to be blasphemous, or in any way to suggest a denigration of the concept of deity. The linking of God to the biological system is not, to my mind, so much the worse for the idea of God, but so much the better for a greatly enlarged and truer biology. That is surely a less shocking notion than the ideas suggested by the titles of such books as *Radical Theology and the Death of God* and *The Gospel of Christian Atheism*, which have recently been much to the fore in some theological circles. My book is intended more in the spirit of John Robinson's *Exploration into God* (1967); it could in fact be described as the quest of a naturalist in the same direction. Instead of being shocking to those of religious feelings it may, I hope, provide the ground for a rational, biological approach to the idea of God, in a world where an increasing number of people, including some theologians, have come to regard the concept as 'no longer on the agenda'.

If some of my colleagues in biology should be shocked at what

I am suggesting, albeit in the opposite way, I would remind them, by quoting from John Langdon-Davies's book, *Man and his Universe* (1930), that there is a good precedent for it:

> The whole history of science has been a direct search for God, deliberate and conscious, until well into the eighteenth century ... Copernicus, Kepler, Galileo, Newton, Leibnitz and the rest did not merely believe in God in an orthodox sort of way: they believed that their work told humanity more about God than had been known before. Their incentive in working at all was a desire to know God; and they regarded their discoveries as not only proving his existence, but as revealing more and more of his nature ...

At a period when man began to realize that the old Ptolemaic concept of the universe was no longer tenable, it was natural for scientists to search for evidence of the Divine in the new fields being opened up by the discoveries in astronomy; today, with the great advances in our knowledge of evolution theory, genetics and molecular biology, it is into the science of life that those who would pursue a similar aim must direct their steps.

I do not wish, of course, to imply that I am presenting a biology of God in the sense of, say, a biology of fish or of birds; nor am I pretending to offer an entirely biological explanation of the concept of God — far from it. And I hope I may not be thought to be so arrogant as to suppose that in this simple essay, or with my so limited equipment, I have solved the greatest riddle of the universe. I choose the title to emphasize that I am convinced, on the evidence to be presented later, that on the one hand the experience of what may be called God is a very real and important one to a large number of individual members of our species, in both primitive and sophisticated societies, and on the other hand that it has also some fundamental biological connections. *This* is what I mean by the biology of God.

I am not intending to imply that I am writing *the* biology of God in any final sense; my essay is meant to express my belief that there is a basic biological significance in man's experience of the

Divine. The science of life, as I see it, should range from biophysics and biochemistry, at one end of a descriptive 'spectrum', to the study of man's emotional behaviour, both sexual and religious, at the other end of it. My book deals with the spiritual end of this span.

In order to indicate to my scientific colleagues why I maintain that an approach to this problem can be made from a biological position, let me say at the outset that I believe—and this I shall be discussing in chapters 8 and 9—that there are important similarities, not just analogies, between man's attitude to what he calls God, and certain well-established facts in the field of animal-behaviour studies. Now that I have dropped this hint, let me make clear that I have no wish to imply that this animal parallel in any way destroys the reality or power of that element which many personify and call God, and which is revealed in the study of much of man's religious experience. Here is something we are going to look at—something profound, which the evidence appears to suggest is of vital importance to man. I might say in passing that whilst Freud may have given us a valuable clue, concerning this personification, I do not regard his concept of the super-ego as the complete explanation. All this will come later; for the moment I am simply maintaining that the feeling towards Divinity must be as much a part of the biological system as is, say, the feeling of human affection. Mysterious it is; *no more so*, however, than is our consciousness, that state of our awareness that is fundamental for our sense of *being alive*, but which is still ignored by biology because we cannot at present see in what manner it fits into the system.

How, it may be asked, can biology, as a science, deal with religious experience? In reply I must first say that science, of course, cannot, at any rate in its present form, be concerned with the actual inner essence of religion, any more than it can deal with the nature of art or the poetry of human love. What I do believe, however—and this is what I shall be discussing—is that the scientist can make an objective, systematic study of the *written records* of man's religious experience; and that by so doing he may eventually, after long research, not only help towards a better understanding of this remarkable concept of God, but bring a more natural theology (which is a rational study of religion and not, of course, religion itself) into the same realm of philosophic thought to which science itself belongs. Such written accounts of experience have been studied by my colleagues and myself at our Religious Experience Research Unit at Manchester College, Oxford, for the last five years. The scope of this work, now based upon over four thousand records, will be discussed in chapter 10 (p. 183), and the first three volumes of our findings should soon be published.[1] These are the preliminary beginnings of much more extensive studies now being undertaken. The value of the method cannot be judged, I believe, without making a critical examination of these results. I must here, however, make two important points if I am not to be misunderstood.

Firstly, I realize that the written records of those sacred, sub-jective feelings can never reveal their full nature; all the mystics tell us that these experiences are ineffable. This we must recognize and put up with, as an unfortunate but necessary limitation; it is like trying to express in words the emotions evoked by great music or masterpieces of art. Music and fine pictures, however, can be heard and seen by all who have appreciative ears or eyes, and so there is no need for attempted verbal interpretation; few rationalists would deny the reality and importance of art and music in the life of man. Spiritual experiences, from all accounts, appear to be just as real to those who feel them, and if they are to be discussed they must, at second-best, be verbally described.

The second point I must make is that just as a knowledge of the biology of sex does not destroy the love of a lover, so a systematic study of religious experience linked with the world of science through an empirical natural theology need not destroy the rap-ture of anyone's communion with what he feels to be God. The joy implied in the accounts of such experience is entirely different from anything like superstition; it is related to love. We must

---

[1] It is hoped that they will form a uniform series, *Studies from the Religious Experience Research Unit*; details of publication to be announced later.

guard against the danger that in our rational determination to stamp out superstition—and who will deny that it has played its part in religious practices in the past?—we may stifle the spirit of Divine feeling which may, when better understood, come to be recognized as a vital part of man's nature: a part, I believe, as biologically real as is sex. As the anthropologist R. R. Marett said, 'Thanks to the predominance of emotion over reason in it, religious experience is always hot. Gone cold it has gone out. Rationalism can at most serve to temper a flame which it does not light and may easily extinguish.'[1]

The reason why so many people doubt that science can in any way be concerned with religion is that they have come to accept an idea which is nothing more than a dogma: the supposition that everything that is truly scientific must eventually be reduced to physical and chemical terms. This is methodologically false. To make clear this fallacy, I must briefly discuss the very nature of science, and here I find it helpful to draw a distinction between science and natural history.

Natural history, as the term 'history' implies, is a description of nature—a straightforward account based upon accurate observation. *Science* goes further in being the quantitative and experimental analysis of nature's interactions; it represents nature in terms of numbers and measurement, and it puts forward propositions (hypotheses) about nature, to be tested by experiment.

With this latter definition we can have a true science of living things, on a different level from that of physics and chemistry. I am not a vitalist in the old-fashioned sense, for I am sure that all the physical and mechanical actions of the animal body—and the human, too—can be described in physical and chemical terms. I believe, however, with Sherrington, Eccles and others that mental events may belong to a different order, although linked with the physical system. The mystery of the mind–body relationship is still unsolved. As the late Sir Charles Sherrington, perhaps the

[1] *Faith, Hope and Charity in Primitive Religion* (Clarendon Press, Oxford, 1932), p. 15.

greatest investigator of our nervous action, said, 'We have, it seems to me, to admit that energy and mind are phenomena of two categories.'[1]

We can apply the scientific method to the study of certain aspects of living things quite independently of physics and chemistry. Just as important as the physico-chemical analysis of the animal's internal mechanism is the scientific study of the living animal as a whole, looked at in relation to its natural surroundings: the branches of biology which we call *ecology* and *ethology* (the study of animal behaviour).

Physics and chemistry are sciences just because they are based upon statistical laws concerning the behaviour of particles, electrons, atoms and molecules; so also *ecology* is a true science *in its own right*, being based upon the statistical treatment of the interactions of animals as *living wholes*. There is no need for it to be wedded to the unproven hypothesis or *dogma* of materialism; animal bodies may be completely described in physico-chemical statements, but it is as yet merely a pretence to suggest that we understand their mental life in similar terms.

Ecology is not, as some people are inclined to think, just a new-fangled name for natural history—there is a difference, or there should be: the difference between science and natural history to which I have just referred. When we record that a particular kind of fish is confined to warm oceanic water and feeds upon various kinds of shrimps, that is simple natural history—not true ecology.

1 *Man on his Nature* (Cambridge University Press, Cambridge, 1940), p. 318. This is his volume of Gifford Lectures. Some may object, as an eminent biologist did, that a quotation from this source is unfair in that it is taken from Sherrington 'in his more consciously literary moments'. If this should be said again, I would rebut it with a quotation taken from his truly physiological writing: when the International Congress of Physiology met in Oxford in 1947 they republished, as a compliment to Sherrington, his great book, *The Integrative Action of the Nervous System*, which was first published in 1906. Sherrington, nearing the end of his life, wrote a remarkable foreword to this 1947 edition (Cambridge University Press), again emphasizing the apparent duality of mind and matter. He ends with these words (p. xxiv): 'That our being should consist of *two* fundamental elements offers I suppose no greater inherent improbability than that it should rest on only one.'

When, by extensive surveys in a research-ship, we can determine the particular degrees of temperature and saltiness of the water which limit its distribution, and by a vast number of post-mortem examinations can work out the average percentage-constituents of its food at different times of the year, and for fish of different ages, we are then beginning to know something of its ecology — its relationships with the various elements in both its physical and animate environment expressed in quantitative terms. Ecology is converting natural history into science. From such quantitative analyses it hopes in time, step by step, to discover more of the laws operating in the world of living things. We should note, however, that the naturalists are the pioneers discovering the essential facts by observation, preparing the way for the future ecologists.

All the ideas as to the possible nature of what man has called God have been based entirely upon interpretations of his past and present experience. Theologies of the past have shown how highly speculative these interpretations can be. The study, which I envisage as a branch of a greatly widened biology, will be built upon the records of man's experience and upon studies of his behaviour. It will be a science allied to the fields of ecology and ethology. However, before it becomes anything like a science, it will have to pass through a long period of natural history, a period of comparative observations rather than one of quantitative or experimental studies. We must not despise natural history; some of the discoveries by observation have been just as important as those made by experiment and measurement. We should not forget that the greatest contribution that biology has yet made to human enlightenment — the doctrine of evolution — was built up by the observations of those great field naturalists, Darwin and Wallace; only later, in this century, after the rediscovery of Mendel's laws and now the revelation of the marvels of DNA chemistry, has a part of evolution been made into an exact science.

The biology of God really began just over seventy years ago with the work of two great Americans, William James and his pupil Edwin Starbuck. It was in fact Starbuck who, with his book,

The Psychology of Religion (1899),[1] induced William James to follow him with his more famous study, *The Varieties of Religious Experience*, published in 1902.[2] For me, these two, James and Starbuck, stand out in our subject as the great pioneers, like Darwin and Wallace in the launching of the theory of evolution. Starbuck begins his book with these words: 'Science has conquered one field after another, until now it is entering the most complex, the most inaccessible, and, of all, the most sacred domain — that of religion. The Psychology of Religion has for its work to carry the well-established methods of science into the analysis and organisation of the facts of the religious consciousness, and to ascertain the laws which determine its growth and character.' And a little later in the same introduction he says, 'The study of religion is today where astronomy and chemistry were four centuries ago.' William James, carrying the subject further, wrote the greater book, but it was, as he acknowledges, a study based largely upon the material collected by Starbuck. Their methods, however, were never followed up, except by the social anthropologists working among the more primitive peoples; I think it likely that we know more about the religious feelings of South Seas islanders and certain tribes of Africa than we do of the religious experience of the inhabitants of our own Western cities of today. It is in the footsteps of James and Starbuck, whose work we shall discuss in chapter 6, that my colleagues and I at our Religious Experience Research Unit are now humbly trying to follow.

Our methods are not unlike those of the ecologists, and like them, we too must found our future science upon a natural history of careful observation. I have spent the greater part of my life, when not teaching as a professor, researching into the ecology of life in the sea; I believe this is a good preparation for our new endeavour. All marine ecology is, of course, built upon the pioneer work of the naturalists, and the ecologist himself must continually be collecting new facts of natural history to form the raw material

[1] 2nd edn: Walter Scott, London, 1901.
[2] Longman, Green & Co., London.

for his later, more quantitative and experimental studies. Let me quote from a public lecture I gave over thirty years ago,[1] for it will also show that what I have now embarked upon is not just the product of a recent senile whim:

> Perhaps I may make a confession. I have worked hard at marine ecology, but I have done so only partly because I have had a desire to benefit the fishing industry; I have this desire most sincerely, but also I have felt that I have been working towards a better understanding of animal relationships and making contributions to the development of general principles in ecology ... I will go further – I will confess that perhaps my main interest in ecology is the conviction that this science of inter-relationships of animals and their environment will eventually have a reaction for the benefit of mankind quite apart from any immediate economic one. I believe that one of the great contributions of biology in this century to the welfare of the race will be the working out of ecological principles that can be applied to human affairs: the establishment of an ecological outlook. I believe the only true science of politics is that of human ecology – a quantitative science which will take in not only the economic and nutritional needs of man, but one which will include his emotional side as well, including the recognition of his spiritual as well as his physical behaviour[2] ... I believe what

[1] My inaugural lecture as Regius Professor of Natural History in the University of Aberdeen, published under the title, *Natural History Old and New* (1942; now out of print). The theme was more fully developed in my Essex Hall Lecture, *Science and the Quest for God* (Lindsey Press, London, 1951).

[2] At this point I briefly referred to Mass Observation, as a pioneer attempt towards such a study of religion; this system of survey, inaugurated by Tom Harrisson, later gave us the book, *Puzzled People: a study in popular attitudes to religion, ethics, progress and politics in a London borough* (Victor Gollancz, London, 1947), and later still (1961), in *Britain Revisited* (also Gollancz), Harrison gave us a chapter entitled 'For God's Sake!' in which he came back to a survey of religious attitudes. These were beginnings hardly out of the natural-history phase but nevertheless important pioneer steps towards such a future ecology now being attempted, and discussed later in chapter 10, p. 193.

Professor Joad said the other day [that was in 1942] to be profoundly true: that the unconsciously frustrated desire for spiritual experience is no less important than the unconsciously frustrated sex upon which the psychoanalysts have laid so much stress.

Professor Joad was, of course, saying very much what Aldous Huxley had said before him, as quoted earlier in this chapter. I believe it is indeed urgent for our civilization that we should satisfy these unappeased and frustrated desires with a spiritual philosophy that can be seen to be in harmony with the modern scientific outlook.

You may well wonder, if I felt this to be so some thirty years ago, why was it that I postponed my active attack upon this problem for so long. That is a reasonable charge. The fact is, whilst I felt this urgency, I was also (and still am) a convinced Darwinian; it took me all that time, with some hard thinking and a searching of the literature, before I was really satisfied that the spiritual side of man could be reconciled with the Darwinian doctrine of natural selection (and more recently with that of the DNA genetic code). It had at first seemed that the firm establishment of neo-Darwinism could point only to a doctrine of materialism. This had been a powerful reason for the abandonment of religion by so many in the intellectual world. I eventually became convinced that the two could be combined. Before I can explain the nature of this reconciliation, however, I must first discuss modern evolution theory and this I shall do in the next chapter. Here I have only been concerned with introducing our outlook and method of approach.

2. The animal and chemical background

The Christian world was certainly disturbed when Copernicus and Galileo shattered the medieval dream of man's abode being at the centre of the universe; greater still was the shock when Darwin and his followers showed that man was not separately created but was descended from ape-like ancestors who in turn were part of a long line of evolving animals.

We now know that organic evolution has been going on for some two to three *thousand million* years, with modern man being in existence for barely a quarter of a million; and as for his civilization, it can be measured in a paltry few thousand.

Evolution is not, of course, only a theory, as some elderly, sheltered people may perhaps still imagine; it is as much a reality as are the facts of geography. There is now a remarkably complete account of all the main changes which have taken place in the long, past sequence of animals and plants; and this is no imagined history built by inference from other evidence, but an actual record, in the form of fossils excavated from the sedimentary rocks laid down in the past successive periods in which they lived and died. The course of evolution is now plotted on *time*-charts covering the last five hundred million years, every bit as real as the maps within an atlas.

We can trace modern man, *Homo sapiens*, and that extinct side-line race of the Neanderthals, back to Mousterian man of some hundred thousand years ago, to his pre-Mousterian forebears, and still further back to those famous fossils from Java and Peking belonging to the *Homo erectus* (= *Pithecanthropus*) group. These may perhaps be linked with the smaller-brained, but still man-like, creatures (*Australopithecus*), of two million and more years ago, being unearthed in Africa, although this is not yet certain for *H. erectus* has now been discovered there at an equally early date. Some thirty million years earlier the human family diverged from the primitive ape-like forms, and another fifty million years carries us back through the lemur-like ancestors to the very beginnings of the primate stock, to little arboreal mammals no larger than the tree-shrews of today. Back and further back we can journey on our time-charts of the fossil record to the very earliest mammals and to their forebears, the mammal-like reptiles. Earlier still we can see how the reptiles themselves sprang from the primitive, newt-like amphibians which in turn can be traced back to those air-breathing fishes which left the water for the newly risen land in those far-off days of some three hundred million years ago. These fish were highly organized, vertebrate animals whose evolution from the simplest forms of life must have taken perhaps ten times as long as that of the period we have just considered. All this lineage from fish to man is recorded fact. The part that is theory relates to the way in which it has come about; and more and more of this theory is being established by experiment.

This record of our past, whilst showing clearly that we are indeed one with this long, unbroken chain of life, perhaps fails by itself to convey the real significance of this unity. We are one with these early forms of life in a peculiarly intimate way, which is not always obvious to those who are not biologists.

Our bodies, like those of all plants and animals, are made up of material in a continuous state of chemical activity. As soon as this reaction stops we die. There can be no doubt that physically we are complex chemical machines which run by a dual system. Our energy is not, of course, derived from burning fuel under a boiler or from igniting it in a cylinder but from a similar process going on, as it were, within the very cranks and pistons of our engines. Elementary biology tells us that one side of this dual system is the building-up of the elaborate substances characteristic of the particular species, whether man or maggot, from the simpler products of digested food; the other is the breaking-down of these substances by a burning-like oxidation *within* the tissues to provide the vital driving-energy, particularly that of muscular movement. In the young, the building-up process is the stronger and we witness growth. For the greater part of our life the two activities are in balance; gradually, however, the building-up declines and can no longer keep pace with the wearing-out, and we see the onset of old age leading to the final breakdown of death. But here is a marvel; not quite the whole of our body is necessarily so condemned.

We know that every animal's body develops by a vast proliferation of cells derived by the repeated division of the single, fertilized parent egg. It is a strictly orderly process in which nearly all of the cells, but not quite all, become modified in various ways to serve as liver, kidney, muscle, brain-cells and so forth; all those *specialized* cells wear out and die. The exceptions are the germ-cells which appear to be potentially *immortal*; if they and their descendant germ-cells are not killed by accident, starvation, attack or disease, they have the chance to survive and carry forward the hereditary factors, the genes, to the following generations – on and on into the future, apparently for ever. We who are living today are the result of billions and billions of generations of germ-cell survivals in the past; and not only are we handing on the genes, but we are indeed a continuation of that actual chemical reaction – *the very same one* – which was started and, while undergoing some changes in its nature, has never stopped since life began thousands of millions of years ago. We are a part of the *same living organism* that breathed and pulsated with activity all those eons ago. Millions upon millions of bodies have carried forward the stream of life that is now *us*. These bodies have worn out and died, generation after generation; they have been thrown aside like dilapidated broken perambulators, but the babies they carried – the eggs and sperm – unless inadvertently killed, became, when united, the new vehicles carrying forward the next generation, and so on – ultimately, to *us*. You and I are one with the primordial, protean speck of life, just as we are each individually one with the egg that developed within our mother's womb.

This, our lineage, if we do not ourselves destroy it, seems likely to continue into the future for an even longer period to come. All this is no mythological story. It is a reality to which all our ideas of religion, of God—what for example was God doing in this vast stretch of time?[1] – and of our spiritual side of life, must be seen to be related. It is the material mechanism of our creation, but is it the whole truth?

We inhabit a puzzled world; people may still feel religion in their hearts but find their minds deciding that such yearnings must be the product of a childish wishful thinking.

Let us now turn to the generally accepted biological view as to how evolution is brought about. Present-day theory is essentially Darwinian, or perhaps better expressed as neo-Darwinian: the combination of Darwinism and Mendelian genetics in its modern form. Darwin was not, of course, the first to put forward views on evolution; his predecessors, however, failed to convince the scientific world or influence general thought, and it was not until he presented both a reasonable theory and an overwhelming mass of evidence as to the reality of evolution in *The Origin of Species* in 1859 that the change came. The basis of this theory is the principle of natural selection;[2] although it is so well known, the theory can usefully be summarized as the starting-point of our discussion.

All animals and plants differ from one another in all sorts of ways; no two individuals of the same species are exactly alike in their inherited make-up, except in the rare and accidental cases of identical twins. There are also small differences such as may be caused by the influence of the environment during the growth of the individual, but these, not being inherited, are of little direct

[1] This is a question we must ponder on, and one which the new 'process theology', based upon the philosophy of Whitehead, attempts to answer, as we shall see in chapter 11 (p. 204).

[2] The theory of natural selection was put forward quite independently by Charles Darwin and Alfred Russel Wallace; it was, however, the great marshalling of facts in its favour by Darwin, more than twenty years' work, that justifies it being termed Darwinism, but let us not forget Wallace's share in and contribution to the theory.

consequence in evolution; it is only with the former that we are concerned at the moment. All organisms reproduce at such a rate that there is intensive competition for the available supplies of food —only a small proportion can survive to reach reproductive maturity. Some varieties will be more successful in this struggle for life and will tend to survive rather than others—to be, as Darwin said, selected by nature—and so contribute more to posterity; the less efficient strains will tend to be eliminated and will consequently appear less often in the ancestry of future generations. Thus the average characteristics of the members of a population of any species will gradually change with the passage of time; whole *populations* are slowly evolving towards better adaptation to their surroundings.

It was not only the fact that man was not separately created which made evolution such a shock to the religious world; worse still was the form of the Darwinian theory, for it swept away the arguments from design, which since the days of Paley's *Natural Theology* (1802) had appeared to present the unanswerable argument to prove the existence of a Deity. The mechanism of a watch implies a designer, and so it was thought that all the intricate structures and beautiful adaptations of animal and plant life must also point to a Divine artificer. All that was now gone—natural selection appeared to explain it all. Just as Laplace had said about the working of the solar system, 'I have no need for the hypothesis of God,' so the naturalists began to say the same in regard to the living world.

Here it may be well to dispose of a criticism one sometimes hears from those who say they cannot see the wholesale destruction going on in nature that is implied by the Darwinian doctrine of the struggle for existence. There could be no better answer than that made by Wallace in his book, *Darwinism* (1889), taking the sparrow as his example. Usually a sparrow lays six eggs in a clutch and has two or three broods in the year; in captivity a sparrow if kept healthy will live for over fifteen years. Let us be conservative, said Wallace, and suppose that they only live ten years and only produce ten young a year. If all these young grew up to lead a natural breeding life and if on an average half of them are females, a simple sum (a geometric progression) will show that in ten years' time, for every pair of sparrows today, there would be over twenty-four million. Yet we know that the sparrows are not usually on the increase. This, of course, does not mean that for every two sparrows over twenty-four million will die in the next ten years, because, out of each ten offspring per year, to keep the balance right, there will be a loss, on an average, of eight or nine. In the case of the sparrow we are demonstrating an eighty- or ninety-per-cent destruction per year; over thousands and thousands of years this gives plenty of scope for selection. Now the sparrow's reproductive rate is not large for animals in general; there are many insects that lay a thousand eggs, and this is nothing compared with the fecundity of many fish: the codfish lays a million eggs and the halibut five million! The destruction of life and the struggle for survival is indeed great.

In evolution, death is as 'vital' as birth. Without it, and the consequent continual replacement by new variations in the populations for selection to act upon, there could be no progressive change. In nature, of course, death is usually brought about by predation, pathogenic organisms or physical catastrophes; if these agencies fail to terminate the organism's life after a reasonable spell of reproductive activity, then the natural wearing-out in the process of senile decline brings it to an end. It might almost be said perhaps that senility ending in death is itself an adaptation for evolutionary progress.

The nature of inheritance, upon which modern evolution theory so much depends, was not known to Darwin. The great discovery of Gregor Mendel, although published in 1865, remained unnoticed by the scientific world until it was brought to light in 1900. It is clear, however, that Darwin realized that his theory could only be concerned with the selection of *inherited* variations, for his great book, The Origin of Species, bears the following alternative title: *The Preservation of favoured Races in the Struggle for Life.* Mendel was the first to show that inheritance is particulate; in other words that all the heritable variations are caused by differences in discrete factors, or genes as they later became called, which are handed on from one generation to another in the germ cells. The form of any animal or plant is determined by the combined action of all its genes—the so-called gene complex—together with those smaller and uninheritable effects already mentioned, which may result from the influence of the environment. Now the genes from time to time undergo sudden, spontaneous and apparently random changes in their form, technically termed mutations, which alter their effects and so provide, in combination with other genes, the great range of variations upon which natural selection can act.

When the process is described and considered in such terms it is no wonder that so many biologists have come to the view which may be summarized in the words of Dr G. G. Simpson, one of the world's leading authorities on evolution; in his Terry Lectures at Yale University in 1949, published under the title of *The Meaning of Evolution*,[1] he says (p. 230), 'it does seem that the problem is now essentially solved and that the mechanism of evolution is known. It turns out to be basically materialistic ...' Later in the same work Dr Simpson says (p. 277), '... as the geneticist's studies progressed they were providing the last major piece of the truth so long sought regarding the causes of evolution.'[2]

It is always unwise to say 'the last major piece of truth'. Since these words were uttered has come that most spectacular discovery in molecular biology concerning the nature of this genetical element in the evolutionary system: a discovery which makes the whole system appear to many minds to be even more materialistic,

[1] Oxford University Press, London, 1950.

[2] It is perhaps only fair to indicate Dr Simpson's views regarding the mystery of the universe. In the same volume, on p. 278, he writes: 'There is neither need nor excuse for postulation of nonmaterial intervention in the origin of life, the rise of man, or any other part of the long history of the material cosmos. Yet the origin of that cosmos and the causal principles of its history remain unexplained and inaccessible to science. Here is hidden the First Cause sought by theology and philosophy. The First Cause is not known and I suspect that it never will be known to living man. We may, if we are so inclined, worship it in our own ways, but we certainly do not comprehend it.'

if that were possible, than it was thought to be before. I refer to the work of those two brilliant Cambridge scientists, Drs Watson and Crick, both Nobel Prize-winners.

Firstly, they have shown us that the genes are made up of giant molecules of a substance known for short as DNA (deoxyribonucleic acid) with a remarkable spiral structure—the famous 'double helix'. This is not just a speculation, for it has been magnificently vindicated by the results of X-ray diffraction analysis and other experimental tests. Its detailed chemical structure, fascinating as it is, need not concern us here. Secondly, they have established that these molecules have an enormous source of variation caused by different arrangements of certain chemical units which are of four kinds and, in tandem pairs, link the two sides of the double helix together. There may be a thousand such links in a single molecule. Further, they have shown that these units provide a specification in the form of a code—the genetic or DNA code as it is called—determining the inherited form of every developing individual organism. Just as the telegraphic Morse Code is made up of combinations of only two symbols—dots and dashes—in a limited number of arrangements, so the DNA code is made up of a much greater range of possible combinations by using four different symbols: the four chemically different kinds of links just mentioned, but in a vastly greater number of possible permutations. Now the arrangement of these is altered from time to time within the giant molecule, apparently by chance, to provide the mutations which change the code to give rise to differing genetic strains.

How does the code operate? It interacts through other nucleic acids (in a manner which is chemically too technical to be entered into here) to lay down those main building-substances of the body, the proteins. These proteins of so many different kinds vary one from another by an even greater array of possible combinations and permutations than those in the DNA; these are provided by *twenty* different kinds of amino-acid units which may be linked together in all sorts of ways and sequences in their hundreds of thousands to build the great protein molecules. As Crick has said, the genetic code is the dictionary which relates the four-letter language of the DNA with the twenty-letter language of the proteins.

Now here is something that closely links up with what we have been saying about the continuous chemical activity in the evolutionary stream of life, for it is remarkable that there is little or no essential difference in the general form of the DNA molecules at different stages in this long evolutionary history from the lowest organisms to man; it is only the details of their coding arrangements that are different. Even in bacteria the system is essentially the same. A still more extraordinary feature of the DNA molecules is their surprising power of reproducing exact copies of themselves. This amazing ability of molecular reduplication – which is continually going on – gives the prodigious forward surge of organic growth and reproduction; it is this reproductive pressure which forces the ever-increasing populations of animals *and men* into every conceivable place that will give them the barest of livings. This and the sex drive are at the root of all population explosions.

Certainly this great DNA discovery appears at first sight to make Darwinian evolution a materialistic system. Dr Crick ended an article on the genetic code, written for the general public soon after his discovery, with these words: 'From every point of view biology is getting nearer and nearer to the molecular level. Here in the realm of heredity we now find ourselves dealing with polymers [i.e. chain-molecules] and reducing the decisive controls of life to a matter of the precise order in which monomers [i.e. the units in the chain] are arranged in a giant molecule.' He talks of the 'decisive controls of life', but is that really true? Certainly the genetic code – together with the effects of the environment – appears to be governing the form of an *individual's* physical body. But do these chance variations of the code really govern evolution? Many are inclined to think so. Jacques Monod says in his book, *Chance and Necessity* (1972; p. 110), 'since they constitute the *only* possible source of modifications in the genetic text, itself the *sole* repository of the organism's hereditary structures, it necessarily follows that chance *alone* is at the source of every in-novation, of all creation in the biosphere'.

It is indeed the random DNA mutations and the chance inter-play and recombinations of the genes (in the remarkable shuffling process which takes place in the formation of the germ-cells, generation after generation) that provide the almost endless range of variation upon which natural selection acts. This is their essential role in the evolution system which could not work with-out them; it is, however, a fallacy to suppose that they control the course of its direction. It is *selection* that *guides* the process, and selection is far from random. Whilst most evolutionists today actually recognize the truth of this, it is still widely thought that we as good as know all there is to know about the various selec-tive agents and that these again appear to point to an entirely materialistic system. I believe, however, that this is another fallacy, and that a most vital selective agent has, except by a very few, been overlooked on account of its somewhat subtle nature. If this selective agent is indeed as important as I think it is—and this is what I have to show—then it must present us with a very dif-ferent picture of the process.

Since the argument I am coming to concerns the action of this selection, I must first say a little more about the nature of the pro-cess. There are still some critics of Darwinian theory who try to maintain that selection could never itself create novelty, because it depends on the weeding-out of the less fit. I want first to show how very creative it can be. Two main types of selection are readily recognized; that by the physical environment as, for ex-ample, when mammals with thicker fur tend to survive better in colder climates than those less well-provided, and that by the action of predatory enemies or competitors.

It is some of the effects of predation that provide us with such remarkable examples of the creative powers of selection. Consider for a moment all the wonderful adaptations involving colour-patterns, shape of body and even behavioural postures which to-gether make an insect resemble in every detail some natural object, say a leaf or a twig. Much more subtle, however, than these exact copies are the camouflage devices found in many mammals, birds and fish, as well as insects, that counteract the effects of the play of light and shade upon the body and so destroy its appearance of solidity; and to this system are often added over-lying patterns which destroy the body's outline and thus, concealing its shape, make it merge into a variety of backgrounds. These are indeed devices which employ all the tricks of shading, and tone-values — and sometimes the principles of illusion — that are usually known only to the artist and appear to be masterpieces of imaginative skill. Such creative 'artistry' could only have been produced by some sensory agent outside the animal concerned, because camouflage-designs only have significance when viewed at *some little distance*. The selective agents in such examples are indeed their predators which, more often than not, fail to capture those variations which are the better likenesses to natural objects or present the better optical illusions; this is not armchair-theorizing, for it has been beautifully demonstrated through experiments made in the field by the students of animal behaviour,[1] and not just in the laboratory. Such remarkable 'designs' began, of course, as variations presenting slight chance resemblances or illusions just sufficiently effective to be misleading; then, by further chance changes over long periods of time, they were gradually improved by the continued tendency towards survival of those which were slightly more deceptive.

In a different way, selection by the physical environment can be just as 'inventive', as witness the different devices found in the form of seeds for their aerial distribution; parachutes, autogyros and gliders — designs which might have come straight from Leonardo's sketch-books — have all been produced, by the gradual selection of those random variations which turned out to be better suited to such dispersal. It is not difficult to see how such aerodynamic perfection gradually took place. Chance variations would provide normally smooth seeds, which fell to the ground, with a few hairy projections; caught by the wind, these would be

[1] See for example the chapter on 'Studies of Camouflage' in Professor Niko Tinbergen's book: *Curious Naturalists* (Country Life Limited, London, 1958).

scattered a little more widely than the smooth ones to give slightly better chances of survival in covering a greater variety of ground. Seeds which were even more hairy would do better, and those odd varieties that had hairs at only one end of the seed would have better buoyancy and tend to float in the air for even longer, and gradually after thousands and thousands—indeed millions—of years the almost-perfect parachute is formed to carry our dandelion and thistle seeds across the countryside. By a similar process the gyrating seeds of the sycamore or the gliding seeds—wonders of design—of certain conifers would be produced. It is selection that gradually guides evolution, and not the random genetic changes which, as we have seen, supply the almost endless range of variations upon which it can act; if given time—and there is plenty of time—selection (of different kinds) can produce all the adaptational wonders of the living world.

Selection is certainly the key to the physical side of evolution. Because so many of these truly remarkable adaptive creations can be shown to be produced by the selective powers of either the physical or the living environment, so many biologists seem to feel that there is surely no need to look further; they become blind to other possibilities. The kind of selection which I believe has been almost entirely overlooked is one to which I have given the name of 'behavioural selection'. So important is it in relating evolution theory to the spiritual side of man, that it deserves a chapter to itself; and to this we shall now proceed.

3. Behaviour and evolution

In summarizing the generally accepted, present-day views on evolution theory, I briefly made the point that it is essentially the changes in the average characteristics of populations that mark the course of evolutionary progress of any species towards better and better adaptation to its surroundings and ways of life. We must not just think of lines of individuals. Throughout any inter-breeding population there is a continual interchange of genetic material going on with the passage of time: what biologists so expressively call gene-flow.

The magnitude of this genetic flux is brought home to us if we consider the question which H. G. Wells asked in one of his sociological studies: how many ancestors may we have had living at the time of the Norman Conquest? We have had, of course, two parents, four grandparents, eight great-grandparents, sixteen great-great-grandparents and so on. Now if we take an average period for a generation as 30 years, i.e. from one birth to the next in the chain, there will be 30 such generations in the 900 years going back to 1066. The possible number of ancestors we might have had thirty generations ago is, of course, $2 \times 2 \times 2 \times \ldots$ thirty times, or expressed mathematically 2^{30} (i.e. 2 to the power of 30) which is no less than over a *thousand million* (1,073,741,824 is the exact figure); and this might suggest that it is possible that *each* individual alive today in our overcrowded Britain *could* have had this number of ancestors at that time. The total population of Great Britain, however, in the reign of Queen Anne was said to be only five millions and at the time of the Norman Conquest it was probably much less. What does it mean? It can only mean that most of us have more likely than not shared the same ancestors many times and that we are all more closely related to each other than we ever suspected.

We may be surprised at the extent of this gene-flow within our own species during what is, in relation to evolution's time-scale, a very short period indeed; man, however, on account of his greatly lengthened period of childhood and his relatively small number of offspring, is a slow breeder compared with most other animals. Consider how much greater will be the gene-flow in the populations of a more rapidly-breeding animal: many birds and mammals become mature in a year and have a much larger number of offspring; some insects become mature in a few weeks and, as we have already noted, many lay a thousand eggs. Vast populations are evolving under the action of selection, slowly changing their average form as those members with the less efficient combinations of genes tend to be reduced in numbers and those with combinations giving better adaptations to their circumstances come into the ascendancy. When the environment changes, as it surely does with the passage of time, or if a species may extend into new terrains, or yet again if an animal may change its way of life, so are slightly different gene-complexes favoured by selection.

No one will deny that animals living under natural conditions may come to change their behaviour; such new habits may no doubt often be due to alterations in their environment, such as a failure of food supplies or the destruction of breeding sites and so on, but sometimes they may be formed through the animals themselves discovering new ways of life. They are inquisitive, exploratory creatures. Among the higher vertebrates—the birds and mammals—a new piece of behaviour, perhaps, for example, in the gathering of food, if adopted by one or two individuals and then seen by others to be advantageous, will gradually spread by copying through the community and be passed on from parent to offspring. We see in fact, in birds and mammals, the beginning of what might be called tradition. In any population of animals among which there has come about a change of habit there will turn up sooner or later individuals having small variations in structure which will make them more efficient in relation to this new behaviour; over a period of time these kinds will tend to survive rather better than those less well-equipped in this particular respect, and so the composition of the population will gradually change.

As an illustration let me use an imaginary example that I have used before:[1] that of birds which mainly lived by picking off insects from the surface of tree-trunks. If, perhaps in some period of shortage, one or two more enterprising individuals started probing with their beaks into cracks in the bark and found that they could get more insects by doing so, and then developed this new habit, they might be copied by others of the same species, and so gradually we would see a change of behaviour spreading through the populations. This is not just supposition. Our common bird, the great tit (*Parus major*), took to opening the tops of milk-bottles left by the milkmen on their customers' doorsteps, and so getting at the rich cream at the top; this new behaviour spread rapidly across the country, apparently by copying, and extended right through the populations of Europe.[2] At first the milk-bottle tops were cardboard lids; later, however, in an attempt to defeat the tits, the dairies introduced the metal caps. Were the tits beaten? — not a bit of it. Here, indeed, we see the result of enterprising exploratory behaviour spreading throughout the range of the species where milk-bottles are available. Soon the great tits were being copied by another species, the smaller blue tit (*Parus caeruleus*).

Then there is the new habit developed by the greenfinch (*Ligurinus chloris*) which recently took to attacking the seeds of the shrub, *Daphne*; beginning in the north of England, this new behaviour has since been seen to spread southwards county by county, again presumably by being copied and passed on.[3] A more remarkable example is the behaviour observed by Jane Goodall and her husband Hugo van Lawick who saw and photographed Egyptian vultures picking up stones in their beaks and then hurling them with such force at ostrich eggs that they broke the shell

---

[1] *Proc. Linn. Soc. Lond.*, vol. 168 (1957), pp. 85–7.
[2] R. A. Hinde and J. Fisher, *British Birds*, vol. 44 (1952), pp. 393–6.
[3] Max Petterson, *Nature*, vol. 134 (1959), p. 649.

and allowed the vultures to eat the contents. This proved not to be just an isolated instance, for they set out two ostrich eggs at a site some sixty miles away and waited to see what would happen; sure enough, before long, a pair of these vultures appeared and performed the same, almost tool-using, act.[1] This must surely be a new habit developed in the first place by some more enterprising individuals. I have myself watched the large Dominican gulls (*Larus dominicanus*) stealing eggs from the colony of jackass penguins on Dassen Island off the coast of South Africa and carrying them in their widely-opened beaks to drop them upon a flat rock from a height of some forty feet; they then swoop down to feed on the yolk and developing young.[2] Or again, there is the Californian sea-otter which habitually feeds by using a stone to break open sea-urchins and various forms of shellfish, to say nothing of the well-known practice of the thrush breaking its snails on an 'anvil' stone.

The beautiful studies by Drs Itani and Kawai of the social life of wild monkeys in Japan show the copying of new behaviour-patterns such as potato-washing spreading through the colony and being transmitted from one generation to another.[3] Recently Professor Tinbergen has drawn attention to two different methods of opening mussel-shells employed by those wading birds, the oyster-catchers; these are not genetically determined but represent two separate traditions of feeding which are passed on by parent to offspring.[4]

After this digression to contemporary examples showing that the development of new behaviour-patterns and their spread are very much a reality, I will now return to my original hypo-thetical example of birds probing into the bark of trees for insects. If this new habit became well established in the species and, being more profitable, replaced the old practice of pecking insects off

[1] *Nature*, vol. 212 (1966), pp. 1468–9.

[2] *Great Waters* (Collins, London, 1967), p. 248.

[3] J. Itani in *Primates*, vol. 1 (Inuyama, 1958), pp. 84–98, and M. Kawai, ibid., vol. 6 (1964), pp. 1–30.

[4] The Croonian Lecture for 1972, *Proceedings of the Royal Society*, Series B, vol. 182 (1972), pp. 395–6.

the surface, then any members of the population with a gene-complex providing a beak slightly better-adapted to such probing would have a better chance of survival than those less well-equipped. A new shape of beak would be evolved as a result of a change of habit. When I first discussed this I had thought, as I said at the time, that I was merely recalling the views which had been put forward by Mark Baldwin and Lloyd Morgan at the turn of the century.[1] Now, some people tell me that I am reading too much into Baldwin's views and that what I am saying is really something different.[2] Most people, however, when I discuss it, tell me I am simply talking pure Darwinism and that I am just making a fuss about nothing. This is where I disagree and insist that there is a real, if subtle, difference which is fundamental to our understanding of the evolution process. I shall try to explain why.

Because a change of habit is often occasioned by changes in the environment, it is generally supposed, I think, that any selection due to such a change of habit is one differing only in degree, but not in kind, from other forms of Darwinian selection. This for me is the crux of the whole issue; I think they are radically different. I realize, of course, that it is the differential mortality in the population which brings about the survival of the more efficient type of beak in our example, and that this is obviously mediated by various factors in the environment killing off a higher proportion of the less efficient forms; nevertheless the real *initiating agent* in

[1] Whilst I first briefly mentioned these views in my Presidential Address to the Zoology Section of the British Association in 1949 (*Advancement of Science*, vol. 6, p. 221), I expressed them in my Essex Hall Lecture of 1951 (published as *Science and the Quest for God*, The Lindsey Press, London) as follows:

Their views [i.e. Baldwin's and Lloyd Morgan's] could, I think, if re-stated in modern terms, be expressed very briefly something like this: gene combinations better suited to allow a fuller expression of the animals' habits may tend to survive in preference to those gene combinations which do not give such full scope to its pattern of behaviour. Here we see coming back the idea of change of habit affecting bodily structure—but not, as Lamarck held, through use and disuse of the body, but through a form of Darwinian selection ... Here we see the possibility of *changing behaviour* modifying the course of evolution.

[2] I have further discussed the relation of my views to those of Baldwin and Lloyd Morgan at some length in *The Living Stream* (1965), pp. 161 ff.

the process is the new behaviour-pattern, the *new habit*. I believe the case for regarding this 'behavioural' type of selection as different in kind from other forms of natural selection can be maintained. Although new habits may, as I have said, frequently result from environmental changes, they are by no means always so formed; among vertebrates it must often be the restless, exploring and perceptive animals that discover new ways of living, new sources of food, just as the tits discovered the food value of the milk bottles or the vultures took to breaking ostrich eggs. This searching, inquisitive type of behaviour has no doubt been fostered and developed by selection just because it pays dividends.

To continue with birds' beaks, it was Darwin, who, in his famous account of his voyage in H.M.S. *Beagle*, discussed the finches of the Galapagos Islands and pointed out the gradation in size and shape of the beaks of the different species. David Lack, who followed Darwin to the islands more than a century later to make a special evolutionary study of these birds, shows in his book, *Darwin's Finches* (Cambridge University Press, Cambridge, 1947; p. 60), how the beak-differences between most of the genera and subgenera are clearly correlated with differences in their feeding methods. 'This is well borne out', he says, 'by the heavy, finch-like beak of the seed-eating *Geospiza*, the long beak of the flower-probing *Cactornis*, the somewhat parrot-like beak of the leaf-, bud- and fruit-eating *Platyspiza*, the woodpecker-like beak of the woodboring *Cactospiza* and the warbler-like beaks of the insect-eating *Certhidea* and *Pinaroloxias*.'

Which is the more reasonable explanation of these adaptations: that chance mutations in beak-shape *first* occurred in the population causing such birds to seek new food more suited to their new beaks, or that competition drove some of these birds to develop new feeding habits so that, when chance mutations produced more efficient beaks within these populations, they tended to survive rather than those less well-adapted to the new food? Shall we not agree that the second explanation is the more likely?

Now among these Galapagos finches is to be found a piece of behaviour which indeed supports the conclusion we have just reached, for here we come upon one of the most remarkable examples of the exploring, perceptive behaviour among birds: that shown by the woodpecker-finch, *Camarhynchus pallidus*. This is the bird that actually uses a tool; it selects a cactus-spine or a twig of just the right size to poke insects out of the cracks in the bark of trees. Surely chance mutations alone did not lead to this new habit, any more than they could lead to the behaviour of the Egyptian vultures we have just mentioned.

No doubt it must be the mutations affecting the connections in the nervous system which will later convert such learnt behaviour into instinctive actions; this incidentally is indeed a puzzle, for here is something a little different from the selection of those chance variations in beak-shape which are better suited to new habits in feeding. I introduce this slight digression as a particularly compelling example of the development of new feeding habits: new behaviour, moreover, which in this case not only influences the form of the beak by such selection, but the instinctive way in which the bird uses its beak to pick up and handle 'a tool' as an aid to feeding. I don't believe that anyone yet knows exactly how such a change from learnt to instinctive behaviour actually takes place, but clearly some genetically controlled modification of the nervous system must be established.

Why do I say 'clearly it must'? Because there are examples that seem to tell us so. For instance, the young of some species of birds have to be *taught* their characteristic song by hearing their parent sing—if reared away from their parent they cannot render the species tune; on the other hand there are many other species of bird whose young will automatically sing their correct song if brought up away from members of their kind. In some way, yet to be discovered, behaviour that had originally to be learnt generation after generation has been fixed into an instinctive automatic nervous action—presumably by the natural selection of suitable alterations in the nerve connections; let us be honest, however, and admit that we don't yet know exactly how this fixation takes place—the incorporation of something like a musical score into the molecular genetic code. It is well that we should realize that there are still many problems waiting to be solved regarding the detailed mechanism of evolution. We must not, however, carry this digression further (I have devoted a whole chapter to such puzzles in my book, *The Living Stream*); let us return to the main thread of our argument.

Consider for a moment the remarkable diversity of beaks among birds in general: compare, for instance, the beaks of the snipe, the curlew, the falcon, the spoonbill, the flamingo, the pelican, the cross-bill and the humming-bird, to mention only a few. Can it really be maintained that it is *more likely* that random mutations forced these various groups of birds into their different modes of life rather than that they first developed different feeding habits which then led gradually, by this behavioural selection, to beaks which were better and better adapted to their ways of life? Must it not be admitted that it is change of habit which is the dominating factor influencing such selection? And if we had been considering the different kinds of legs and feet of birds would we not have come to a similar conclusion?

I believe that the same principle will apply to the evolution of all the higher vertebrate animals and particularly the mammals, which have developed so may new ways of life such as digging in the ground or climbing trees for food, diving into water after fish —indeed some becoming entirely aquatic as the whales—or flying like the bats. Does a terrestrial animal by chance get webbed feet and then take to the water to use them? Of course not. We can imagine the ancestors of the otter, before they took to swimming, watching fish in shallow water, and one, more enterprising than the rest, diving in and catching a fish, repeating the process and so developing this new way of hunting. It would be copied by others farther up the stream so that before long this new habit of aquatic feeding might spread through the population. Even now the young have to be taught to swim by their parents. Once it became a well-established way of life, new chance mutations giving webbing to the feet would make swimming more successful, so that those possessing this advantage would tend to survive better than others. This would be a change brought about *within* the Darwinian system—but one originating in a change of behaviour, through the animal's inquisitive exploratory activity. All the major adaptations which distinguish the main diverging lines of animal evolution are essentially, I believe, examples of what I would call *behavioural selection*. All this I have discussed in detail in *The Living Stream* (1965).

While I had briefly put forward my views in 1949, 1951 and 1957 (see footnotes on pp. 38 and 40), a number of other biologists have independently been coming to similar conclusions. Dr R. F. Ewer[1] emphasizes the same effect, saying that 'behaviour will tend to be always one jump ahead of structure, and so play a decisive role in the evolutionary process.' Professor C. H. Waddington points out that 'an animal by its behaviour contributes in a most important way to determining the nature and intensity of the selection pressures which will be exerted on it'.[2] Ernst Mayr, one of the greatest American authorities on evolution, has been coming to similar views, and in 1970 sums up his conclusions thus: 'Changes in behaviour, such as a preference for a new habitat, food, or mode of locomotion, may set up new selection pressures. Much evidence indicates that most major evolutionary shifts (the origin of higher taxa) began with a behavioural shift.'[3] In the same year even Jacques Monod, in his *Le Hasard et la nécessité*, was saying the same thing; I quote from p. 121 of the English translation, *Chance and Necessity* (1972): 'It is also evident that the initial choice of this or that kind of behaviour can often have very long range consequences, not only for the species in which it first appears in rudimentary form, but for all its descendents, even if they constitute an entire evolutionary subgroup.'

Is not evolution theory beginning to look rather different from what it appeared to be in the discussion at the end of the last chapter, and still appears to be in the minds of so many people

[1] *New Biology*, vol. 13 (Penguin, London, 1952), pp. 117–19, and *Acta Biotheoretica*, vol. 13 (Leiden, 1960, pp. 161–84).

[2] *Nature*, vol. 183 (1959), pp. 1134–8.

[3] *Verhandlungen der Deutschen Zoologischen Gesellschaft*, vol. 64 (1970), pp. 322–336.

today? I hope I have made it clear that I am not in any way underrating the importance both of the physical environment and the action of predators, as powerful selective agents—indeed in the last chapter I particularly pointed out their remarkable creative powers; here I am stressing an additional selective force which I believe to be equally creative and which actually operates *within the populations* of the species concerned—one that is acting through the animal's mental life, through their behaviour. This is a selective agent within the recognized neo-Darwinian system but one which, to my mind, makes a radical difference to it.

Here I can imagine some of my colleagues saying that, although I have shown the importance of behaviour as another selective force, it does not really make any philosophical difference to one's attitude towards evolution; it must be just as materialistic a process, they will say, as was Darwinism without it, because they believe that the animal's mental life is nothing but a reflection, an epiphenomenon, of its physico-chemical nervous action which in turn is solely the product of environmental selection. But is it?

Here is the crux of the matter, and the possibility of a new view. This epiphenomenon concept is no more than a speculative and, to my mind, an unlikely hypothesis; its presentation as a materialistic 'theory' of evolution is but another unwarranted dogma. Why do I think it unlikely? Because in the first place it completely ignores the probability, nay the near-certainty, that at any rate the higher animals, the mammals and birds, are beings with a good deal of *conscious* behaviour, and secondly because, for the reasons to be developed later, I cannot think it likely that consciousness will ever be reduced to just those physico-chemical terms as we now understand them. I have already (p. 18) stated my agreement with Sherrington, Eccles and others in this respect. Consciousness must certainly have its link, in the mind-body relationship, with the physico-chemical nervous action, but just how? It is one of the greatest of all puzzles.

Can anyone who has kept and become fond of a dog, a cat or a horse believe that they are unconscious organic machines? Can we read such accounts as Mrs Joy Adamson's friendship with her lioness in her book *Born Free* (1960), or of Gavin Maxwell's affectionate otters in his *Ring of Bright Water* (1960), or again of Miss Len Howard's studies of *Birds as Individuals* (1952), and be in any doubt that there is as much, or almost as much, ground for regarding such animals as conscious as we have for attributing this quality to our fellow men? Lacking the reasoned thought and intelligence of ourselves, they will, of course, have nothing like the same conception of their surroundings as we have through our education and tradition.

It is almost taboo to discuss the question of consciousness in biological circles; yet what could be more fundamental to our existence? In the field of consciousness, as we experience it, lie all our feelings of purpose, love, joy, sorrow, the sense of the sacred, the sense of right and wrong, appreciation of beauty, indeed all the things that really matter in life. 'Scientists', as Sir Peter Medawar so well reminded us in his Reith Lectures, *The Future of Man* (1960, p. 62), 'tend not to ask themselves questions until they can see the rudiments of an answer in their minds. Embarrassing questions tend to remain unasked, or if asked, to be answered rudely.' Fortunately, however, there are a few who are prepared to face these embarrassments. Professor C. H. Waddington, in *The Ethical Animal* (1960, p. 63), says that 'As soon as one places the problem of free will in juxta-position with that of consciousness, it becomes apparent that it cannot be solved either by manipulation of our existing physico-chemical concepts ... We need ideas which depart more radically from those of the physical sciences ...'

I was delighted that that great scientist, the late Sir Cyril Hinshelwood, gave such prominence to the question of consciousness in his last Presidential Address to the Royal Society, that of 1959.[1]

It is surprising that biological discussions often underestimate human consciousness as a fundamental experimental datum. In science we attach no value to unverifiable deductions, or to empty qualitative statements, but nobody defends the neglect of experimental data. Among these we cannot validly disregard those of our own consciousness except by a deliberate abstraction for which we must assume responsibility, and which we should not forget having made ...

He now proceeds to show that we are in fact all the time trying experiments—not, of course, in a laboratory sense but nevertheless experiments—in our relations with other people by informing, asking, ordering, obeying, resisting and so on with various emotions and observing the results. The hypothesis that other people have an inner life not unlike our own is tested again and again in the daily experiments we make with them; it enables us to register correspondences at point after point in so intimate a way that we accept the hypothesis, if not as absolute truth, then as something nearly as good. And then Hinshelwood says, 'with most of the basic conclusions of science I am in no position to demand more'. After more discussions of the problem he continues, 'There is at present no obvious answer to the question of what kind of advance can possibly be hoped for in the problem of psycho-physical concomitance. This, however, is no reason for giving up thought which at least helps to avoid the kind of errors so easily made both about physics and about biology when the problem is ignored ...'

I think it likely that we cannot hope to solve the problem if, as scientists, we continue to look at it only from the physico-chemical side. And on logical grounds I can see no reason why we should draw a line at some arbitrary point in evolutionary time between the higher members of the primate stock, the ancestors of man, who are conscious beings, and those earlier 'more animal' members whom we might, in shallower thought, have imagined (as many people have apparently so imagined in the past) to be creatures lacking this sense of awareness.

Professor Michael Polanyi makes[1] an important distinction by dividing knowledge into two main kinds; and by so doing

[1] *Personal Knowledge* (Routledge & Kegan Paul, London, 1958).

emphasizes that man's mental life is not only in one important and obvious respect radically different from that of his animal ancestry, but is in another more fundamental way much nearer to the animal world than perhaps has ever been thought before, even by the most confirmed evolutionists. His two kinds of knowledge are (1) *explicit knowledge*, that which is formulated in words, maps, mathematical symbols, etc., and (2) *tacit knowledge*, that which is not so formulated, for example the knowledge of what we are in the act of doing or experiencing before we express it in words or symbols. When we go for a country walk by ourselves we gain a knowledge of the scenery through which we are passing and we appreciate its beauty without necessarily describing it to ourselves in words; only later, on getting home, we may give a verbal description of it.

The more primitive forms of human knowing—those forms of intelligence which man shares with animals—are situated, says Polanyi, behind the barrier of language. Animals have no speech (beyond systems of communication by signs and sounds); the towering superiority of man over the animals is almost entirely due to his development of language. Speech enables man to formulate ideas, to reflect upon them, and communicate them to others. Babies up to eighteen months or so are said to be not much superior to chimpanzees of the same age; only when they learn to speak do they leave the apes far behind. Even adult humans, however, show no distinctly greater intelligence than animals, so long as their minds work unaided by language. 'In the absence of linguistic clues, man sees things, hears things, feels things, moves about, explores his surroundings and gets to know his way about very much as animals do.' Man, of course, with his tradition of explicit knowledge and the long extension of the period of his growing up, and so learning by speech-communication, has a vastly larger conscious conception of the nature of his environment than any animal could possibly have; nevertheless we have no right to assume that there has been a radical break in evolution with the sudden creation of conscious awareness at some point in early human history. It perhaps may not be far from the truth to

think of the conscious awareness of the higher animals to be somewhat like that of little children.

My bringing in Polanyi's views at this point may appear at
first sight to be somewhat of a digression from our main argument.
I discuss them at some length because I believe that they do *con-
clusively prove* that there is such a state of consciousness in at any
rate the higher vertebrate animals; furthermore, such a demonstration of their conscious actions is, I believe, of the greatest
importance for our appreciation of the part played by behaviour
in the course of Darwinian evolution. Whilst I shall be referring
again to Polanyi's ideas later in the book, it is here in relation
to conscious behaviour that they must be given a specially important place. When I say he has proved this point, the reader
will want to be given chapter and verse; and he may ask, 'Has he
proved it by experiment?'

Michael Polanyi is a scientist who was elected to his Fellowship
of the Royal Society for his brilliant work in chemistry more than
thirty years ago; he is also a renowned philosopher and Emeritus
Professor of Social Studies in the University of Manchester.
Whilst his philosophy has all the characteristics of crisp scientific
argument, it is not by experiment that he has proved that animals
are creatures of conscious awareness, but by the force of inescapable
logic. We have just seen (p. 46) that so eminent a scientist as the
late Sir Cyril Hinshelwood regarded the reality of human consciousness as experimentally demonstrable, not in the laboratory
sense, however, but in the frequent testing of the hypothesis in the
daily experiments in communication we make with our fellow
men. We cannot do this in the same way, or at any rate with
equal force, with animals who lack speech. It is by reasoning that
Polanyi shows that conscious, *tacit* knowledge must *always* precede
the explicit knowledge which distinguishes man from the rest of
the animal world.

Polanyi suggests that, since what he calls tacit knowledge
appears to be 'a doing of our own lacking the public, objective,
character of explicit knowledge', it may be objected by some that
it lacks the essential quality of knowledge and perhaps should not

be called knowledge at all. This, however, he believes to be mistaken. In *The Study of Man* (1959), he goes on to show that tacit knowledge is in fact the dominant principle of all knowledge, and that its rejection would, therefore, automatically involve the rejection of any knowledge whatever. He points out that the essential *logical* difference between the two kinds of knowledge lies in the fact that we can critically reflect on something explicitly stated, in a way in which we cannot reflect on our tacit awareness of an experience. In passing let us note the importance of this for our own particular theme. Science and descriptive natural history are both explicit in their nature, whereas religion, like art, is essentially in the field of tacit knowing and feeling. It is well known, as already noted, that all those who have had any profound religious experience find it almost impossible to convert it into explicit communicable terms. Herein lies a real difficulty in the research into religious experience which I shall be discussing later on, for we can only evaluate and compare explicit statements.

In order to illustrate the logical difference between the two kinds of knowledge, Polanyi proceeds to compare the tacit and explicit elements of the same operation in a very illuminating way. He quotes Tolman, who has worked so much on the behaviour of rats in mazes, as saying that a rat gets to know its way about a maze *as if* it had acquired a mental map of it. He goes on to say that observations on human subjects suggest that a man, however intelligent, is no better at maze-running than a rat, unless assisted by notes, whether these are remembered verbally or sketched out in a drawing. Man, of course, can make such notes, and the advantages of a map are obvious; in addition, however, a man has, with his explicit knowledge, the power of reflecting critically upon such a map, checking its validity with reality and seeing if perhaps at some point it may be inaccurate. If it is a map he has previously made himself, it is telling him something he has put down before; it is like playing back, for criticism, something he said before. Nothing like this can take place at a pre-articulate level. If we have only a mental memory of a fairly familiar region, and we then lose our way, we can only correct our mistake by plunging from one view of a scene to another. Knowledge held in this inarticulate manner he calls *a-critical*.

Those who are only used to the scientific way of looking at the world may now be somewhat shocked at the next step that Polanyi takes. Can we go further, he asks, and show that at all mental levels it is the *tacit* powers of the mind which are decisive? He believes we can, and goes on to suggest that not only are the purely tacit operations of the mind processes of understanding, but the understanding of words and symbols is also a tacit process. As he says a little later, 'our whole articulate equipment turns out to be merely a tool-box, a supremely efficient instrument for deploying our inarticulate faculties'.[1] When we try to understand something, we exercise our tacit powers in search of a better intellectual control of the matter in hand. We seek to clarify something said or experienced, and to move from one position which we feel to be uncertain to another we find more satisfying. 'And this,' Polanyi emphasizes in italics, '*is how we eventually come to hold a piece of knowledge to be true.*' Or again he says, 'All human knowledge is now seen to be shaped and sustained by the inarticulate mental faculties which we share with the animals.'

Before I leave Professor Polanyi's exciting ideas, I may perhaps be excused if I give just one more quotation to present a suggestion he makes, which may well be of importance to our later studies: not only may the tacit powers of animals be greater than our own, but those of children may outshine those of adult life.

It is of course impossible to compare exactly the level of tacit performances involved in the works of human genius, with the feats of animals or infants. But we may recall the case of Clever Hans, the horse whose powers of observation far exceeded those of a whole array of scientific investigators. They believed the animal was solving problems set out on a blackboard in front of it, while it was actually taking its clues for correct answers by watching the involuntary gestures made by the scientists themselves in expectation of these

[1] *The Study of Man* (Routledge & Kegan Paul, London, 1959), p. 25.

answers. Remember also how readily and how well children learn to read and write, compared with hitherto illiterate adults. There is enough evidence here to suggest that the highest tacit powers of an adult may not exceed, and perhaps actually fall short of those of an animal or an infant, so that the adult's incomparably greater performances are to be ascribed predominantly to his superior cultural equipment. Genius seems to consist in the power of applying the originality of youth to the experience of maturity.[1]

As speech developed in man, it was accompanied by a rapid increase in the size of the brain; verbal communication would give those with better speech facilities a greater advantage (both tribes and individuals), so that natural selection would constantly, generation after generation, be tending to preserve those who had better, more complex and larger areas of association-centres in the cerebral cortex, with which to produce more and more explicit forms of language and consequent powers of reasoning. All this happened, as we have seen from the fossil evidence available, in an extremely small fraction of time compared with the long history of animal evolution. The resulting explicit statements of knowledge and the culture to which they have given rise, while so important and so novel, can hardly have introduced some entirely new element that was not present in the universe before. The field of human consciousness has, of course, been enormously enlarged, but this, as I have already stressed, cannot itself have produced this fundamental state of awareness. I agree, of course, that the complex human personality has indeed been built up in some such manner as the psychologists suggest, although the advocates of the different schools still differ very much amongst themselves as to the exact nature of the process. Personality, however, is not the same as consciousness. I shall be arguing later that some, at any rate, of the elements which go to make up religion – the sense of the sacred, the numinous and the feeling of being in contact with some power other than the self, are unlikely in themselves to be

[1] *The Study of Man*, pp. 18–19.

products of the explicit system, although only that system can give a verbal expression of them. They are, I believe, more likely to be part of a tacit, inarticulate, extra-sensory knowledge of a part of the universe to which consciousness belongs: a mystery certainly, but no more so than is the link which undoubtedly exists between consciousness itself and the biological system.

Polanyi's distinction between explicit and tacit knowledge marks the real division between man and the other animals, not consciousness. While we alone have the means of an explicit expression of our thoughts, and so the powers of logically discussing them with fellow members of our race, in the tacit emotional field there can be no sharp division between us and our animal ancestors.

Surely it is not unreasonable to suppose, as I have suggested, that the new habits which may develop in the higher animals, and lead to such behavioural selection as I have been discussing, may indeed be the result of their conscious exploratory actions. This is why I believe that the concept of behavioural selection makes such a difference to our views on Darwinian evolution and its philosophical implications. We are not only one with the animal kingdom in a physico-chemical sense, we are one with it in our emotional life as well. On this emotional side, from the evidence of the records of their behaviour, can we doubt that animals experience conscious delight? Dolphins which have been close companions in an oceanarium, but then separated for a time, exhibit, when brought together again, such mutual excitement and exuberant play with one another that it must surely indicate conscious joy. Julian Huxley, in his *Memories* (1970, p. 61), describes how as a young man he first saw porpoises disporting themselves round the bows of a ship, 'obviously enjoying their leaping and racing, just as the herons at Avery Island which I saw some years later enjoyed their aerial flight-games. I realized how stupid the behaviourists were in denying any subjective emotional experience to animals.' Does not the delight of a dog on being taken out for a walk, or its expression of loyal devotion as it rests its head in our hands, show every appearance of a consciously felt emotion?

I should record that the idea of consciousness playing a part in evolution was included as part of a single paragraph in a book by Professor H. W. Conn, *The Method of Evolution* (Putnam's, New York and London), in 1900. He relates it (p. 313), as I have done, to Mark Baldwin's theory of organic selection in the following terms:

> This conception of the action of selection evidently makes consciousness a factor in evolution. It has always been claimed by the Lamarckian school that consciousness aids in the process of descent. It has sometimes been supposed that by this claim is meant that by conscious efforts an animal can modify its structure; but such a conception has certainly not been held by scientists in recent years. Consciousness may, however, lead to the use of organs or to the adoption of new habits, and, if the view we are now considering be sound, such use of organs, or such habits, leads to the development of acquired characters which enable the individual to live in new conditions more successfully, until after a time congenital variations take their place. Consciousness thus becomes an indirect factor in evolution.

I was quite unaware of this book until my own *The Living Stream* (1965) had gone to press; I was able, however, before publication, to add an addendum note (on p. 179) giving this same quotation.

Where do we draw the line, if indeed we must, between our spiritual life and the emotional side of animal behaviour? Such a question may seem outrageous, but let us pause for a moment before casting it aside. Animals, being without explicit thought and reasoning powers, can, of course, have no formulated ideas regarding anything like a religious concept; this is not what I mean. Any consideration of the beginnings of religion we must leave till a little later. Under the headings of man's spiritual life, however, I would place in addition to his religious feelings, his joy in a quest or in the moment of discovery and his love of natural beauty and the arts. Whether animals have any appreciation of the beauty of their surroundings we have, of course, no means of knowing, and so perhaps a consideration of the arts seems irrelevant.[1] However, what of man's love of adventure? Is not that perhaps linked with the restless, inquisitive, exploratory nature of animal life? Somehow, out of the process of evolution, has come the urge that drives a man to risk his life in climbing Everest, in reaching the South Pole or exploring the moon, just as in the past it sent more primitive men in frail canoes across the ocean. Is it altogether too naive to suggest that this drive, this curiosity, which is really at the heart of all true scientific seeking, has had its beginning in some deep-seated aspect of animal behaviour which has played a fundamental part in this process of life?

I hope I have said enough to suggest that Darwinian evolution need no longer be considered an entirely materialistic doctrine. It can only be so regarded if we either deny the part played by conscious behaviour or deem consciousness itself to be no more than an illusory by-product of an entirely mechanistic system. I maintain that there is no reasonable support for either view and that to proclaim them as a part of well-established science is not only an unwarranted assumption but is most likely a misrepresentation of the nature of life and of man, and so a danger to our civilization.

[1] It 'seems irrelevant', I have said; perhaps, however, in a footnote I may add that I have a hunch that just conceivably it isn't. I remember watching a television film of the private life of one of the Australian bower-birds, with that well-known artist, naturalist and man of action, Peter Scott, acting as commentator. We saw the male bird placing a brightly coloured flower-petal into the decorated side of the bower through which he would later drive the female during courtship stimulation. He put it into one position and then stood back looking at it for a moment with his head cocked on one side; then taking it up again he placed it in another position, and after having another look he went off apparently satisfied. 'Just as I do myself when painting a picture,' said Peter Scott, or words to that effect. There are, of course, some species of bower-birds which do actually 'paint' the branches forming the walls of their bower in bright colours from the juices of berries and fruits which they crush in their beaks, and at least one species uses a small wad of bark (like using a tool) to smear the stain on, as if with a paint-brush. This latter practice is described by A. J. Marshall in his book *Bower-Birds* (Oxford, 1954), p. 51. Again, do the female birds of paradise or tropical pheasants get only a sexual thrill when they see the glorious displays of their suitors, or is there an aesthetic element as well?

Those who have studied the history of evolution theory will know how in the last hundred years the prevailing views as to its operation have changed and changed again. Towards the end of the last century, Darwinism had gone into eclipse because at that time the old idea of blending inheritance seemed to preclude the possibility of natural selection being an effective force, and so the theory of de Vries that evolution proceeded by sudden jumps – large mutations – tended to take its place. The rediscovery of Mendel's laws in 1900, whilst actually sweeping away the obstacle of blending inheritance, appeared at first sight to give further support to de Vries's views; but Darwinism came back stronger than ever when it was realized how perfectly it fitted in with the Mendelian system of particulate inheritance and how impossible it would be for de Vries's larger mutations to form viable new strains. I merely refer to such changing views in order to suggest that we should not imagine that the last word on the mechanisms of evolution has yet been said. As I have already hinted, these matters are not of just academic interest; they *do* affect civilization, and at times the lives of millions of people. To emphasize the point I will cite another example of a widespread, mistaken view, which has indeed done just that.

It had often been implied that the action of natural selection must *always* make a race of animals or plants fitter in its struggle with its environment. Professor J. B. S. Haldane, in his *Causes of Evolution* (lectures given early in 1931 and published the following year), was perhaps the first to give prominent attention to this fallacy – 'a fallacy which', he says (p. 119), 'has been responsible for a good deal of poisonous nonsense which has been written on ethics in Darwin's name, especially in Germany before the war and in America and England since'. He was of course referring to the First World War, and writing before Hitler came to power, but the poisonous nonsense he speaks of was that which largely influenced the German outlook leading to both conflicts. Haldane clearly showed that there are many subtle ways in which competition between members of the same species may lead to the selection of features that eventually must spell ruin to the race.

Some of these features, however, are more obvious, such as the weapons evolved for combat between rivals of their own kind. 'The geological record', he says, 'is full of cases where the development of enormous horns and spines (sometimes in the male sex only) has been the prelude to extinction. It seems probable that in some of these cases the species literally sank under the weight of its own armaments.' That is indeed a lesson for mankind today.

Our philosophy of evolution, therefore, is certainly more than an intellectual exercise; it is vital for our future. Man is the animal we should know more about than any other species; our knowledge is incomplete without a study of all aspects of his experience. I shall have a little more to say about evolution theory when we come to consider (on p. 211) some of the ideas being developed in a new philosophy of religion which is now being called 'Process Theology'.

4. The coming of man and the emergence of belief

Professor Polanyi's distinction between the two kinds of knowing, as explained in the last chapter, has shown us that it is the development of speech and the consequent powers of explicit, linguistic reasoning that mark man off so sharply from the rest of the animal world.

Whilst reasoning and language developing together have fostered invention in tool-making and its spread by copying through the populations, the making of tools is not in itself a unique characteristic of man. Not only do some animals use various objects such as the twigs and stones as tools, as we have already seen (p. 29), but the chimpanzee actually trims a small branch to make an efficient instrument for extracting termites from ant-hills for food; it fashions a tool for a particular purpose.[1] It is the development of language, giving rise to the wide dissemination of knowledge and experience, and its transmission from generation to generation, that has led to the tremendous increase in the power of tradition which has now changed the very nature of evolution itself. We have come to quite a new stage in the process, that which Sir Julian Huxley has designated, and so rightly stressed, as the psycho-social phase.

Evolution is no longer proceeding entirely by Darwinian selection acting upon the wide range of inherited variations in the populations—nor even by what I have called behavioural selection—but by the handing-on of knowledge and ideas and their

---

[1] Jane van Lawick-Goodall, *In the Shadow of Man* (Collins, London, 1971), pp. 43–5; she also describes how they use sticks to prize open boxes (p. 91), and crumple up and partly chew leaves to form a 'sponge' for sucking up water for drinking (p. 97).

subsequent development. Knowledge is continually being added to and passed on: at first it was transmitted only by speech, but then in writing, next in printed books and now by all manner of new means of communication. Whilst man is still subject to some forms of natural selection through, for example, the action of pathogenic organisms, these are being continually reduced as man gains almost complete dominance over his environment and conquers one disease after another. Instead of the Darwinian system, we see emerging this new verbal transmission of acquired experience and ideas. A new step, quite unlike anything preceding it, has been taken in the history of creation and so marks a division between man and the rest of the animals at least as great as that separating the animal and plant kingdoms. And, in geological time, how very recent it is.

In my former discussion of evolution theory I left out any mention of Lamarck (except in the brief footnote reference on p. 40), because his theory had been shown to be wrong. Why then do I introduce him at this point? Because in a strange way the great change in evolution that we are here discussing is a change-over from Darwinian selection to a process which in certain respects is almost Lamarckian in character. The essence of what Lamarck taught was that changes in the environment may cause an animal to change its habits and so come to exercise its body in new ways; so he thought that parts of its body might be altered, as when muscles may increase in size through greater use, and likewise that other parts, less used, might tend to dwindle. It was these physical changes in the body, *acquired characters* as they were called, that Lamarck supposed would be inherited and so provide the mechanism for his theory; whilst he was proved to be wrong in this, for all attempts to demonstrate such inheritance have failed, we should in passing acknowledge the greatness of his vision in emphasizing the importance of change of behaviour in the evolution process. (He published his *Philosophie Zoologique* in 1809, the year of Charles Darwin's birth.) What we are now witnessing is the transmission of *acquired knowledge*, skill and experience, not by genetic inheritance but by tradition.

No one could have more veneration for Darwin than I have, yet, because Lamarck has been so much misunderstood and abused—an eminent colleague of mine writes of 'the disreputable theory of Lamarck'[1]—I confess that I find a certain perverse amusement in the realization that we ourselves, in our new phase, are now evolving in a manner which is far more Lamarckian than Darwinian, although not quite in the way that Lamarck had imagined. This has been so well expressed by Sir Peter Medawar in his Reith Lectures,[2] when he brought home to us once again how relevant is a true knowledge of our evolution for a proper understanding of human affairs.

> ... In their hunger for synthesis and systematisation, the evolutionary philosophers of the nineteenth century and some of their modern counterparts have missed the point: they thought that great lessons were to be learnt from similarities between Darwinian and social evolution; but it is from the differences that all the great lessons are to be learnt. For one thing, our newer style of evolution is Lamarckian in nature. The environment cannot imprint genetical information upon us, but it can and does imprint non-genetical information which we can and do pass on. Acquired characters are indeed inherited. The blacksmith was under an illusion if he supposed that his habits of life could impress themselves upon the genetic make-up of his children; but there is no doubting his ability to teach his children his trade, so that they can grow up to be as stalwart and skilful as himself.

In an earlier essay[3] he discusses the fundamental distinction between the 'Springs of Action' in mice and men. He points out that mice have no traditions, or very few ones, as can be shown by breeding them in such a way that each individual in successive generations is separated from its parents from the moment of

[1] Professor C. D. Darlington in his foreword to a reprint of the first edition of Darwin's *Origin of Species* issued by Watts (London, 1950).

[2] *The Future of Man* (Methuen, London, 1960), p. 98.

[3] 'Tradition: the evidence of Biology', in *The Uniqueness of the Individual* (Methuen, London, 1957), p. 141.

birth; when this is done there is 'no loss of their mouse-like ways'. He then makes his most telling point. 'The entire structure of human society as we know it', he says, 'would be destroyed in a single generation if anything of the kind were to be done with man.' Tradition, he emphasizes, is 'a biological instrument, by means of which human beings conserve, propagate and enlarge upon those properties to which they owe their present biological fitness, and their hope of becoming fitter still'. The question I shall be asking later on is to what extent have the traditions of religious belief and practice been such biological instruments in the development of human culture.

This change-over in evolution from a process dominated by Darwinian selection to one governed by the handing-on of acquired knowledge and skills, is surely the development of the very process which we have seen beginning among the higher animals, with the dissemination by copying and the passing-on from one generation to another of new modes of life — indeed the beginnings of tradition. With them it led by behavioural selection to advantageous changes in bodily structure; the same process has occurred in the ancestry of modern man, but in addition to giving him his erect posture and more sensitive and flexible hands for better tool-making and the manipulation of objects, such selection has been largely concerned with picking out those variations in brain-structure which provide better equipment for his growing powers of linguistic communication, reasoning and inventive skill. Later on (in chapter 9) I shall be referring to the importance of man becoming a carnivore and a hunter in relation to this development of mental power; logically such a discussion might well have come here, but it happens that it has special relevance to a subsequent argument, and so I reserve it till then. Here we may just note it in passing.[1]

[1] I am not entering here into any discussion of some earlier ideas I put forward in 1960 in the *New Scientist*, vol. 7, pp. 642–5, and in the *Listener* for 12 May of that year. I there suggested that man had passed through a semi-aquatic phase for perhaps some twenty or more million years in the Miocene and Pliocene after leaving the trees and before taking up a hunting life on land again; I seriously believe that this phase of life can alone explain a whole host of his peculiar

Many biologists have commented on the remarkable speed with which man obtained his increased brain-capacity. I would suggest that this acceleration of the selective process was brought about in much the same way as was that of the rapid evolution of the different stocks of early mammals, when taking up their new modes of life at the end of the age of reptiles; they came under a powerful behavioural selection to bring about a relatively rapid bodily change which would fit them for all their different new ways of life made possible by the recent departure of the reptiles. In the same way when man opened up an entirely new field of activity – this time one of unprecedented mental life – he came under a similar selection-pressure related to his new behaviour-patterns.

It was that remarkable man Alfred Russel Wallace, co-founder with Darwin of the theory of natural selection, who first realized the fundamental change that had taken place with the coming of man's mental evolution. He put forward his views as early as 1864, only five years after Darwin's *Origin of Species* and seven years *before* Darwin's *The Descent of Man*. Unfortunately Wallace published his paper, 'The Origin of Human Races and the Antiquity of Man Deduced from the theory of Natural Selection', in a new journal, the *Anthropological Review*,[1] which very soon ceased to exist and so is only to be found in relatively few libraries; as a consequence few people today seem to know of its existence. Because of this I make no apology for quoting him at some length, although I have already done so in my now out-of-print book, *The Divine Flame*. Wallace was a genius of a magnitude

---

characters, including his loss of hair, layer of subcutaneous fat, erect posture, underwater swimming powers, possession of the diving reflex, etc. All this, however, has little bearing on my present argument except that I believe it led him to change from a vegetarian to a carnivorous diet and so, after learning tool-making from the use of stones from the shore, he became, with his spears, a hunter on the land. It will, I hope, form the subject of a subsequent volume for which I have been collecting evidence for many years; in the meantime Mrs Elaine Morgan in her book, *The Descent of Woman* (Souvenir Press, London, 1972), has added to my hypothesis some interesting ideas of her own.

[1] Vol. 2, pp. clviii–clxx.

that has not yet, I believe, been fully appreciated. This is what he wrote:

> Thus man, by the mere capacity of clothing himself, and making weapons and tools, has taken away from nature that power of changing the external form and structure which she exercises over all other animals ...
>
> From the time, therefore, when the social and sympathetic feelings came into active operation, and the intellectual and moral faculties became fairly developed, man would cease to be influenced by 'natural selection' in his physical form and structure; as an animal he would remain almost stationary; the changes of the surrounding universe would cease to have upon him that powerful modifying effect which it exercises over other parts of the organic world. But from the moment that his body became stationary, his mind would become subject to those very influences from which his body had escaped; every slight variation in his mental and moral nature which should enable him better to guard against adverse circumstances, and combine for mutual comfort and protection, would be preserved and accumulated, ... and that rapid advancement of mental organization would occur, which has raised the very lowest races of man so far above the brutes ...

Surprise has sometimes been expressed that the languages of even the most primitive peoples of today are relatively well formed in their verbal structure, and that there are in fact no languages in the world which we might regard as being at a distinctly lower evolutionary level than others. By this I am meaning the structure of spoken language and not, of course, the production of literature as a creative and expressive art.[1] It would seem probable that when anything like a language developed from a more primitive communication by sounds and

[1] A discussion of this, together with the views of various authorities, is given in C. H. Waddington's *The Ethical Animal* (Allen & Unwin, London, 1960), p. 145.

signs it would at once have great survival value; thus, as the form of primitive languages came under the influence of natural selection, those peoples with the less efficient forms of speech would continually tend to be eliminated and so all the early stages in the process would be lost. It would indeed be a part of what Wallace has referred to as 'that rapid advancement of mental organization'. Let the eloquence of Wallace continue in his summary of human evolution:

At length, however, there came into existence a being in whom that subtle force we term *mind*, became of greater importance than his mere bodily structure. Though with a naked and unprotected body, *this* gave him clothing against the varying inclemencies of the seasons. Though unable to compete with the deer in swiftness, or with the wild bull in strength, *this* gave him weapons with which to capture or overcome both. Though less capable than most other animals of living on the herbs and the fruits that unaided nature supplies, this wonderful faculty taught him to govern and direct nature to his own benefit, and make her produce food for him when and where he pleased. From the moment when the first skin was used as a covering, when the first rude spear was formed to assist in the chase, the first seed sown or shoot planted, a giant revolution was effected in nature, a revolution which in all the previous ages of the earth's history had had no parallel, for a being had arisen who was no longer necessarily subject to change with the changing universe — a being who was in some degree superior to nature, inasmuch as he knew how to control and regulate her action, and could keep himself in harmony with her, not by a change in body, but by an advance of mind.

Here, then, we see the true grandeur and dignity of man ... He has not only escaped 'natural selection' himself, but he actually is able to take away some of that power from nature which, before his appearance, she universally exercised.

And here Wallace foresees a prospect, which we, living a hundred years later, realize is only too likely to come to pass, and which those of us who are lovers of nature can only contemplate with horror. 'We can anticipate', he said, 'the time when the earth will produce only cultivated plants and domestic animals; when man's selection shall have supplanted "natural selection"; and when the ocean will be the only domain in which that power can be exerted, which for countless cycles of ages ruled supreme over all the earth.'

I have briefly mentioned the importance of man becoming a carnivore and a hunter, and have said that I shall be referring to this phase later on; here let us just note that it was Alfred Russel Wallace again who first pointed out the significance of this. In his book, *Darwinism* (1889), he writes (p. 459):

> The anthropoid apes, as well as most of the monkey tribe, are essentially arboreal in their structure, whereas the great distinctive character of man is his special adaptation to terrestrial locomotion. We can hardly suppose, therefore, that he originated in a forest region, where fruits to be obtained by climbing are the chief vegetable food. It is more probable that he began his existence on the open plains or high plateaux of the temperate or sub-tropical zone, where the seeds of indigenous cereals and numerous herbivora, rodents, and game-birds, with fishes and molluscs in the lakes, rivers, and seas supplied him with an abundance of varied food. In such a region he would develop skill as a hunter, trapper, or fisherman, and later as a herdsman and cultivator, — a succession of which we find indications in the palaeolithic and neolithic races of Europe.

Now let me return to tradition and draw attention to another side of it in the evolution of man, one which had, I think, been largely overlooked until it was brought forward very forcibly by Professor C. H. Waddington in his book, *The Ethical Animal*. He maintains that this new cultural system, the passing-on of acquired experience through the coming of speech, can only

c

work successfully, not merely if there is developed the means of offering the information to the new generation, but also if the *members of the new generation are made to receive it*. The new-born infant has, as he says, to be 'moulded into an information acceptor', in fact to be made 'ready to believe (in some general sense of the word) what it is told'. The mechanism of information transfer cannot work successfully until the human being has been turned by evolution into someone 'who goes in for believing'. He further points out that the development of an infant 'into an authority acceptor'—an entertainer of beliefs—'involves the formation within his mind of some mental factors which carry authority, and that it is some aspects of these same authority-bearing systems that are responsible for his simultaneous moulding into an ethicizing creature'.

If what he is suggesting is true, and I must say that it seems to me most reasonable, then here is another important link between the biological system and the evolution of religion: the process of building into the mind of man a *capacity for belief*. We have been evolved into beings who tend to believe what we are told in our childhood. We are beings prone to be amenable to indoctrination, to take on trust what we are taught at our mother's knee, to be liable to become conditioned at an early age to any particular religious faith; it is all part of the new system of tradition, one of the latest developments in the long chain of biological evolution. Perhaps some may feel that this demonstration of the likely origin of the will to believe is yet another blow against religion, so let me say at once that, in the light of other evidence to be presented later, I do not feel this to be so at all—in fact the very reverse. It may well make us reconsider—and I hope it does—the validity of traditional dogmas; these, however, are not the essence of what I mean by a spiritual faith. And from what Waddington himself writes I think he would feel the same; in referring to the cultural development which differentiates our life today from that of our Stone-Age ancestors he says, 'It includes spiritual and intellectual changes as well as those concerning materials and tools.'

Having made the point that a great deal of social transmission takes place at a time when the recipient is much too young to attempt to verify the truth of what he is being told, Waddington makes an interesting comparison between this new social transmission of tradition and that of the mechanism of heredity. Just as in the latter process inefficient or even lethal genes are often transmitted and then eliminated from the stock by the action of natural selection, so in the new socio-genetic system erroneous information may be passed on and at first accepted but then later rejected by the individual after attempts at verification show that what he has been taught cannot be made to fit with the facts as he finds them. This is particularly so in the present age with the rapid development of science and social studies, and their exposition in the press and in books for the general reader, quite apart from what is now taught in schools; we witness the revolt of the teenagers against what they are taught in their early childhood. Tradition, more than ever before, is being subjected to the selective processes of a critical scepticism.

Waddington stresses all the time the biological approach, as I do, but he emphasizes this approach more particularly to philosophy and to man's moral, ethical behaviour rather than to religion itself; nevertheless he says that the points he is making are 'certainly not without importance from a religious point of view, or viewed as factors in man's spiritual life'. For philosophy, he regards the contributions from biology as far more relevant than anything physics has to offer concerning the ultimate nature of matter. I certainly agree with him.

In a further discussion of the evolutionary steps which must have taken place before the system of cultural socio-genetic transmission became possible, Waddington goes on to consider the psychological modifications that must have been made within the mind of man. In all pre-human animal societies, as far as we know, the authority-bearing entity is, like the pack-leader, external to the recipient individual. In human communities, however, whilst there is such external authority in one form or another, there is also something very different in the nature of each person. In the process of early development there comes about an 'internalization' of authority; it becomes built into the very mental make-up of man, so that within the individual there are two parts, one which acts as teacher and the other as the taught. 'Conscience', says Waddington, 'may, as we well know, become a stern internal authority.' And he goes on to discuss some aspects of this authority which may be termed ethical. 'Going in for ethics', he says, 'is for man an integral part of the role of the taught or the authority-acceptor, without the existence of which his cultural socio-genetic evolutionary system could not operate.'

A little later he says that any discussion as to how this state actually comes about must rest heavily on the work of Piaget and of Freud and his successors. The psycho-analytical theories of the latter will be considered in our discussion of psychology and religion in chapter 6; it is the findings of the former which clearly have the greater relevance to Waddington's views. Piaget recognized two important processes in child development. The first is what he terms the 'moral constraint of the adult', that is of the parent, or other person in charge of the child, giving commands which must be accepted. Waddington quotes Piaget as saying, 'It seems to us an undeniable fact that in the course of the child's mental development ... the respect felt by the small for the great plays an essential part; it is what makes the child accept all the commands transmitted to him by his parents and is thus the great factor of continuity between the different generations.' The second process which comes later is that of co-operation with other children as equals.

It is with the first process that Waddington is especially concerned, and he draws attention to the great importance which Piaget attaches to what he calls 'respect' and then says that term is 'perhaps rather too palid and innocent for the mental factor which is actually involved'. He goes on to point out the close similarity between the role which Piaget attributes to 'respect' and the role he himself assigns to what he has called the authority-bearing systems within the mind. While Piaget argues that such systems are essential for the first appearance of the moral consciousness, Waddington is saying that in addition they are equally essential for disposing the new-born individual to be a recipient of the socially transmitted information. Waddington then shows that Piaget realizes that the term 'respect' is actually inadequate to describe what he finds, by quoting the following illuminating passage: 'It is a fact that the child in the presence of his parents has the spontaneous feeling of something greater than and superior to himself. This respect has its roots deep down in certain inborn feelings and is due to a *sui generis* mixture of fear and affection which develops as a function of the child's relation to his adult environment.'[1] Is there not something here to be compared with that complex of awe and devotion which may often be so characteristic of man's attitude to what he calls God?

Waddington then goes on to consider the doctrines of Freud and his followers. Whatever we may think about the validity or importance of Freud's concept of the Oedipus complex, and this we shall discuss in a later chapter, Waddington makes it clear that the phases of personality-development in which the Oedipus situation is involved are not among the very earliest to occur. They are, he says, 'too late to be directly relevant to the initial moulding of the new-born infant into an "ethicising" being'. Here we must leave him and his ideas regarding the biological conversion of our species into the ethical animal: a creature who first, in his early stages, becomes an information-acceptor — a believer — and then during development undergoes the process which he calls the 'internalization of authority', giving him a conscience. Ethics and morality have frequently been associated with this or that form of religious doctrine, but they are by no means the same thing as religion. Remembering what Polanyi,[2] Medawar, Wallace, Waddington and Piaget have taught us about some of the changes that have taken place in the emergence of man and his mental life, let us now move on to man the religious animal.

[1] J. Piaget, *The Moral Judgement of the Child* (Kegan Paul, London, 1932), p. 379.
[2] See previous chapter.

5. *Religion in the making*

Like the beginnings of language, the origin of religion is lost in the past; and we can only speculate as to how it may first have arisen. We have seen the paramount importance of language in establishing man in his dominant position and how it seems likely, at a fairly early stage in his new system of evolution by the development of tradition, that he became converted into a congenital believer of what he was told as an individual in early life; not that any particular belief, any more than any particular language, would itself be inherited, but that there would be an inborn propensity for the young to believe whatever they might be told by their elders. And man developed a conscience, which was, as Waddington says, a psychological internalization of authority.

Now, related to this, have come views concerning the origin of religion put forward by another biologist, Professor V. C. Wynne-Edwards, in his Herbert Spencer Lecture, on 'Ecology and the Evolution of Social Ethics', which I heard him deliver in Oxford.[1] 'Children', he said, 'have no reason to question what they are taught about the existence of a supernatural world, and the inculcation of moral principles and codes of conduct has traditionally been reinforced by fostering at the same time a belief in divine powers that are beyond challenge and bid us to regard morality as sacred; together these form the foundation for religion.' He has been much impressed, as I have been, by the work of Émile Durkheim who, in his *Elementary Forms of the Religious Life* (trans. J. Swain, 1915), came to the conclusion that religion is eminently a social-collective phenomenon; this is an important element but, as I shall presently explain, it would seem to me to

[1] Now published in *Biology and the Human Sciences*, ed. J. W. S. Pringle (Oxford University Press, Oxford, 1972).

be only part of the truth. Religion, on the evidence of experience, is, I believe, much more than this; nevertheless I would certainly agree with Wynne-Edwards that it may be a most powerful reinforcement of the social code. 'Over a vast area of behaviour,' he says, 'conformity with the social code depends on self-discipline; and in the absence of religious reinforcement, especially the fear of a divine all-seeing eye and retribution from heaven, self-discipline is enforced rather weakly, or not at all, by the common desire to conform with public opinion and avoid incurring censure.'

Certainly, for the development of the communal life of the tribe such a moral code—essential for making altruistic behaviour have precedence over an individual's selfish desires—would be most important; in saying this, however, I must not be thought to imply that I regard either altruism or a moral code as paramount constituents of religion. Nevertheless a moral code is certainly necessary for the establishment of communal life and this would be greatly strengthened if it could be reinforced by an association with a supernatural power, which would add the fear of some dreadful retribution to that of the displeasure of the tribal authority. This indeed we have seen so well displayed in our own civilization which we like to think of as most advanced. Who can doubt that the fear of hell fire, eloquently preached for so long from many pulpits until only a few generations ago, was a powerful persuasion towards adherence to the code of the ten commandments? Both the force and function of religion in bringing about this phase of traditional and tribal life in the new social system cannot be denied; and we shall discuss more evidence for this in chapter 9. Just as sex has played such a vital part in the older mechanism of evolution, by bringing about a continual reassortment of the genes generation after generation, so perhaps that remarkable behavioural pattern of religion has played a significant part in this newer human evolution just because it has indirectly fostered the spirit of altruism upon which the preservation of society so much depends. If both are biologically important it is no wonder that religion, like sex, arouses such deep emotional reactions. 'One cannot too often recall', wrote Sir Richard Livingstone,[1] 'the profound words of Pascal, "It is the nature of man to believe and to love: if he has not the right objects for his belief and love, he will attach himself to wrong ones." ' Whilst there are innate forms of altruistic behaviour in animals lower down the scale, can the very different voluntary altruism within our own society be maintained without a traditional religion? If the power of religion fails through disbelief, can civilization, or indeed our very species which is now dependent upon this new type of traditional evolution, survive? We have already been reminded (p. 46) that competitive forces *within* particular species may lead to their extinction.

Because with hindsight we can now see the great ulterior advantage of attaching a superhuman sanction to man-made codes of behaviour, does it necessarily follow that the idea of some power which *appears* to the individual to be beyond his conscious mind must be a convenient illusion? We must indeed be suspicious when we know what tricks the subconscious mind can play; should we, however, dismiss out of hand the possibility that what we call religion may have behind it some other deep reality? So far this is only speculation. When so much is at stake, however, must we not make every effort to examine the evidence before we decide, on supposed rational grounds, that it can only be a fallacy? It is obvious, of course, that the particular form which this or that theological doctrine may take is unlikely in itself to be true when so many of them appear to contradict one another; theology and its doctrines, however, do not make up the real essence of religion. Is it not possible, in spite of the fantastic ideas which have been associated with it, that there may indeed be a profound truth at the back of religion which has made it the force it has been in the development of man's society? In addition to any psychological effect produced by evolution to support a social code necessary for the adoption of an altruistic culture, could it not be that there is in man's experience a deeply felt contact with a power which he feels to be sacred and from which he

[1] *Some Tasks for Education* (Oxford University Press, London, 1947), p. 27.

is able to draw strength and encouragement in his actions, and further that his culture could not in fact have been achieved without its having some reality? This is what has to be explored. When I speak of a deeply felt power, or indeed call it a spiritual power, I do not separate it from the biological system as I conceive it, any more than I would separate human love, the mystery of consciousness or the emotional appreciation of beauty from it. To me all of these are as much a biological reality as is the molecular structure of the living tissues, but widely different from them; clearly they must be linked with the physico-chemical system of nervous activity, but in a way which at present we do not understand. There is much in the universe that we still cannot fully grasp, such as for example the true nature of time, and even of gravity which we take so much for granted; and perhaps, if it exists (and I believe the evidence is strong), what we call extra-sensory perception. The purpose of this book is firstly to discuss what, if any, may be the evidence to support the view that there is some profound reality behind religion, and secondly to urge that like any other hypothesis it must be made the subject of prolonged and thorough research, before—quite apart from personal conviction—it can be either accepted or rejected on an intellectual level.

Let us now look at what scholarship has brought to light about the origins of religion, and begin with the work of those naturalists of mankind—the social anthropologists. The present century has seen a marked change in their studies. The observers of today, unlike their predecessors, are no longer content just to visit this or that tribe and report upon what they can gather from interviews through an interpreter and the attendance at certain ceremonies; they go and live with the people, thoroughly learn their language and enter into their way of life before they attempt to give any account of their social and religious behaviour. In the early days the enthusiastic pioneers were the great collectors of facts from all parts of the world, but they mainly gathered their information at second hand, and today are generally regarded by their successors as the 'arm-chair anthropologists'. We are told that with one exception no anthropologist conducted field studies until the end of the nineteenth century.[1] They were the ardent theorists; their views about the origins of religion, however, have not stood up to the test of modern research. The two outstanding figures of this period were Sir Edward Tylor who derived religion from animism and Sir James Frazer who thought it developed from magic. How are they regarded by some of the leading workers of today? The late Sir Edward Evans-Pritchard, who was Professor of Social Anthropology at Oxford, writes,[2] 'Sir Edward Tylor ... laid it down as an axiom that the idea of God is a late conception in human history ... and this was so much taken for granted that no one would listen when Andrew Lang, and after him Wilhelm Schmidt, pointed out that, as far as the most primitive peoples in the world today are concerned, the evidence points to the opposite conclusion.' Regarding Sir James Frazer, Dr Godfrey Lienhardt, Lecturer in African Sociology at Oxford, whilst praising his remarkable achievement in showing 'the possibility of a wide-ranging comparative study of religion which would reveal underlying similarities between "advanced" and "savage" beliefs', and the value of his massive work, *The Golden Bough*, as an encyclopaedia and bibliography, nevertheless says that 'Frazer's broad general idea of the universal scheme of psychological evolution, from magical thought to religious belief, from religious belief to scientific thought, has not proved in itself to be of any great value.'[3]

The views which were developed by Dr R. R. Marett, Reader in Social Anthropology at Oxford, at the beginning of this century are, I believe, much more important and mark the beginning of the more modern outlook. He made a sharp break with the ideas of Tylor and Frazer, pointing to a general experience felt by primitive man all over the world: a feeling of his being in contact with a power that helps him in his life. He says:

[1] E. Evans-Pritchard, *Social Anthropology* (Cohen & West, London, 1951), p. 72.
[2] *The Institutions of Primitive Society* (a series of broadcast talks) (Blackwell, Oxford, 1956), p. 2.
[3] *Social Anthropology* (Oxford University Press, London, 1964), pp. 33-5.

It is the common experience of man that he can draw on a power that makes for, and in its most typical form wills, righteousness, the sole condition being that a certain fear, a certain shyness and humility, accompany the effort so to do. That such a universal belief exists amongst all mankind, and that it is no less universally helpful in the highest degree, is the abiding impression left on my mind by the study of religion in its historico-scientific aspect.[1]

In a later work he writes:

When it is a question of a more or less definitely religious rite of the primitive pattern, we should be wrong in assuming any consistent doctrine to underlie the performance ... A play of images sufficiently forcible to arouse by diffused suggestion a conviction that the tribal luck is taking a turn in the required direction is the sum of his theology; and yet the fact remains that a symbolism so gross and mixed can help the primitive man to feel more confident of himself— to enjoy the inward assurance that he is in touch with sources and powers of grace that can make him rise superior to the circumstances and chances of this mortal life.[2]

Now compare his views and those being developed at the same time quite independently, and from a very different angle, by Émile Durkheim and his sociological colleagues in France. I have already briefly referred to his *Elementary Forms of the Religious Life*, in relation to the recent lecture by Professor Wynne-Edwards; the quotations I make are from the translation by J. W. Swain (1915). His general conclusion is 'that religion is something eminently social', and that its rites are a manner of acting which takes place in assembled groups in order to excite, maintain or recreate certain mental states within such groups. Whilst his ideas on totemism need not concern us, for

---

[1] *Psychology and Folk-lore* (Methuen, London, 1920), p. 166.
[2] *Head, Heart and Hands in Human Evolution* (Hutchinson, London, 1935), p. 17.

they are by no means universally accepted, so many of his other conclusions are indeed held in respect by the anthropologists of today. Godfrey Lienhardt, in his *Social Anthropology* (1964), writes on p. 40:

> ... French sociologists of Durkheim's school established convincingly that social tradition moulds the individual conscience more fully than even the most self-conscious members of a society usually recognize. Different societies exhibit different *patterns* of thought, different 'collective representations' as the French called them, and these collective representations are the object of specifically sociological study ... Social anthropology has become a study of such differences in proportion, aiming finally perhaps — in Durkheim's own words — 'to reach the scientific facts under the level of the unscientific'.

Lienhardt also pays warm tribute to Marett, in his Preface, 'especially in the field of religion'.

I want particularly to point out the similarity of Durkheim's conclusions to those of Marett regarding the effects of religion, although his approach and explanation are quite different. We have just heard Marett say that religion makes primitive man feel more confident of himself, that it gives him an assurance that he is in touch with 'powers of grace that can make him rise superior to the circumstances of this mortal life'. Durkheim, in his concluding chapter, writes (p. 416):

> The believer, who has communicated with his god, is not merely a man who sees new truths of which the unbeliever is ignorant; he is a man who is *stronger*. He feels within him more force, either to endure the trials of existence, or to conquer them. It is as though he were raised above the miseries of the world, because he is raised above his condition as a mere man; he believes that he is saved from evil, under whatever form he may conceive this evil. The first article in every creed is the belief in salvation by faith.

He goes on to say that it is hard to see how a mere idea could have this efficacy: however much we may consider such a god worthy of being loved or sought after, it does not follow that we ourselves feel stronger afterwards. By the religious act there must, he believes, be some releasing of energies superior to those we ordinarily have at our command, and 'some means of making these enter into us and unite themselves to our interior lives'. For him it is not just an interior force but something that comes from outside the self, that *enters in to us*—a power that is generated by the assembling of members of the tribe or cult for religious exercises:

> Whoever has really practised a religion knows very well that it is the cult which gives rise to these impressions of joy, of interior peace, of serenity, of enthusiasm which are, for the believer, an experimental proof of his beliefs. The cult is not simply a system of signs by which the faith is outwardly translated; it is a collection of the means by which this is created and re-created periodically. Whether it consists in material acts or mental operations, it is always this which is efficacious.

He then goes on to make this important statement:

> Our entire study rests upon this postulate that the unanimous sentiment of the believers of all times cannot be purely illusory. Together with a recent apologist of the faith [William James] we admit that these religious beliefs rest upon a specific experience whose demonstrative value is, in one sense, not one bit inferior to that of scientific experiments, though different from them.

Here we see him, like James to whom he has just referred, agreeing that the reality of religion rests upon the evidence of experience. He goes on to say much more about the development of religion as a social force. Many, who perhaps have not read Durkheim sufficiently carefully, have thought, I believe, that his theory of religion is one linking it simply to a *mechanistic* interpretation of the evolution of man as a social animal. Nothing could be further from the truth, as is clearly shown when he says, 'it is necessary to avoid seeing in this theory of religion a simple restatement of historical materialism: that would be mistaking our thought to an extreme degree'. He then explains what whilst he regards religion as something essentially social, and believes that social life depends upon its material foundation just as an individual's mental life depends upon his nervous system, there is what he calls a *collective consciousness* which is, he says, 'something more than a mere epiphenomenon of its morphological basis, just as individual consciousness is something more than a simple efflorescence of the nervous system'. This indeed is his idea of God, and he makes it clear in one of the last paragraphs of his book (p. 444) that he considers it to be a power which is beyond the individual.

> ... the collective consciousness is the highest form of the psychic life, since it is the consciousness of the consciousnesses. Being placed outside of and above individual and local contingencies, it sees things only in their permanent and essential aspects, which it crystallizes into communicable ideas.

What a phrase that is—the consciousness of consciousnesses. It reminds me of a remarkable passage by that eminent biologist, Professor J. B. S. Haldane (one which I shall refer to again on p. 206), where he says, '... if the co-operation of some thousands of millions of cells in our brain can produce our consciousness, the idea becomes vastly more plausible that the co-operation of humanity, or some sections of it, may determine what Comte called the Great Being'.

Durkheim's views on religion are important to us particularly for the emphasis he places both on the *evidence of experience* and— in company with Marett—on the feeling that man has of being under the influence of *a power that raises him above the miseries of the world*. He is surely wrong, however, in thinking that such feelings are only to be gained through social gatherings; other evidence will show that such collective actions are not essential to their manifestation. Let us recall those well-known words of Professor A. N. Whitehead:

> Religion is what the individual does with his solitariness ... and if you are never solitary, you are never religious. Collective enthusiasms, revivals, institutions, churches, rituals, bibles, codes of behaviour, are the trappings of religion, its passing forms. They may be useful, or harmful; they may be authoritatively ordained, or merely temporary expedients. But the end of religion is beyond all this.[1]

And William James had indeed emphasized this very point a quarter of a century earlier; in his *The Varieties of Religious Experience* (p. 31), after explaining that he will not be dealing with institutional religion, ecclesiastical organization or systematic theology, he writes (and the italics are his), 'Religion, therefore, ... shall mean for us *the feelings, acts and experiences of individual men in their solitude, so far as they apprehend themselves to stand in relation to whatever they may consider the divine.*'

I have heard quoted in support of Durkheim's view the famous saying of the founder of the Christian religion, which begins, 'When two or three are gathered together in my name ...'; it should be remembered, however, that he was also reported to have said, 'When thou prayest, enter into thine inner chamber and having shut the door, pray to thy Father which is in secret ...' We shall see from the evidence, I believe, that what may be called spiritual awareness has not been confined to just one of these two approaches.

In returning to Marett for a moment, there are two further points to make. One is that he emphasized that the components of awe, fear, admiration and wonder are so often found to be combined in primitive religions; these, as we shall see on p. 89, are in fact the main elements that go to make up what the German theologian Rudolf Otto much later termed the sense of the

[1] *Religion in the Making* (Cambridge University Press, Cambridge, 1926), pp. 16–17.

numinous,[1] or, as expressed in the title of the English edition of his famous book, *The Idea of the Holy*. The other is that he called attention to the fact that the passions and practices associated with religion are by no means always a good thing, and have at times led societies into terrible by-ways; he ends one of his Gifford Lectures, *Faith, Hope and Charity in Primitive Religion*[2] (p. 90), with these words:

> Thanks to the grosser forms of the sacrificial rite, the middle religions—not those of savages so much as those of the half-civilized peoples—reek of blood like a shambles ... As psychologists, then, we must not be content to speak together in whispers about the lust or the cruelty that found their way into the religious complex together with the noblest of the human tendencies. Let us honestly proclaim that religious emotion is ambivalent, exciting the mind at once for better and for worse. At times, then, man is apt to think that he has reached the heights when he has merely touched the lowest depths of his spiritual nature.

I now come to two modern and quite outstanding examples of research into the religious feelings of peoples of primitive culture, made by anthropologists who went to live with the tribes they studied and got to know them so well that they could analyse their thoughts and behaviour to a remarkable degree. The peoples concerned are neighbouring, cattle-herding tribes, the Dinka and the Nuer, of the Southern Sudan. I doubt if there exist any more careful studies of the intimate religious life of social groups of present-day people than the accounts of these two tribes; indeed, I doubt the existence of any comparable studies: not since, I believe, the remarkable records of the tribes of Israel in the Old Testament have we had anything like them. Through the painstaking work of two eminent social anthropologists we now know

[1] Marett's discussion of this first appears in an essay in *Folk-lore* in 1900 which was reprinted in his volume, *The Threshold of Religion* (Methuen, London, 1909), whereas Otto's volume, *Das Heilige*, was not published until 1917.

[2] Clarendon Press, Oxford, 1932.

more of the religious feelings of these particular peoples than we do of those of any social communities, either urban or rural, in our modern Western society. Just as the researches of the students of animal behaviour are showing us the springs of action of animals living under natural conditions, so it is that these examples of field anthropology are illuminating for us the nature of religious experience in its unsophisticated state. Among the Dinka and Nuer tribes we find religion developed apparently from their own *experience* and not by contamination from external missionary sources. In just a few paragraphs it is impossible, of course, to give anything more than the merest sketch of the nature of their religious life, but enough, I hope, to indicate its significance for our discussion; these two pieces of field research are, I believe, key studies in the development of our natural-history approach to the idea of God.

I will take the Dinka religion first because it is, I feel, not so highly developed as that of the Nuer; the study was made by Dr Godfrey Lienhardt, Lecturer in African Sociology at Oxford, and published in his book, *Divinity and Experience: The Religion of the Dinka* (Clarendon Press, Oxford), in 1961. The essence of their religion is the existence of a spiritual element which they encounter in many different forms in their surroundings and life; Lienhardt calls them *Powers* rather than spirits, but they are not to be thought of as forming a separate 'spirit-world' of their own. The Dinka think in terms of a broad division into 'that which is of men' and 'that which is of Powers', and their religion is concerned with the interrelations of these two different natures in the single world of their own experience. When talking about their religion they most frequently use a word (*nhialic*) which literally means 'up' or 'above' and may sometimes be used for 'the sky', but it is also referred to as 'creator' and 'father', and prayers and sacrifices are offered to it. For some purposes it could well be translated as God, yet this, as Dr Lienhardt points out, will hardly do, for while it is used sometimes to mean a Supreme Being, it can also denote the collective activity of a multiplicity of beings; he therefore translates it as Divinity.

This seems to be the core of Dinka religion – the belief that their world of experience is permeated with Divinity; it is, Lienhardt says, concerned with 'a relationship between men and ultra-human Powers, between the two parts of a radically divided world'. Although they speak of sky-Powers, for them Divinity is one; if they knew what it meant, they would, says Lienhardt (p. 156), 'deeply resent being described as "polytheistic"'. And again he says (p. 157), 'Divinity ... transcends the individual ... This theme is frequently stressed in Dinka invocations and hymns:

> ... and you, Divinity, I call you in my invocation because you help everyone and you are great towards [in relation to] all people, and all people are your children ...'

Here then we again find this feeling of receiving help from a power, from Divinity, beyond the self.

The religion of the neighbouring tribe, the Nuer, examined with so much understanding by Professor Sir Edward Evans-Pritchard in his book, *Nuer Religion* (1956), has developed on to a higher and more philosophical plane than that of the Dinka. With the Nuer individual prayer and communication with the Deity is a common practice, whereas for the Dinka, who as a rule make group supplications, individual prayer is a rarity. It is indeed extraordinary that the Nuer, with so simple a culture, should have reached such a high level in their religion and that they should, as far as we know, have done so quite independently of any contact with Judaism or with Christian influences. Their philosophy, essentially of a religious kind, 'is dominated by the idea of *Kwoth*, Spirit'. This, as it cannot be directly experienced by the senses, is defined by them only by referring to its effects and by the use of symbols and metaphors. If the Nuer are asked what Spirit is thought to be like in itself, they make no claim to know. 'They say', writes Sir Edward, 'that they are merely *doar*, simple people, and how can simple people know about such matters? What happens in the world is determined by Spirit and Spirit can be influenced by prayer and sacrifice. This much they know, but no more; and they say, very sensibly, that since the

European is so clever perhaps he can tell them the answer to the question he asks.'

He goes on to discuss different aspects of Nuer religion, and a little later (p. 317) says:

> We can say that these characteristics ... of Nuer religion indicate a distinctive kind of piety which is dominated by a strong sense of dependence on God and confidence in him rather than in any human powers or endeavours. God is great and man foolish and feeble, a tiny ant. And this sense of dependence is remarkably individualistic. It is an intimate, personal, relationship between man and God ... In prayer and sacrifice alike, in what is said and in what is done, the emphasis is on complete surrender to God's will.

The final paragraph of his book is of particular interest for us:

> We can, therefore, say no more than that Spirit is an intuitive apprehension, something experienced in response to certain situations but known directly only to the imagination and not to the senses ... Hands are raised to the sky in supplication, but it is not the sky which is supplicated but what it represents to the imagination ... If we regard only what happens in sacrifice before the eyes it may seem to be a succession of senseless, and even cruel and repulsive acts, but when we reflect on their meaning we perceive that they are a dramatic representation of a spiritual experience ... Though prayer and sacrifice are exterior actions, Nuer religion is ultimately an interior state. This state is externalized in rites which we can observe, but their meaning depends finally on an awareness of God and that men are dependent on him and must be resigned to his will.

Before leaving the social anthropologists I must refer to the Riddell Memorial Lectures[1] delivered in 1934–5 by Bronislaw Malinowski. They are particularly interesting because they show

[1] *The Foundations of Faith and Morals* (Oxford University Press, London, 1936).

a change in outlook of one of the most prominent anthropologists in the first half of the century, one who had for so long appeared as a materialistic rationalist. Malinowski was clearly much influenced by the calamity of the First World War and still more by the events which followed it; he was giving his lectures soon after Hitler came to power. Speaking of anthropology as the comparative science of human cultures, he says the student of human institutions is feeling less and less inclined to confine himself to the so-called primitive or simple cultures: 'he draws on the savageries of contemporary civilization as well as on the virtues and wisdom to be found among the humbler peoples of the world'. For him the real 'scientific task of anthropology' is to reveal the fundamental nature of human institutions, including religion, through their comparative study. He explains in his Preface that whilst he cannot accept any particular revealed religion, Christian or not, even an agnostic has to live by faith— 'in the case of us, pre-war rationalists and liberals, by the faith in humanity and its powers of improvement'. This, however, was a faith 'as rudely shaken by the war and its consequences as that of the Christian', so that he finds himself in the same predicament. He goes on later to express his view that it is no easier for an atheist to study religion than for a deeply convinced believer: the former finds it difficult to study seriously facts which appear as a delusion or a trickery, whilst the other will be looking only for evidence of his own special 'truth'. He pleads for an agnostic, humble 'approach to all the facts of human belief, in which the student investigates them with a sympathy which makes him almost a believer, but with an impartiality which does not allow him to dismiss all [other] religions as erroneous whilst one remains true'. This, surely, is the way in which religion should be examined in the modern world.[1] Malinowski (p. 2) gives us this striking passage:

[1] Ninian Smart in his recent book, *The Religious Experience of Mankind* (Collins Fontana Library, London, 1971; p. 13), makes much the same point which he sums up in the sentence, 'The study of religion is a science, then, that requires a sensitive and artistic heart.'

Beliefs, which we so often dismiss as 'superstition', as a symptom of savage crudeness or 'prelogical mentality', must be understood; that is, their culturally valuable core must be brought to light. But belief is not the alpha and omega of religion: it is important to realize that man translates his confidence in spiritual powers into action; that in prayer and ceremonial, in rite and sacrament, he always attempts to keep in touch with that supernatural reality, the existence of which he affirms in his dogma.

'*His confidence in spiritual powers*' – how reminiscent this is of what all those anthropologists who have studied religion with sympathy have found to be so important. In his final lecture (p. 59), Malinowski shows us how far he has come from the thought of his earlier period: '... religion fulfils a definite cultural function in every human society. This is not a platitude. It contains a scientific refutation of the repeated attacks on religion by the less enlightened rationalists.'

Let us now compare these statements by anthropologists with some by other writers. If it should be felt that this chapter is becoming too much of an anthology of quotations, I can plead that here I am gathering and presenting the evidence upon which I shall later build: collecting views as specimens in the natural history of religion. As a link with the anthropologists let me begin with those of William James to whom Durkheim had referred in the paragraph cited above (p. 77). I shall presently be discussing James's work in relation to psychology but will here make a brief quotation from the philosophical postscript which he added to *The Varieties of Religious Experience*; it represents his summing-up, after he had examined so many examples of such experience:

If asked just where the differences in fact which are due to God's existence come in, I should have to say that in general I have no hypothesis to offer beyond what the phenomenon of 'prayerful communion', especially when certain kinds of incursion from the subconscious region take part in it, immediately suggests. The appearance is that in this phenomenon something ideal, which in one sense is part of ourselves and in another sense is not ourselves, actually exerts an influence, raises our centre of personal energy and produces regenerative effects unattainable in other ways ... I am so impressed by the importance of these phenomena that I adopt the hypothesis which they so naturally suggest. At these places at least, I say, it would seem as though transmundane energies, God, if you will, produced immediate effects within the natural world to which the rest of our experience belongs.

Here he picks out the same factor that has been so prominent in the accounts of primitive religion: that power or influence, call it what we will, that *raises our centre of personal energy, and produces regenerative effects unattainable in other ways*. Now let us compare this statement with one made by another psychologist, Professor Sir Frederic Bartlett of Cambridge, who was giving the Riddell Memorial Lectures in 1950, nearly half a century after James's Gifford Lectures:

I confess that I cannot see how anybody who looks fairly at a reasonable sample of actions claiming a religious sanction can honestly refuse to admit that many of them could not occur, or at least that it is highly improbable that they would occur in the forms in which they do, if they were simply the terminal points of a psychological sequence, every item in which belonged to our own human, day to day world. I am thinking not of the dramatic and extraordinary actions which people who write books about religion mostly seem to like to bring forward. They are rare anyway. I remember the ways of life of many unknown and humble people whom I have met and respected. It seems to me that these people have done, effectively and consistently, many things which all ordinary sources of evidence seem to set outside the range of unassisted humanity. When they say 'It is God working through me,' I cannot see that I have either the right or the knowledge to reject their testimony.[1]

To the naturalist who has an open mind and is not tied to the dogmas of either materialism or theology it may well seem significant that there is an extraordinary similarity in the nature of religion in its simplest form among whatever people — primitive or sophisticated — it may be found. Here is some factor in human life that appears to have a profound effect, something which, if man responds to it, provides him with a power over his difficulties that he might not otherwise have and gives him a feeling of confidence and courage in the face of adversity. Is not this very different from being only a reinforcement of a social code? As I have already said, I do not for a moment deny that religion has often been used as such a reinforcement; what I am suggesting is that fundamentally it has a much deeper significance.

Whatever we may prefer to call this something — whether spiritual power, or God working through us, or psychological motivation — here would seem to be a very significant feature in the make-up of our species. It is the essence of what Aldous Huxley called the Perennial Philosophy, taking the term from Leibniz: 'the metaphysic that recognizes a divine Reality substantial to the world of things and lives and minds; the psychology that finds in the soul something similar to, or even identical with, divine Reality; the ethic that places man's final end in the knowledge of the immanent and transcendent Ground of all being — the thing is immemorial and universal'.[2] His book is a remarkable natural history of the universality of this Highest Common Factor, as he also calls it; since it was first committed to writing more than twenty-five centuries ago, 'the inexhaustible theme', he says, 'has been treated again and again from the standpoint of every religious tradition and in all the principal languages of Asia and Europe'.

---

[1] *Religion as Experience, Belief, Action* (Oxford University Press, London, 1950), p. 35.
[2] *The Perennial Philosophy* (Chatto & Windus, London, 1947), p. 1.

Let us remind ourselves of the universality of this sense of dependence upon a spiritual power. Apart from the example – the supreme example for Christians – of the New Testament, where in the literature of the world will we find man's realization of this assistance more beautifully expressed than in the poetry of the Book of Psalms? 'The Lord is my shepherd ...' (Psalm 23) – 'Restore unto me the joy of thy salvation; And uphold me with thy free spirit' (Psalm 51). Here it is also in an early Stoic prayer: 'Lead me, O God, and I will follow, willingly if I am wise, but if not willingly I still must follow.'[1] Or in the Taittiriya Upanishad of Hinduism: '... if a man finds the support of God, he is free from fear;'[2] or from the Sikh Guru Arjun (1563–1616): 'In whatever he does, the man of God acts with a heavenly air/caught from the constant companionship of God.' (Mascaró, p. 47.) Yet again, take this from the Sufi poets of Islamic mysticism in Persia as exemplified by Jalalu D-Din Rumi: 'What punishment is greater, than to dwell afar from thy Face? Torture not thy slave, tho' he be unworthy of Thee!' (Green and Gollancz, p. 233.) Then from Taoism comes 'He who has his roots in Tao shall never be uprooted. He whom Tao embraces shall never be lost.' (Mascaró, p. 86.)

The similarity of this feeling in so many different faiths was well summed up in the words of Mahatma Gandhi:

> I claim to be a man of faith and prayer, and even if I were to be cut to pieces I trust God would give me the strength not to deny Him, but to assert that He is. The Mussulman says, 'He is, and there is no one else.' The Christian says the same thing, and so does the Hindu. If I may venture to say so, the Buddhist also says the same thing, only in different words. It is true that we may each of us be putting our own interpretation on the word 'God'. We must of necessity do so; ... (Mascaró, p. 101.)

[1] *God of a Hundred Names: Prayers of Many Peoples and Creeds*, collected and arranged by Barbara Green and Victor Gollancz (Gollancz, London, 1962), p. 156.

[2] *Lamps of Fire; From the Scriptures and Wisdom of the the World*, chosen by Juan Mascaró (Methuen, London, 1961), p. 113.

In view of his opening sentence it is well to record that his last words as he was dying under the assassin's bullet are reported to have been 'He, Ram! He, Ram!' ('Ah, God! Ah, God!' – Green and Gollancz, p. 223.)

We have been quoting from the great religions of the world: do they not have a similar ring to the feelings which the anthropologists have found among much more primitive peoples? Look back for a moment to p. 82 and see the translation by Lienhardt direct from the Dinka language: '... and you Divinity ... you help everyone and you are great towards all people, and all people are your children ... ' Or let me now quote a translation by Evans-Pritchard of a Nuer prayer: 'God, thou (who) knows how to support [or care for] souls, support [or care for] our souls' or again, another Nuer expression translated as 'God who walks with you that is, who is present with you'.[1]

Whilst we have been stressing the common feeling of dependence, we should note that there *are* differences. For example, William James draws a contrast between the emotional moods of the Stoic and the Christian. He says that when Marcus Aurelius reflects upon the eternal reasons at the back of things there is a 'frosty chill' about his words which one only rarely finds in Jewish and never in Christian religious writings. Compare, he says, the Roman Emperor's 'If gods care not for me or my children, here is a reason for it,' with Job's cry, 'though he slay me, yet will I trust in him.' For the Stoic, the *anima mundi* is there to be respected and submitted to, 'but the Christian God is there to be loved'.

In any study of religion mention must be made of the concept which the German theologian, Rudolf Otto, called the numinous. He wrote on it at length in his book, *Das Heilige*, published in 1917 (translated as *The Idea of the Holy*, Oxford University Press, London, 1923). Since it has had considerable influence in theological circles I think it well to point out that it is not something only experienced by those embracing the more sophisticated faiths; it appears to be something much more primitive. I have

[1] *Nuer Religions*, pp. 26 and 8.

already briefly mentioned that Marett discussed this same feeling in primitive religion; I will now quote from his first account of it published in 1900:

> ... we must I think ... admit the fact that in response to, or at anyrate in connection with, the emotions of Awe, Wonder, and the like, wherein feeling would seem for the time being to have outstripped the power of 'natural', that is reasonable, explanation, there arises in the region of human thought a powerful impulse to objectify and even personify the mysterious or 'supernatural' something felt, and in the region of will a corresponding impulse to render it innocuous, or better still propitious, by force of constraint, communion or conciliation.[1]

This, I believe, expresses the main core of Otto's concept of the numinous. For Otto the numinous has an objective reality and should not, he says, be regarded as a subjective feeling in the mind; when he speaks of the feeling of the numinous he really means a form of awareness which he would say was neither that of ordinary perceiving nor ordinary conceiving, but a peculiar apprehension of this mystical something—*the* numinous. He insists that it is not itself an emotion like an affective feeling of love, joy or fear; it is something which, he says,

> ... is to be found, in the lives of those around us, in sudden, strong ebullitions of personal piety, ... in the fixed and ordered solemnities of rites and liturgies, and again in the atmosphere that clings to old religious monuments and buildings, to temples and to churches ... we shall find we are dealing with something for which there is only one appropriate expression, '*mysterium tremendum*'. The feeling of it may at times come sweeping like a gentle tide, pervading the mind with a tranquil mood of deepest worship.[2]

[1] See footnote on p. 80.
[2] *The Idea of the Holy* (2nd edn, Oxford University Press, London, 1950), p. 12.

Having quoted Otto's views, we should not forget that William James, writing earlier, expressed this somewhat differently. He stressed that whilst we speak of religious love, religious fear, religious awe, or joy and so forth, they are only man's natural emotions directed to a religious object: for example, he says 'religious awe is the same organic thrill we shall feel in a forest at twilight or in a mountain gorge; only this time it comes over us at the thought of our super-natural relations'.[1] Having said this we should also recall that Otto, as an Appendix to his English edition (p. 215), quoted a remarkable passage from Ruskin describing experiences in his youth felt whilst on the banks of a mountain stream which made him 'shiver from head to foot with the joy and fear of it'; these experiences, says Otto, 'are purely numinous in character'.

It is most likely that different people experience what Otto calls the numinous in different ways according to their varying psychological make-up. One of the components Otto gives prominence to is the 'element of awfulness' — the sense of mystery — which for some people appears to merge into a sense of dread or fear. More important, for I think they are more generally felt, are the feelings which may be grouped under what he calls the 'element of fascination'.

He points out that both the elements of the mysterious and of fascination, in their highest development, lead to mysticism; and he realizes that the numinous is not experienced only by Christians. In discussing the rapture of Nirvana in Buddhism he says that it is only in appearance a cold and negative state; it is actually felt in consciousness 'as in the strongest degree positive', and 'it exercises a fascination by which its votaries are as much carried away as are the Hindu or the Christian by the corresponding objects of their worship'. He tells us of a conversation he had with a Buddhist monk who had been putting before him the arguments for their 'theology of negation' — the doctrine of Anatman and 'entire emptiness' — and how at the end of the discussion he had

[1] *The Varieties of Religious Experience* (Rev. edn, Longmans, Green & Co., 1922), p. 27.

asked him, 'What then is Nirvana itself?' After a long pause came at last the single answer, low and restrained, 'Bliss — unspeakable.'[1]

Gandhi, in discussing the evidence for God's presence, said, 'There is an indefinable mysterious Power that pervades everything. I feel it, though I do not see it. It is this unseen Power which makes itself felt and yet defies all proof, because it is so unlike all that I perceive through my senses. It transcends the senses.'[2]

These feelings of indescribable bliss are, of course, characteristic of all mystical experience. The testimony of the mystics must form a large contribution to the natural history of religion. I take that for granted. An important feature of the whole experience, common to the mystics of all great religious traditions is, in the words of Professor Grensted, 'the complete and self-authenticating character of the "sense of presence" which accompanies it'.[3] Apart, however, from the real mystics, those exceptional characters who reach the higher flight of vision, there are many more who give us the same essential testimony. 'It will be found', said Dean Inge, 'that men of pre-eminent saintliness agree very closely in what they tell us. They ... have arrived at an unshakeable conviction, not based on inference but on immediate experience, that God is a spirit with whom the human spirit can hold intercourse ...'[4]

Elsewhere Dean Inge[5] made a plea for the recognition of a third line of Christian thought which he believes should be regarded as separate from the two main types called Catholic and Protestant, but yet penetrating into them. 'Mysticism and the Christian Platonism which is the philosophy of mysticism', he says, 'are at home in all branches of Christendom.' The influence of this third line of thought has, he believes, been much neglected. Is it not, indeed, related to the *mysterium tremendum* of Otto and, further back, to those similar elements of more primitive religions, as Marett has shown us?

[1] *The Idea of the Holy*, p. 39.
[2] J. Mascaró, op. cit., p. 54.   [3] *The Psychology of Religion* (1952), p. 96.
[4] *Lectures on Christian Mysticism* (1899), p. 326.
[5] *The Platonic Tradition in English Religious Thought* (Longmans, Green & Co., London, 1962).

He points out the remarkable fact, revealed by study of comparative religion, that a new spiritual enlightenment came to all the civilized peoples of the earth in the millennium before Christ: first felt in Asia, but then in Greece and Southern Italy in the sixth and fifth centuries B.C. It is the recognition of what seemed to them to be an unseen world of eternal values behind the material world of the senses. It was this mystical faith, held first by the Pythagoreans, that Plato developed to give it a firm foot-hold in the west. From its revival in the Neoplatonism of the Roman Empire, it passed into the theology and philosophy of the Christian Church. Dean Inge shows how, after its eclipse in the Dark and Middle Ages, it burst out with a new and exuberant life in the Renaissance writers, appearing again in the seventeenth century with the little group of Cambridge Platonists; later, with the movement of emancipation following the French Revolution, came 'the remarkable outburst of Platonism in English poetry ... the names of Shelley, Wordsworth and Coleridge will occur to everybody, and the last two of these were, and wished to be, considered, religious teachers.'

At the end of his two-volume the *Philosophy of Plotinus*, Inge gives a valuable summary of Neoplatonic characteristics which I feel have a special relevance for our natural history of religion. Among other things, he says, 'Neoplatonism ... floats freely of nearly all the "religious difficulties" which have troubled the minds of believers since the age of science began. It is dependent on no miracles, on no unique revelation through any historical person, on no narratives about the beginning of the world, on no prophecies of its end ... and it requires no apologetic except the testimony of spiritual experience ...'

The Platonic tradition brought us to Wordsworth, who in turn brings us to a consideration of the 'Worship of Nature' — to borrow the phrase from the title given by Lord Clark to the eleventh in his series of brilliant television-programmes on Civilization.[1] He begins it by reminding us that for almost a

[1] *Civilization: a personal view* (B.B.C. Publications and John Murray, London, 1969), p. 269.

thousand years the chief creative force in Western civilization was Christianity. 'Then in about the year 1725,' he says, 'it suddenly declined and in intellectual society practically disappeared.' In his previous contribution, which he called 'The Smile of Reason', he had shown how the Christian inspiration was being eroded by science and philosophy. 'Of course', he continues, 'it left a vacuum. People couldn't get on without a belief in something outside themselves, and during the next hundred years they concocted a new belief which, however irrational it may seem to us, has added a good deal to our civilization: a belief in the divinity of nature.'

The love of nature is mixed with the wonder of it. It is this sense of wonder which is the source of inspiration of the true scientist as much as it is for the artist. The late Professor Walter Garstang, the zoologist, wrote[1] of Wordsworth:

> His delight in Nature was closely akin to that which has inspired many naturalists, and his early sympathy with science was so clearly indicated that a slight turn of Fortune's wheel at the critical period of his life might well have made a naturalist of him instead of a poet. In 1785, when a happy schoolboy of fifteen, he eulogised from his Lakeland home:

> > those Elysian plains
> > Where, throned in gold, immortal Science reigns,
> > And where Truth teaches
> > 　　　　　　　the curious soul
> > To search the mystic cause of things
> > And follow Nature to her secret springs.

After recounting the period of scepticism and hopelessness which came to Wordsworth after his return from France at the time of the Revolution, Garstang goes on to show how he had to regain his earlier vision of the all-embracing unity of things be-

[1] 'Wordsworth's Interpretation of Nature', *Nature*, vol. 117 (Supplement, 16 Jan. 1926), pp. 1–8.

fore he could accomplish anything. His achievement in poetry came only after he had once again obtained 'a true view of life as a whole, of man in relation to Nature, even as a part of Nature'. After referring to the arguments which illustrate this in Words-worth's *Prelude*, he goes on to say

Nature, indeed, was to Wordsworth a universal symphony, a harmony of infinitely varied elements, appealing to man through every sense and gateway to the heart ... The musical analogy crops up incessantly:

No sound is uttered, — but a deep
And solemn harmony pervades
The hollow vale from steep to steep
And penetrates the glades.
A soft eye-music of slow-waving boughs.

I am sure that a sense of a Divine element in the universe be-comes more real to countless lovers of the countryside through nature herself than through formal religious practices based upon any dogmatic theology. The 'belief in the divinity of nature' was manifest not only in literature but in art; no one could know this better than Lord Clark himself who, after pointing out that both Turner and Constable appeared at the same time, goes on to say that 'Wordsworth's real kinship was not with Turner but with Constable ... They both grasped nature with the same physical passion ...' After saying they both loved their own places, and never tired of the things which had entered their imaginations as children, he quotes Constable as saying, 'The sound of water escaping from mill-dams, old rotten banks, shiny posts and brickwork — these scenes made me a painter — and I am grateful.'[1]

Art certainly comes into a natural history of religion. That great scientist, the late Sir Cyril Hinshelwood O.M., President of the Royal Society, who was also an artist (although perhaps

[1] Op. cit., p. 280.

only his close friends knew that he painted, and painted very well),
said this:

> Men draw and paint, carve and model because they feel an
> inner need to do so. This inner need is an elaboration of the
> urge to explore, grasp and understand what is around them;
> to control these things, indeed, though not in the crude sense
> of exerting magic power, but in the deeper one of making
> them part of the self ...
>
> There is a profound human instinct to seek something
> personal behind the processes of nature: and people are led
> both by intellectual and by emotional paths to the contem-
> plation of religious questions ... in their desire for com-
> munion with the universal and personal they pursue what I
> suppose through the ages they have meant by the vision of
> God ...[1]

In all these considerations we are certainly faced with a great
mystery. Is there something showing itself through nature —
something like the numinous which Otto believed to have an
objective reality beyond the individual and yet to be felt by
means other than through the physical senses? Clearly our impressions of objects, colours, sounds and scents which may give
us those Wordsworthian feelings in regard to nature, reach us
through our sense organs. And even the most elementary knowledge of science will tell us that these apparently solid bodies,
colours, sounds and so on do not actually exist in the form in
which we seem to see and hear them; they are in reality whirling
particles or waves of energy. It is the picture produced by the
rays of light focused on the retina — and *modified* in the brain —
that we see, not the outside world as it really exists. Objects
would seem to take solid form and beauty only in the mind. The
lens of the camera, of course, also focuses the light-vibrations to
give us the picture which we recognize as a representation of the
three-dimensional world of our experience.

[1] *The Vision of Nature* (Fifteenth Eddington Memorial Lecture, Cambridge
University Press, Cambridge, 1961), pp. 12 and 29.

I would now like to make a slight digression to compare the beauty of the world as seen by man, with that seen by animals. We have already noted (p. 34) how the same artistic principles which are apparent to man have also been at work in the evolution of the complex patterns of animal camouflage, i.e. were produced in Darwinian fashion by the action of other predatory creatures. The devices of illusion which deceive animal perception are exactly the same as those which fool the mind of man. The colours, shape, fragrance and supply of nectar of the flowers have been brought to perfection by the same gradual process of selection; this time, however, it is brought about by the greater success of those that are the more attractive to the insects which, in visiting them to get the honey, bring about their essential pollination. Different colours and different scents appeal to different types of insects or birds; the blues and purples appeal more to the bees, whereas the yellows are more attractive to the two-winged flies; and humming-birds go for the red and orange blossoms of the tropics. Let us note once more that these forms of selection are again brought about by an appeal to the *senses* of animals; is it not perhaps significant that the shapes and colours so essential to the beauty of the flowers, beauty which so excites our own aesthetic pleasure, were brought about—long before man sought to improve them by selective breeding (actually millions of years before man himself appeared)—by the attraction they have had for other sentient animals. I may at first be laughed at if I suggest that the same quality of beauty which enraptures the nature-lover and the cultivator of flowers may be there in the very heart of the natural world—part of its mental system—part of what I would call its signs of Divinity. Solomon in all his glory was not arrayed liked the lilies of the field; and they are the product of insect selection!

Just as the glories of a sunset, the scent of wild thyme, or the sound of the wind rushing through the long, dried grass on a hillside may fill us with a natural joy, so also the light through coloured glass, the smell of incense, the music of a choir or organ may similarly be the means of creating the sense of the numinous within us. Are they not, then, both – the numinous and the love of nature – simply subjective emotions confined to the individual mind? Most psychologists and philosophers of today would say yes. Let us, however preposterous such a proposal may appear to be, for the present keep an open mind on this question. I have a feeling, a hunch, that perhaps there was more in that part of the philosophy which Plato gave the world – namely the concept of the general ideas – than most of us moderns think.

There could hardly be a better summary of Plato's main thesis than that given by Sir Richard Livingstone.

> ... his philosophy starts in a logical problem; how, in the changing manifold world around us, are we to attain knowledge? How do we know that these pieces of wood of different shapes, which we call tables, are tables? In virtue of what do we call beautiful the countless different things to which we apply the word? The reply is: we have this knowledge in virtue of a general 'idea' of a table, and a general 'idea' of beauty; these 'ideas' exist not on earth, or for our senses, but for our minds, and, to Plato's mind, have a higher reality than the fleeting objects of sense.
>
> ... Why do we take pleasure in beauty – a beautiful face, violets scattered along a hedge foot, the words of a great poet? What value have these beautiful things? These are real problems ... For Plato, Soul controls the world and is the supreme reality. It exists, entirely pure, as God; but it is also present in all living things, more dominant in some than others, though in all mixed with and impeded by earthly elements.[1]

Before coming specifically to his concept of ideas, let us note how Plato's philosophy of the supreme reality (or God) being in all living things has its relation, as Dean Inge emphasized, to the springs of religious feeling. We shall come back to this when we consider the new branch of theology (new since Inge's day) – that of the so-called process theology – in chapter 11 (p. 204).

[1] *The Pageant of Greece* (Clarendon Press, Oxford, 1923), p. 284.

What I am now about to suggest, regarding his philosophical scheme of ideas, is highly speculative. So long as we realize this, there perhaps is no harm in it, for speculation is the fuel of progressive thought; in science it is by the testing of hypotheses, their rejection or acceptance, that advance is made. Surely we cannot believe that in 1975 we have solved all the problems relating to mind, consciousness, religious feelings and the appreciation of beauty. Now supposing, just supposing, that there should be found to be something – and when we come to the curious field of parapsychology we shall be discussing this – something in the notion of shared subconscious mental elements, perhaps like the collective unconscious postulated by Jung, in which over long periods of time common ideas have been built up with the evolution of conceptual thought, is it not just possible that Plato's world of ideas may in fact be *really there*, existing beyond our individual minds in a continuing pool of ideas shared subconsciously, in a kind of telepathic way, between the living members of the race? Individuals would come and go, but the subconscious mental stream of shared ideas of what is beautiful or good, or red or blue, or even of God, goes on. I am only pleading that, however fantastic the original speculations of Plato may be thought at present to be, we should not yet dismiss them out of hand. Let us keep an open mind. It is just possible that they might form a really important part in our future biology of God.

We must now turn to what the psychologists have to say about religion and the idea of God, and come back a little later to a further consideration of its possible origin and significance when we have looked more closely at certain biological facts, particularly those relating to animal behaviour.

6. The impact of psychology

Evidence such as that which I sketched in the last chapter has failed as yet to make any considerable impression on the uncommitted intellectual world for two main reasons. One is the still widely-held idea already discussed, that the Darwinian theory necessarily points to materialism, a view which I hope I have shown is by no means inevitable; the other, which has proved to be an even greater block to the consideration of religion as a possible reality, has come from psychology and particularly that of the psycho-analytical school associated with the name of Freud.

The destructive force of these Freudian ideas lies in the fact that they not only recognize the feelings we may have of being in contact with some higher element above the normal self—a personal-like element which some may call God—but they actually point to it, claiming, however, that it is really something else: something not distinct from, but a part of, our own mental make-up.

Freud's theory was indeed a shock which was made still more powerful by the marvel of the new world that his psycho-analytical methods had revealed: the hidden world of our own subconscious being. He did not 'discover' the subconscious mind as is so often implied in some of the more popular writings; he uncovered it. Its existence had been well recognized and much discussed before his time, but it was he who, as it were, took the lid off to show us its complex, and seemingly in part most unpleasant, character and to demonstrate its influence on our lives. It was the impact of these surprising new doctrines that nipped in the bud the growing recognition of the work of two earlier psychologists who were beginning to influence religious thought in the first decade of this century: William James and Edwin

Starbuck, to whom I briefly referred in my opening chapter (p. 20) as the pioneers in the systematic study of religion. We must consider them before coming to Freud and the other psycho-analysts, and then we shall see (p. 107) how it was that Freud effectively delayed the development of the ideas of James and Starbuck which at first had seemed to hold out so much promise.

Edwin Starbuck was Professor of Psychology at Stamford University when he wrote *The Psychology of Religion* (1899), but earlier he had been James's pupil at Harvard. In writing a preface to this book James relates how Starbuck had tried to interest him in a study of religious feelings by using the questionnaire method and how James had tended at first to pour cold water on it; he did so because he thought that 'an undue number of answers from egotists lacking in sincerity might come', and further that 'so few minds have the least spark of originality that answers to questions scattered broadcast would be likely to show a purely conventional content', and so on. He then goes on to say that, having read a large proportion of Starbuck's raw material and the proofs of his book, he had completely revised his views and now considered that the results amply justified his methods. So impressed, indeed, was James that he was fired to make his own classic studies, although not on such statistical lines. He acknowledges in the introduction to his own book that his work was largely based upon the records of the experiences which Starbuck had collected and subsequently made available to him.

I will only sketch the nature of Starbuck's work. It is essentially a study of the growth of religious consciousness and a large part of it compares the emotional feelings of those who, during adolescence, experience a sudden conversion and those who undergo a more gradual religious development without any such dramatic change. In the case of conversion, what comes out so clearly is a changed relationship to the world; he finds three main types of attachment: the desire to help and have love for other persons, to have a closer relation to God (sometimes expressed as 'to Christ'), and a closer relation to nature. He summarizes his results as percentages of the total number of cases in which any such changes in relationship were mentioned in the records of experience; we see how remarkably similar are the figures for the two sexes: for boys the percentages for the three types of change mentioned are 70, 47 and 34 respectively, and those for girls are 70, 49 and 31.[1] He points out that they express the lowest possible estimate since they represent only those examples in which the feeling was sufficiently prominent to receive explicit mention. 'It is clear', he says, 'that an immediate result of conversion is to call a person out of himself into active sympathy with the world outside ...', and to become 'one with the Power that makes for Righteousness'.

In his statistical analyses Starbuck is beginning to move towards a science. He gives graphs comparing the number of conversions taking place among boys and girls of different ages; while that for the boys shows a more or less steady rise and fall with a peak at the age of 16, that for the girls is by no means so regular. Starbuck suggests a possible biological difference: that in female adolescence there may be more complex physiological conditions relating to conversion than in boys. From his study of those who experience no such sudden crisis, but nevertheless recall points in their development when spiritual awakenings began, he concludes that conversion is not a unique experience but has its correspondence in the common events of religious growth. Going on to the religious life of adults, he summarizes his findings from his studies of their experience by saying that 'the line along which religion grows, when represented in terms of feeling, is expressed as dependence, reverence, sense of oneness with God, and faith', and that these feelings 'all express relation between the self and the larger life outside'.

In passing from Starbuck to William James we should note that both were dealing with material which was almost without exception Protestant in nature and predominantly of an evangelical kind. It is important, as James himself has said,

---

[1] In some cases a person might mention a new awareness of, say, both God *and* Nature so that the percentages given add up to more than a hundred.

that similar collections should be made from Catholic, Jewish, Mohammedan, Buddhist and Hindu sources; and, of course, from those who do not profess allegiance to any particular faith. As we shall see in chapter 10 (p. 183), this is part of the developing programme which my colleagues and I are now undertaking in the new Religious Experience Research Unit at Oxford.

James's *The Varieties of Religious Experience* is perhaps the greatest single contribution yet made in the scientific spirit to the natural history of man's religious life. Whilst much of it, too much perhaps, deals with the more abnormal side of man's religious development, he sketches out a broad chart of the field and presents his own conclusions. The fact that various psychologists and philosophers have so many different ways of conceiving what religion is—relating it to dependence, fear, sex, the feeling of the infinite and so on, should, he says, make us doubt whether what is called the 'religious sentiment' can really be one specific thing; he regards it as a collective term, embracing many sentiments which may be aroused in alternation, and sees in it nothing of a psychologically specific nature.[1]

Later on (p. 53), he says that 'were one asked to characterize the life of religion in the broadest and most general terms possible, one might say that it consists of the belief that there is an unseen order, and that our supreme good lies in harmoniously adjusting ourselves thereto'.

After giving a number of examples of the feeling of God's close presence, he goes on to discuss 'the convincingness of these feelings of reality'. They are, he maintains, as convincing to those who have them as any direct sensible experience can be and are usually much more convincing than 'results established by mere logic ever are'. In discussing the opposition in philosophy between such mysticism and rationalism, we see the importance which he himself placed on the subconscious mind before the influence of Freud; after praising the rationalistic system for

[1] See his views already summarized on p. 91, in relation to the idea of the numinous.

giving us among other good things the fruits of physical science, he says (p. 73):

> If you have intuitions at all they come from a deeper level of your nature than the loquacious level which rationalism inhabits. Your whole subconscious life, your impulses, your faiths, your needs, your divinations, have prepared the premises, of which your consciousness now feels the weight of the result; and something in you absolutely *knows* that that result must be truer than any logic-chopping rational-istic talk, however clever, that may contradict it.

James wrote a great deal about the subconscious although he often called it the subliminal mind, taking the phrase from F. W. H. Myers who — again before Freud — spoke of a threshold (*limen*) of consciousness, a level above which sensation and thought must rise before it can enter into our conscious life. 'Perceiving', said Myers, 'that these submerged thoughts and emotions possess the characteristics which we associate with conscious life I feel bound to speak of a *subliminal consciousness*.'[1] Myers developed his ideas particularly in relation to psychical research, whereas James, although deeply interested in that subject,[2] was specially concerned with the bearings of the sub-liminal mind upon religion. 'In it', he writes (p. 484), 'arise whatever mystical experiences we may have ... In persons deep in the religious life, as we have now abundantly seen, — and this is my conclusion, — the door into this region seems unusually wide open; at any rate, experiences making their entrance through that door have had emphatic influence in shaping religious history.'

James has much to say regarding two types, the 'healthy-minded' and the 'sick soul', sometimes referring to them by the

[1] *Human Personality and its Survival of Bodily Death* (Longman, Green & Co., London; published posthumously in 1906, but written before 1900, the year he died), p. 15.

[2] Gardner Murphy and Robert O. Ballon, *William James on Psychical Research* (The Viking Press, New York, 1960).

terms used by Francis Newman,[1] the *once-born* and the *twice-born*. 'In their extreme forms ... the two types', he says, 'are violently contrasted ... ' but those 'human beings whom we oftenest meet are intermediate varieties and mixtures'. It is just the same with Jung's psychological types of extraversion and introversion, and indeed they are most likely related, as suggested by Professor Grensted.[2] By the *extravert* Jung meant, of course, the more outward-looking individual mainly interested in the outer objective world, and the other, the *introvert*, is the more inward-looking person, turned in upon himself to dwell more upon his own subjective feeling. In giving examples of the state of the sick soul James quotes extracts from Tolstoy and Bunyan and points out that they could and did find something welling up within them by which such extreme sadness could be overcome: 'a stimulus, an excitement, a faith, a force that re-infuses the positive willingness to live'. Is there not something here which may be of biological significance?

It is, of course, impossible in just a few paragraphs to do more than suggest something of the sweep and scope of James's book; in leading up to his conclusions I will quote an earlier passage where he has again been discussing the *subconscious*. After declaring that the whole development of Christianity in inwardness has consisted in the greater and greater emphasis attached to the crisis of self-surrender, he goes on to say (p. 211):

Psychology and religion are thus in perfect harmony up to this point, since both admit that there are forces seemingly outside of the conscious individual that bring redemption to his life. Nevertheless psychology, defining these forces as 'subconscious', and speaking of their effects as due to 'incubation', or 'cerebration', implies that they do not transcend the individual's personality; and herein she diverges

[1] Francis Newman was the brother of Cardinal Newman, but almost his direct opposite in being eager for a faith which would include whatever is best in all the historical religions.

[2] *The Psychology of Religion* (Oxford University Press, London, 1952), p. 60.

from Christian theology, which insists that they are direct supernatural operations of the Deity. I propose to you that we do not yet consider this divergence final, but leave the question for a while in abeyance ...

Here James touches on what is surely the most important issue. Do these forces which play so vital a part in man's religious life belong only to his subconscious mind or do they indicate some extra-sensory contact with some Power beyond the self? That is the question. If the findings of so-called parapsychology should come to be recognized as true – if they should indicate that mental activity does indeed extend beyond the localized mind, either conscious or subconscious – would they lend any support to the latter view? It is these '*if's*' that are so tantalizing; we shall consider them again later on p. 121.

Towards the end of his book, after discussing mysticism and the more psychological and philosophical aspects of his subject, James returns to this crucial problem – do those religious forces, or do they not, transcend the individual's personality? He writes:

> ... confining ourselves to what is common and generic, we have in *the fact that the conscious person is continuous with a wider self through which saving experiences come*, a positive content of religious experience which, it seems to me, *is literally and objectively true as far as it goes*. If I now proceed to state my own hypothesis about the farther limits of this extension of our personality, I shall be offering my own over-belief ...
>
> The further limits of our being plunge, it seems to me, into an altogether other dimension of existence from the sensible and merely 'understandable' world. Name it the mystical region, or the supernatural region, whichever you choose. So far as our ideal impulses originate in this region ... we belong to it in a more intimate sense than that in which we belong to the visible world, for we belong in the most intimate sense wherever our ideals belong. Yet the unseen region in question is not merely ideal, for it produces effects

in this world. When we commune with it, work is actually done upon our finite personality, for we are turned into new men, and consequences in the way of conduct follow in the natural world upon our regenerative change ... But that which produces effects within another reality must be termed a reality itself, so I feel as if we had no philosophic excuse for calling the unseen or mystical world unreal.

God is the natural appellation, for us Christians at least, for the supreme reality, so I will call this higher part of the universe by the name of God.[1]

We are reminded here of the views of another psychologist, Professor Sir Frederic Bartlett, whom I quoted on p. 86. The whole tenor of James's massive study points to the reality of man's contact with a Power beyond the conscious self; of this he gives innumerable examples. 'It would seem', he wrote (also p. 86), 'as though transmundane energies, God, if you will, produced immediate effects within the natural world to which the rest of our experience belongs.'

The year when this was published was 1902. The century opened with the hope of a new natural theology, one based upon psychology and the systematic study of man's experience, which might provide a faith in harmony with the scientific age. James's explanation was rapidly gaining ground. The conversions of St Paul or St Augustine were seen as the emergence into consciousness of the results of 'unconscious cerebration'. 'It all seemed simple enough,' wrote Professor Grensted. 'The full complexity of the process, which the development of Freud's analytic theories was to reveal, did not then appear.'[2] It was Freud and the calamity of the First World War that for the time being stifled the influence of James, and made so many leaders in religion abandon all hope of a natural theology and turn to the new dogmatism of Karl Barth, who, as we shall see presently (p. 198), denied man's reason in matters of religion and pinned

[1] p. 515 (italics in the original).
[2] *The Psychology of Religion* (1952), p. 53.

his faith on the Scriptures as the very word of God. The threads however are being taken up again.

Before coming to Freud's revolutionary ideas concerning the subconscious, it may be well to remind ourselves of the important part played within our *conscious* mind by what we call our sentiments. We are all aware of the three elements which are continually being linked together in a chain of conscious mental activity. There is *cognition*, our knowledge or awareness of some object, or maybe some abstract idea; then there is our feeling about such an object or idea, such as pleasure or fear, which is better called an *affective state*, rather than feeling, so that it will not be confused with the organic sensations of say 'feeling tired' or 'feeling hungry', and third in the chain comes our purposive action or *conation* as it is technically called. An example of such a chain would be that we notice (cognition) some evidence of, say, carelessness or cruelty, which makes us feel angry (the affective state) and we decide to do something about it (conation). Now our character or personality largely depends on our sentiments and our affective or conative dispositions. By disposition we mean our tendency to experience a particular type of conscious state in certain circumstances, such as being angry in the example just given. Our sentiments are our acquired affective dispositions in relation to particular objects or actions, as in being always made angry by carelessness or cruelty. Our distinct sentiments are not thought to be inherited, like an instinct, but to be acquired and developed as a result of experience.

The overwhelming importance of the growth of the sentiments for the character and conduct of individuals has been well stressed by Professor William McDougall.[1] 'In the absence of sentiments our emotional life would be a mere chaos, without order, consistency, or continuity of any kind; and all our social relations and conduct, being based on the emotions and their impulses, would be correspondingly chaotic, unpredictable and unstable.' Whilst every adult has a variety of sentiments, there

[1] *An Introduction to Social Psychology* (15th edn, Methuen, London, 1920), p. 159.

is usually one, or only a small number, which are dominant and round which the lesser ones are organized; these major sentiments will be of various kinds in different people, such as personal ambition, love of home and family, devotion to research, love of sport or a country life and so on. It is here that religion may form an outstanding feature in a person's life. 'When we know what a man's dominant sentiments are, we know a great deal about his character.'[1]

People of similar intelligence and knowledge may react quite differently in the same circumstances, as we may often see in discussions round a committee table; they have different dispositions and sentiments, or, in other words, they differ in personality. We have already referred to the two main personality-types distinguished by Jung, the *extravert* and the *introvert*; each of these he divided into four sub-types according to whether thinking, feeling, sensation or intuition were more prominent in a particular person's way of life. While we must not attempt to follow these distinctions here, we should not forget their likely importance in the interpretation of religious behaviour. Although the sentiments appear to be acquired in development, it seems that individuals vary very much in their propensities towards certain types of personality; it is now being suggested by several psychologists that the tendencies towards this or that type may perhaps be linked with inherited physical characteristics.

Now let us return to the subconscious. Whilst it had already been much discussed by some other psychologists, Freud was its great explorer; it was he who, by the new techniques he employed, discovered so much of its nature that we did not know before. From his study of mental patients, particularly those suffering from hysteria, he developed his new ideas and then, by putting them to the test, effected cures which appeared to support much of their validity. He showed that our subconscious mind is full of impulses which have been repressed so that we are no longer aware of them; although they do not enter our conscious thought,

---

[1] Rex and Margaret Knight, *A Modern Introduction to Psychology* (6th edn, University Tutorial Press, London, 1959), p. 190.

they may nevertheless influence our lives in an unsuspected manner.

We have to distinguish between suppression and repression. We are continually suppressing impulses of a minor kind as when we refrain from doing something we want to do because we feel it may inconvenience other people; such suppression is harmless. If, however, we continually suppress the more powerful impulses, this may lead to their repression: to their being kept locked away in our subconscious, hidden yet able to affect our behaviour in various subtle ways. Some of these are what the psychologists call *rationalizations*: chains of argument, often specious, invented by our minds to justify our performing some particular act, or holding some belief, which is actually motivated by some repressed subconscious cause. Even without such invented rationalizations we are told that much of our ordinary behaviour may reflect our unconscious motives without our being at all aware of it. We should recognize how likely it may be that some of our religious ideas and practice may be influenced in this way, and we should always be on our guard against it.

How much of Freud's contribution is a part of true science and how much untested speculation? Not being a psychologist by training, I should not attempt to answer such a question with any appearance of authority. I can only say that some of his ideas appear to have stood up to the test of experiment, as already stated, when he successfully applied his theories of repression to the treatment of patients; but what of his many other ideas? We must judge them as we come to them and in each instance I shall indicate my own views (for what they are worth) as to their value for our theme.

Freud explains the sense of sin, which plays such an important part in the religion of many people, as being due to the feelings of guilt caused by a repression (or a *complex*, as the Freudians like to call such a repressive system) covering up shame or self-reproach. This may well be so; looking, however, at repression in relation to religion from another angle, we should remember the remark made by Professor Joad, to which I have already referred (p. 23), that the frustrated desires for spiritual experience may be just as important in the subconscious as repressed sex.

There is an alternative to repression. Instead of continually suppressing some powerful impulse, such as a sexual one, to force it into repression, we can divert—or sublimate, to use the technical term—the psychic 'energy' (for want of a better word) into other channels such as art, athletics, social work and so on. Freud actually believed that civilization is the result of this very process: a continual sublimation of the more primitive impulses towards activities of higher social value. Again, this may well be so in part, but it is not, I believe, the whole story.

The main impact of Freud upon ideas concerning the nature of religion comes from his concept of the development of the subconscious in the life of the individual and its relation to the conscious mind. In the new-born child he thought there would be no such division. He looked upon the babe as an out-and-out egoist, full of animal impulses which it strives to satisfy; as these are one by one curbed by the discipline of training, he supposed that they were driven into repression, into a part of the mind which became separated off to receive them: the subconscious. Thus, in his original scheme, there were just these two divisions, with the repressing 'censor' in the conscious part pushing the unwanted impulses into the subconscious. Very soon, however, he realized that this censor could not be entirely conscious because he found by his methods of psycho-analysis, particularly in dream-interpretation, that its action was often of quite a childish kind; when for example such repressed impulses were brought to the surface by analysis, the patient might often find them no longer shocking, except by nursery standards, but in fact amusing.

Freud now divided the mind into three: the *ego*, the *super-ego* and the *id*. The ego, of course, is the rational conscious mind—the self that we are aware of; the id is the unconscious mass of repressed impulses; and the super-ego, taking the place of the censor in his former scheme, is the ruthless repressor which is in part unconscious like the id, and, like it too, is a survival from infancy. The super-ego acts not according to a reasoned system of morality

worked out by the mind, but by a code, often crude and irrational, laid down in the childhood discipline imposed by the
parents or adults in charge: a code accepted without being understood. 'It is in the course of our development', wrote Freud,[1]
'that external compulsion is gradually internalized, in that a special
mental function, man's super-ego, takes it under its jurisdiction.
Every child presents to us the model of this transformation; it is
only by that means that it becomes a moral and social being.'

It is here that we may make an interesting comparison between
the views of Freud and those of Waddington which we have already discussed (p. 67); not only did Waddington suggest that,
in the evolution of culture, the child has been turned into one
who will accept the authority of his elders but that the authority
becomes, by the same selective forces of evolution, incorporated
into the mental make-up of man as his conscience, converting
him into the ethical animal. There is thus, up to this point, some
similarity between the super-ego of Freud and the conscience
envisaged by Waddington as an evolutionary product. Here
again I think Freud makes an important contribution, but very
soon he introduces something markedly different into his scheme
which I find much less convincing and against which there is, I
believe, some substantial evidence.

Largely as a result of their psycho-analysis of *adults*, and based
very little upon the actual observation of children, Freud and his
immediate followers came to believe that in infancy there must
be a period of highly emotional erotic life with feelings of love,
jealousy and hate as powerful as those of later adult life. The infant
boy, they tell us, wants his mother entirely to himself and wishes
the father disposed of, and the girl similarly wants the father; for
a period, they say, the child jealously hates the parent of opposite
sex, but then the mood passes giving way to fear of retaliation
and a desire to propitiate the offended one. This is the supposed
development of the well-known Freudian Oedipus complex. As
the child gets older, it is said that the sexual impulse passes into

[1] *The Future of an Illusion*, trans. by W. D. Robson-Scott (Hogarth Press and
Institute of Psycho-Analysis, London, 1928), p. 18.

latency and feelings of guilt and remorse are likely to develop with a wish for forgiveness. A further important process is thought to take place. The boy wants to be strong and wise like his father and so comes to identify himself with him; he introjects the father-image into himself. Here the father-identification becomes a source of the super-ego: the authority of the father is now built into the mind as a part of the censoring power.

The very early sexuality assumed in this process may be important, but one cannot help wondering in the light of other evidence if it has not been much exaggerated. Is it not possible that Freud and some of his followers have themselves been the victims of the influence of their own subconscious ids? They state that the infant boy commonly gets the idea that the father wants *physically* to destroy his power to love the mother, that is, actually to castrate him. I must say that I find this almost incredible; could the infant at this early age have any idea of castration at all? The evidence against Freud's view of the importance, or indeed of the existence, of this very early sexuality comes from those who have made detailed observations of the infant life of normal children. As already stated, Freud's own evidence came very little from actual child observation, but from his interpretation of adult mental states by psycho-analysis. Professor C. W. Valentine in his *The Psychology of Early Childhood*[1] says that, from the careful study of his own children, he can find 'no evidence whatever... for such an Oedipus complex', and he goes on to show that most of the evidence is directly contrary to it. The girls preferred their mother more than the boys did after the age of about two years when according to Freud they should be turning to the father and the boys to the mother. The first strong attachment of both boys and girls, he says, is for the mother—the nurse and comforter. Later, after the age of two or three, there is some attraction towards the father 'who can enter into their play, and if more severe at times, can provide the most exciting delights'; this, however, showed more in the boys than in the girls whose taste and interests are 'even at this early age

[1] (3rd edn, London, 1945), p. 316.

more in line with the mother's than with the father's'. The extensive work of Jean Piaget on child psychology also gives little support to Freud's ideas associated with his Oedipus complex.

It should also be mentioned that Freud and his followers refer back to the period of early childhood some of those sexual abnormalities which may appear in later life; and that there are some psychologists who would explain a good deal of religious behaviour in terms of these deviations. There are, however, studies other than those of psycho-analysis which I believe have a more important bearing on these possible elements in religion; since these have their roots in much deeper biological levels, they will be better discussed in relation to animal behaviour in chapter 8.

Freud first applied his ideas to religion in his *Totem and Taboo* (1913), where he sought to explain the idea of the internalized father-image as an evolutionary product arising in the beginnings of human culture. Apart from being a speculation derived from theories of early tribal life which have been much criticized by anthropologists, it incorporates the now generally abandoned notion that what goes on in an individual's mental development reflects what has actually happened far back in racial history. This latter idea was based in turn upon a theory which was widely held by biologists at the time he wrote his book but which is now discredited or at least interpreted in quite a different way: the theory of recapitulation. Towards the end of the book he actually admits that this is a far-fetched idea.[1]

Freud's later and more mature ideas regarding the nature of religion deserve more serious consideration. For him the origin of the super-ego as a result of the Oedipus complex and the subsequent development of the child mind is sufficient to explain all of man's religious yearnings and beliefs. These ideas are worked out in *The Future of an Illusion*. Without accepting the Oedipus argument in full, I think it likely that there is a great deal of truth in his concept of the nature of the super-ego being the internalization of external authority; to me, however, it seems more

[1] *Totem and Taboo*, new translation by James Strachey (Routledge & Kegan Paul, London, 1960), pp. 157-8.

reasonable that this process came about in the early evolution or man's cultural system in the manner suggested by Waddington.

Be that as it may, I will say at once that I am not a bit disturbed by the idea that our conception of God as a person—Our Father which art in Heaven—should be based upon our early childhood–parent relationship. I think it likely that Freud has indeed explained a great deal regarding this personification, but I do *not* believe that he has destroyed the power and the glory of religious experience. Freud has not shown to be illusory, as he imagines, the *whole* concept of Divinity; what he has done is to change our ideas from those formed over three thousand years ago, of a great, invisible potentate, Jehovah (Yahweh). It is certainly a fundamental change in our idea of God, but one no more, or no less, radical than that which substituted the Copernican solar system for the optical illusion that the sun went round a central earth.

Today there are members of the Church who are not only able to accept a great deal of Freud's teaching without abandoning their theistic position but find that his doctrines explain some of those features of Christian theology that have hitherto been less attractive to them. One of these is the Rev. Dr R. S. Lee who has made a special study of this theological relationship in his book, *Freud and Christianity* (1948).[1] He believes that some of the theological ideas regarding sin and the atonement can be explained in Freudian terms. In projecting the father upon the world and arriving at the idea of God, man may be inclined not only to carry over the protecting father but also the father as a source of danger—and here he accepts a good deal of the Oedipus complex. 'God is, as it were, the enemy ... counting every transgression against us ... In his eyes we are so bad that there would be no hope of escaping His everlasting wrath if it weren't that His Son is on our side, and, by accepting punishment for our sins while

[1] As witness of the wide range of views now held in the Church of England we may note that Dr Lee, when he published his book, was Vicar of the University Church and was awarded his Oxford D.Phil. for the thesis upon which his book is based.

himself innocent, satisfies the demands of God and procures pardon for us.' This, he goes on to complain, is 'religion much more occupied with sin than with love'.

Whilst we cannot be concerned within the scope of this book with discussing various theological doctrines, whether of Christianity or of other religions, it is interesting from a biological standpoint to see how Dr Lee relates the Freudian concepts of the ego, the super-ego and the id to Christian teachings. He points out that there is a large section of Christianity which concentrates in its moral teaching on developing a sense of sin.

> The Ego is made to feel its unworthiness, its failure to live up to its ideal, and is discouraged in every way from rebelling against the Super-ego. As an acknowledgement of its guilt all sorts of penances are encouraged – rigid discipline of life, fasting, acts of duty. Duty is the keynote of this moral system. The result of this training frequently is to develop a sort of vicious circle. By cultivating a sense of sin and strengthening the dominance of the Super-ego the Ego is made to feel its guilt and unworthiness more intensely. But the more guilty the Ego feels the more strongly the Super-ego attacks it, thereby further increasing the feeling of guilt. So the circle goes on until the Ego is almost paralysed from undertaking novel action. The only brake on the process is obtained through penances and mortification, even to the extent of self-inflicted pain.[1]

Whether or not we believe that the Oedipus complex is as important as the Freudians make out, it does look as if Dr Lee is right in seeing this cultivation of the sense of sin and guilt as an increasing domination of the super-ego. How then does he believe that Christianity can escape from this psychological nightmare? He believes that Jesus taught a different kind of religion, one in which the ego – the real self – must not be so dominated, but must judge by insight what is good. The God of the Pharisees, he says, 'was simply a projection of the unconscious father-image,

[1] *Freud and Christianity* (James Clarke, London, 1948), p. 162.

the core of the Super-ego', as opposed to the real God 'with whom Jesus was concerned and Who could be seen in the lilies of the field, in the farmer sowing his crop, or a father welcoming home a long-lost son, that is, a God discoverable by the Ego'.[1]

In picking out only a few points from his detailed reconciliation of the principles of Freudian psychology with those of Christian theology, I merely want to show how this new psychology may change our attitude to theological problems. I cannot myself pretend to be a psychologist and I am not laying down any dogmatic views. I am only saying that these are ideas which, together with some of those of Jung, must be carefully examined in building any future and more scientific theology. We must be careful, however, not to be carried away in our enthusiasm for this or that hypothesis which appears at first sight to offer some solution to our difficulties; each must be weighed carefully, and as much evidence as possible sought, before we incorporate them into our scheme of thought. Whether we accept them fully or not, the ideas of Freud must make us always on the lookout, lest the arguments we are putting forward in support of this or that belief may be false rationalizations invented by our minds to suggest a reasonable explanation for some view which is really based upon some deeper, hidden and quite different motive.

Having given such prominence to the Freudian theories, I should now turn to those of Jung. Yet, in spite of the view expressed by Professor Grensted that 'In general Jung's psychology has proved far more tractable in the study of religious behaviour than the more rigid and more dogmatic position taken up by Freud and his followers', I must confess that I find it exceedingly difficult to understand him, especially in his works devoted to religion: *Psychology and Religion* (1938) and *Modern Man in Search of a Soul* (1934). He appears to speak in riddles. Particularly do I find it almost impossible to obtain a consistent account of what he really means by his concept of the collective unconscious and the influence of the archetypes. Sometimes he seems to say that this collective unconscious is linking together all

[1] Ibid., p. 153.

individuals *now*, in the present, as when he implies that the individual is (again in the words of Grensted) 'regarded as an out-
cropping of the collective impersonal unconscious'; at other times,
however – and this is perhaps what he usually means – he implies
that our unconscious minds extend back in time and link together
with others in the past as we trace back the branching lines of
our descent, with the archetypes forming basic, far-off ancestral
features. Turning to his autobiography, *Memories, Dreams, Reflections* (1963), one finds it full of religious feeling, but again, at
any rate for me, how intangible it all is. In his chapter on 'Late
Thoughts' (p. 310), he says, 'We know that something unknown,
alien, does come our way, just as we know that we do not ourselves *make* a dream or an inspiration, but that it somehow arises
of its own accord. What does happen to us in this manner can be
said to emanate from mana, from a daimon, a god, or the unconscious.' And then he goes on to say,

> I prefer the term 'the unconscious', knowing that I might
> equally well speak of 'God' or 'daimon' if I wished to express
> myself in mythic language. When I do use such mythic
> language, I am aware that 'mana', 'daimon', and 'God' are
> synonyms for the unconscious – that is to say, we know
> just as much or just as little about them as about the latter ...
> The great advantage of the concepts 'daimon' and 'God'
> lies in making possible a much better objectification of the
> *vis-à-vis*, namely, a *personification* of it. Their emotional
> quality confers life and effectuality upon them. Hate and
> love, fear and reverence, enter the scene of the confrontation
> and raise it to a drama. What has merely been 'displayed'
> becomes 'acted'. The whole man is challenged and enters
> the fray with his total reality. Only then can he become
> whole and only then can 'God be born', that is, enter into
> human reality and associate with man in the form of 'man'.
> By this act of incarnation man – that is, his ego – is inwardly
> replaced by 'God', and God becomes outwardly man, in keep-
> ing with the saying of Jesus: 'Who sees me, sees the Father.'

I find this somewhat obscure; does he mean that what we call God is confined to being a part of the collective unconscious or does he believe that God can as well transcend it? We all remember the famous remark he made when, being interviewed on television shortly before he died, he was asked, 'Do you believe in God?' 'I don't believe,' he replied. '*I know.*' Let me end my chapter by giving one more quotation from Grensted; whilst I doubt if it makes Jung's views any clearer it at any rate emphasizes the need to go further in our studies.

> We have not progressed a step beyond the often criticized conjectures of William James when he stated as his 'over-belief' the view that at the outer margin of the subliminal self we may be in direct touch with a 'more of the same kind', not ourselves, and that we may regard that meeting-place as the sphere of Divine action upon us. There is an obvious similarity between this view and the more elaborate hypotheses put forward by Jung.[1]

It is this feeling of a Power beyond the self, for which we have seen much evidence from primitive religion onwards, that seems to make it so much more than just the censoring authority of Freud's super-ego. I agree that this is also an over-belief, but it is one which is being strengthened both by our new, accumulating evidence of the nature of religious experience, and by the findings of those studies now being grouped together under the term parapsychology. It is to the latter that we now turn in our next chapter.

[1] *The Psychology of Religion*, p. 83.

7. *The parapsychological paradox*

Parapsychology is the modern name for what has generally in the past been called psychical research. I use it because in some minds the older term tends to be associated mainly with investigations into haunted houses, spiritualism, poltergeist manifestations and so forth. Whilst such studies have formed a part of parapsychology, most of the modern research is not at all concerned with these matters.

The majority of workers in parapsychology today are either attempting to provide experimental evidence to substantiate or otherwise the alleged occurrence of what is now usually termed extra-sensory perception (E.S.P. for short) or, if they regard it as already established, as many do, to find out more about its nature and mode of operation. There are thought to be three types of such perception which, as the term 'extra-sensory' implies, are considered to occur without the normal physical organs of sense being involved – in other words to be in some way directly perceived by the mind. These are *telepathy* (or thought-transference, as it was originally called) which is the supposed perception by one person of the thoughts which are in the mind of another, *clairvoyance*, which is the supposed perception of some object or event by other than normal sensory means, and *precognition*, knowledge of future events. Some parapsychologists are also investigating the claims of what is called *psychokinesis* (PK for short) which is distinct from E.S.P. in being the opposite of perception, it being the alleged influence of the mind upon the movement of physical objects.

As I have already indicated, I believe there is sufficient evidence in the records of personal experience – and there is more to come (in chapter 10) – to show that religion, whatever explanation we may give to it, is a very real part of man's nature. Why then, it may be asked, am I bringing in this new factor at all, when it has not yet been recognized as a part of established science? My reason is this. If the evidence can be so experimentally improved as to lead to telepathy being accepted by science as a fact, then it could have a profound effect upon the way the modern humanist world looks upon religious experience. The evidence is indeed increasing, and the purpose of this chapter is to show how the scientific method has been advancing in this very difficult field, and to present some of the more important results.

As I suggested in the last chapter, perhaps the greatest question from the psychology of religion is whether the power that may be called God is entirely within the individual—deep in the sub-conscious—or is it, at least in part, transcendent. If it could be shown beyond doubt that one mind may communicate with another mind by *other* than physical means—that in fact elements of our mental life may extend beyond the physico-chemical structure of the brain—then it would *at least* lend plausibility to the idea that our minds, subconscious or conscious, might be in touch with some larger mental field, possibly like that of the shared subconscious suggested by Jung, beyond our individual selves, or perhaps with something inconceivably greater. It would be an important step towards the scientific recognition of a non-material mental world in which perhaps the numinous — to use Otto's term for the 'mysterium tremendum' of religion—might be thought to lie.

Whilst I shall be dealing mainly with telepathy, we shall see that a consideration of it is not as straightforward as we might at first sight suppose. We soon find ourselves drawn into a dis-cussion of some other curious features which may make the argument appear even more of a digression than I have suggested. Nevertheless whether these other strange things may have a direct bearing on our theme or not, whatever their cause, they indeed tell us—if we are prepared to look at them—that we live in a far more surprising universe than that which the materialists have envisaged.

There are several reasons, certainly four, why so few scientists have been inclined to examine the claims of parapsychology. Firstly, its experimental results cannot yet be repeated at will. Have not the laws of science been built up from observations and experiments which can be repeated anywhere by anyone provided he is working under similar conditions? We can well understand the feelings of those who say they will not consider the findings of this new research until they can always be so repeated. There are, however, many facts of natural history which cannot *always* be demonstrated at will. Animals may usually behave in this or that fashion under particular experimental circumstances, but we cannot be certain that they always will; when this happens we assume that there is something in the animal's behaviour we do not yet understand, and we go on seeking more evidence. Many of the conclusions from the experiments made in the field of animal behaviour depend not upon getting invariable responses but upon there being more positive than negative results in statistically significant proportions. The same is becoming true of parapsychology.

Secondly, comes the question of fraud. There has undoubtedly been deception detected by psychical research among some of those who have claimed to have unusual gifts; this, however, was mainly in the early days before the application of the more rigorous controls. The atmosphere of mystery which surrounds these reported phenomena excites the credulous and makes them easy victims of the charlatans who delight in pretending to have 'supernatural' gifts because it gives them a feeling of superiority and power over their fellow men. This is certainly a most unpleasant side to the subject, but no more so than the corresponding element in the beginnings of chemistry; we know that this great science sprang from the cradle of alchemy, some of whose exponents were genuinely striving after the transmutation of metals and the elixir of life, while others were rank imposters.

The third objection is one which is the most difficult of all to deal with. Those who work in this new field often seem to want a particular result. Surely, say the critics, this cannot be the scientific attitude; are not these experimenters biased? Not that

they willingly distort the evidence to support their case — but unconsciously may they not tend to disregard this, and give undue
prominence to that, and so arrive at false conclusions? If we say
science must only be concerned with experiments about whose
results we have no emotional feeling, then we can never hope to
come to real understanding of living things. Parapsychology does
indeed appear to hold out a promise of results which may release
us from a philosophy of materialism which an intuition seems to
tell us is false. We may be interested in investigating the paranormal for this very reason; if so we would do well to admit it
frankly, and if possible seek the collaboration in our work of
someone who holds quite the opposite view.[1]

The fourth reason why some scientists will not examine the
evidence for telepathy is because they believe it is incompatible
with the rest of science, and therefore must be impossible and so
a waste of time. If we do refuse to look at it for this reason are
we not just as bigoted as those who condemned Galileo for his
experiments and conclusions?

It is the philosophers, rather than the scientists, who up to the
present have looked at the evidence and realized its importance.
Professor H. H. Price, when he was Wykeham Professor of Logic
at Oxford, said, 'Telepathy is something which ought not to
happen at all, if the Materialistic theory were true. But it does
happen. So there must be something seriously wrong with the
Materialistic theory, however numerous and imposing the
normal facts which support it may be.'[2] And the late Professor
C. D. Broad, who was Knightbridge Professor of Moral Philosophy at Cambridge, made the same point.

Telepathy ... is now an experimentally established fact.
There is also ample evidence of sporadic telepathic hallu-
cinations in connection with deaths, accidents, illnesses and
other causes ... Now it is scarcely possible to reconcile with

[1] I have discussed this difficult problem at greater length in my book, *The Living Stream.*
[2] *Hibbert Journal*, vol. 47 (1949), p. 105.

these facts the epiphenomenalist theory of mind and body which is commonly ... assumed without question by most scientists and many philosophers. These facts are therefore of the utmost philosophical importance.[1]

It was another eminent Cambridge philosopher, Professor Henry Sidgwick, who, as the first President of the Society for Psychical Research (which I shall refer to as the S.P.R.) said in his inaugural Address in 1882, '... it is a scandal that the dispute as to the reality of these phenomena should still be going on, that so many competent witnesses should have declared their belief in them, that so many others should be profoundly interested in having the question determined, and yet that the educated world, as a body, should still be simply in the attitude of incredulity.' Since that date—over ninety years ago—this pioneer Society under a long line of distinguished Presidents has, through its members, carried out investigations with the highest standards of scholarship in this difficult field, and published over a hundred volumes of research; yet until quite recently the scepticism or indifference of the intellectual world at large has remained practically unchanged, except for one class of phenomena.

In the first volume of its *Proceedings* the Society gives a list of subjects which it felt it would be important to investigate. The first two are given as follows:

> 1. An examination of the nature and extent of any influence which may be exerted by one mind upon another, apart from any generally recognised mode of perception.
>
> 2. The study of hypnotism, and the forms of so-called mesmeric trance, with its alleged insensibility to pain; clairvoyance and other allied phenomena.

And there follow a number of other subjects, such as apparitions, disturbances in houses reputed to be haunted, an inquiry into the phenomena of spiritualism and so on. Whilst it is with the first item that we are here concerned, it is interesting to note that, of

[1] *Enquiry*, vol. 1 (1948), p. 1.

all the subjects listed, it is hypnotism alone which has so far received general scientific acceptance, and perhaps only because it was found to have important applications in medical and psychiatric practice.

Whilst the phenomena of hypnotism are accepted, I doubt if they are really understood any more than are those in other fields of psychical research. Under hypnotic suggestion a subject can be made to experience an hallucination, in some cases an apparition of a person who is not present but which appears to be as solid as in normal visual perception. The whole field of vision appears to be mentally reconstructed in detail just as is the imagined scene in a vivid dream.¹ Equally interesting and remarkable are those cases in which, for example, a person under hypnosis can be caused to suppose that he is being touched with a red-hot iron when actually only a finger was laid upon his skin. 'The man winced violently, and slowly a blister formed under which there accumulated a large quantity of fluid giving the exact appearance of a blister by heat.'² Although these phenomena and others equally strange are well attested in the appropriate medical journals, they are only very rarely discussed in biological and general scientific circles. When better understood, they must surely throw more light on the problem of the mind-body relationship.

But now for telepathy—and here at the outset I should like to distinguish two types. One is that in which a person is supposed to have extra-sensory knowledge of the thoughts, sometimes quite complex thoughts, in the minds of other people, or maybe an impression of some emotional state of another person in danger, illness or crisis. The other type is that of guessing which of a small number of known objects (or symbols), such as only

¹ *Hypnosis, Fact and Fiction* (Penguin Books, Harmondsworth, 1959), by F. L. Marcuse, Professor of Psychology in Washington State University, and many research papers in the *British Journal of Medical Hypnotism*, especially vol. 10, pp. 35-42, and vol. 11, pp. 41-7.
² Taken from Dr J. A. Hadfield's account in *The Lancet* vol. 2 (1917), p. 678, quoted in Dr D. J. West's *Psychical Research Today* (Rev. edn, Penguin Books, Harmondsworth, 1962), p. 192.

five different kinds of card, another person may be looking at, as in the experiments that have constituted so much of modern E.S.P. research. I wish to emphasize this distinction because, for the reasons I am about to explain, I am beginning to doubt whether the latter type can really be called telepathy at all.

For close on forty years most of the experimental work has been conducted by using the card-guessing technique developed by Professor Rhine and his colleagues at Duke University in America; a vast number of such experiments have now been made in most countries of the world. The great advantage of this technique is that the results may readily be subjected to quantitative statistical analysis. Whilst these at first sight *appeared* to provide statistical support for telepathy, I found myself having misgivings. My difficulty was, and still is, that although I am sure that the statistical tests applied to the card experiments of Rhine and others are demonstrating *card-guessing*, I cannot be sure that they are in fact demonstrating what I myself understand by the term, telepathy. It very soon came as a shock to me, when examining the accounts of the experiments, to find that Rhine and others were getting exactly the same kind of results as they got in their so-called telepathy tests, i.e. above-chance results, when certain subjects were guessing cards entirely by so-called 'clairvoyance' — i.e. guessing the order of the cards in a pack before they have been seen by anyone. In fact, there were more of the latter than the former. I may be prejudiced — I expect I am — but I confess I find it much easier to imagine one mind being in touch with another mind — two elements of a similar kind — than to conceive of a mind being able to know what kind of design is on the underside of a card which has never yet been made visible to any living mental system. The former, if true, is certainly marvellous, but the latter looks like magic.

The difficulty in distinguishing between so-called telepathy and clairvoyance in the card-guessing experiments has recently been well expressed by the Cambridge psychologist, Dr R. H. Thouless, when he writes, 'We do not indeed know whether these are two different processes or whether they are merely two names we give to the same process under different conditions of operating.'[1] And he goes on to say that, while it might be better simply to call them both some form of extra-sensory perception, even this would be objected to on the ground that it implies that the process is some kind of perception. He then suggests that 'One may avoid this implication by coining an entirely new term which carries no implications whatever, and say that a *psi*-process is taking place.' But then he adds, 'If, however, one uses the term "extra-sensory perception", one is more likely to be generally understood.' I see what he means, but we certainly don't understand it, and, as he himself indicates, we don't know that it *is* perception at all.

Since we cannot doubt the above-chance results that have been obtained in what now amount to thousands of experiments carried out in most of the countries of the world, I have sometimes been tempted with an awful thought. It is one I hardly like to admit; yet I think it illustrates our quandary in regard to these card-guessing experiments. Is it possible that what all these experiments with cards are really demonstrating is something very different from most of parapsychology: a measurement of what we *in our ignorance* more usually call luck—that some people *are* in fact, at any rate at times, much luckier, *whatever that may really mean*, at card-guessing than others? Why do I utter such a thought? It is indeed a shocking thing for a scientist to say; I say it *only* because I want to make the point that this should in fact be no *more shocking* to the scientific position of today than the fact now statistically established by significance tests that there *are* a number of people who are able to guess correctly—more often than can be accounted for by the present theory of probability—which cards are which, in a pack they haven't seen. The idea of luck and that of clairvoyance are *equally shocking* to our present scientific view of the universe. Is there something about card-guessing and perhaps the supposed 'influencing' of dice (for most of the psychokinesis experiments have been done with dice)

[1] *From Anecdote to Experiment in Psychical Research* (Routledge & Kegan Paul, London, 1972), p. 35.

which is just as queer as what we call luck, but which scientific law has not yet got hold of?

Then there is precognition, the guessing of cards that would be looked at a few seconds later, which seems equally difficult to imagine, but is apparently demonstrated by just such similar statistics. And there are some people guessing cards who have repeatedly and significantly scored with *below*-chance results—i.e. more often wrong than they should be by chance—a curious and difficult matter to explain. Whilst I think many of us had felt uneasy at the similarity of the evidence for these very different alleged phenomena, it remained for Mr G. Spencer Brown of Trinity College, Cambridge, to suggest the alternative and simpler hypothesis that all this experimental work in so-called telepathy, clairvoyance, precognition and psychokinesis, which depends upon obtaining results above-chance, may really be demonstrating some single and very different principle. He believes[1] that it may be something no less fundamental or interesting—but not telepathy or these other curious things—something implicit in the very nature and meaning of randomness itself. I am not mathematically competent to pass judgment upon his views. Let me say at once, however, that if most of this apparent card-guessing and dice-influencing work should turn out to be something very different from what it is usually supposed to be—something perhaps quite different from Spencer Brown's speculation—it will not have been a wasted effort; it will have provided a mine of material for the study of a very surprising feature of the universe, perhaps something even more fundamental than telepathy!

To reinforce this point, and to get away from the card-guessing, I may in passing briefly mention the remarkable machine devised by Dr Helmut Schmidt,[2] by which subjects who have precognitive ability can guess which of several lamps are going to be automatically switched on entirely at 'random' by the pulses of radiation coming from a piece of radioactive strontium; in other

[1] *Probability and Scientific Inference* (Longmans, Green & Co., London, 1957).
[2] 'Precognition of a Quantum Process', *Journal of Parapsychology*, vol. 33 (1969), pp. 99–108.

words, the machine generates random events without any human intervention. Only a few people out of a hundred gave positive scores, but the three best subjects with whom he worked predicted which bulbs would light up, in a long series of trials, with a performance which could only be obtained by chance with a probability of one in five hundred million. The scientific journal the *New Scientist* (15 Oct., 1969), in commenting on this work, says, 'These experiments are believed to represent as rigorous a proof of the reality of extra-sensory perception as the phenomenon would seem to permit.' The particular significance of these experiments, if confirmed and repeated, would lie in the fact that they appear to show that a human being can actually foretell not just the switching on of a lamp by some person in the future, but can predict the emission of particles at a sub-atomic level, for it is *this* that the lamps are really indicating! A strange universe indeed.

Then what are we to think of coincidences? Are they just *sheer coincidence*, as is usually said, meaning just chance accidental similarities? Or is there something more deeply significant about them as has been suggested by Jung in his principle of 'Synchronicity' or by Kammerer in his so-called 'laws of Seriality'? The views of both of these men have been discussed by Arthur Koestler in his book, *The Roots of Coincidence* (1972). In some experiments I had myself been making to test the possibility of telepathy, using the picture technique, I thought at first I had hit upon a new method of studying spontaneous telepathic effects. It turned out, however, that controls which my colleague, Robert Harvie, and I devised demonstrated equally striking effects by coincidence. Sheer chance? Perhaps, perhaps not. And what do we mean by chance? Arthur Koestler joined us in a discussion of this problem in a more recent volume, *The Challenge of Chance* (1973), in which he presents a remarkable collection of anecdotal cases, and Robert Harvie shows some curious probability effects. In our Religious Experience Research Unit at Oxford we receive a very large number of personal accounts of such experience, and many of them refer to examples of

E

coincidence. In relation to religion it is interesting to recall the saying attributed to Archbishop William Temple: 'When I pray coincidences happen; when I don't, they don't.'[1] There are many religious people who would support his view.

The more one looks at parapsychology the more puzzling it becomes. We may well be in doubt about some of it, but it cannot, I believe, in face of the evidence be entirely dismissed out of hand just because it is so queer. What *are* we to say of it as a whole? We might perhaps describe it as something 'conflicting with preconceived notions of what is reasonable or possible', or again that it consists of 'seemingly absurd though perhaps really well-founded statements'. Both these expressions are selected from the four meanings which are given by the *Concise Oxford Dictionary* (1928) for the word *paradox*; parapsychology is indeed the intellectual paradox of the twentieth century.

Now let us leave this more enigmatic side of the subject and come to what I like to regard as 'real' telepathy: the supposed transmission of thoughts or emotions from one person to another by other than sensory means. It is work in this field that, as I have already suggested, may be important in providing the evidence to convince the psychologists that mental activities do in fact extend outside the limits of the physical brain. Whilst it is proper that we should stress the experimental evidence, it is also right that we should not forget the enormous number of cases of apparently spontaneous telepathy, often over long distances, which are recorded in the volumes of the *Proceedings of the S.P.R.* Such anecdotal examples, however, are only convincing to those who have been directly concerned in them; I have myself had two such experiences (described in *The Challenge of Chance*, p. 12) which I believe can only be explained by telepathy. Having said that, I shall now select three experimental studies each of which approaches the subject from a somewhat different angle. It is only by looking at them in some detail that we can appreciate their significance.

[1] Quoted by Douglas Steere in *Dimensions of Prayer* (Darton, Longman and Todd, London, 1965), p. 85.

First I shall take a long series of investigations conducted by the late L. L. Vasiliev, Professor of Physiology in the University of Leningrad, and described in detail in a book published in Russia in 1962 and translated into English in the following year.[1] They are concerned with telepathic hypnotic suggestion and are in fact an elaboration of some much earlier experiments made in France, to which I must briefly refer, because they and Vasiliev's work confirm one another. In 1886 Professor Janet and Dr Gilbert claimed to have induced hypnotic sleep in 'a healthy peasant woman 50 years of age', by telepathic suggestion carried out at distances of over a quarter of a mile, in 19 out of 25 experiments. Later Professor Charles Richet, the famous physiologist, confirmed their work with the same subject by obtaining successful results in 16 out of 36 trials when the subject was separated from him by a distance of 1 to 2 km.[2] Similar experiments, but over a much shorter distance, were then demonstrated in Russia by Professor K. I. Platonov in 1924 and witnessed by Professor Vasiliev. In 1933 the latter was joined by I. F. Tomashevsky in experiments with two hysteric patients, Ivanova and Fedorova, who had proved to be particularly good at being made to go to sleep and to wake up in response to telepathic mental suggestion. During the tests they were instructed (by ordinary hypnosis) to keep rhythmically squeezing a rubber bulb filled with air and connected to a recording (kymograph) machine. As soon as sleep was induced the oscillations on the graph were reduced to a straight line but began again as soon as the subject was awakened and resumed her squeezing of the bulb. The experimenter marked the graph at the point when he made the suggestion so that the exact time taken to produce sleep could be measured, and similarly with awakening. A series of trials were first made with the experimenter and subject in the same room when the average length of time taken in going to sleep and that of awakening were 6·25 and 2·94 minutes respectively for Ivanova and 1·89

---

[1] *Experiments in Mental Suggestion* (Institute for the Study of Mental Images, Church Crookham, Hampshire, 1963).

[2] Op. cit., p. 75, and Appendix 4.

and 1·67 for Fedorova. Trials were then made with the experimenter in another room and now the corresponding times were 4·05 and 3·67 minutes for Ivanova and 3·87 and 3·60 for Fedorova. (The higher figures for Ivanova in the first series were due to her taking much longer in the first three tests than in the later ones.)

Now comes the more interesting part. Vasiliev tells us that in Russia it was first supposed that telepathy must be produced by some radio-like electromagnetic wave system and that he was only given support for his work when it was thought that it might have military use. He tells us the amusing story of how the authorities were alarmed by reports in a popular French science-magazine alleging (no doubt falsely) that the Americans were using telepathy to communicate with their atomic submarine *Nautilus*. Vasiliev repeated the experiments with the hypnotist enclosed within a metal screening-chamber to cut out any such radiations and subsequently made further tests with the subject also screened but by a different system: the so-called Faraday chamber. In either case the screening was reported to have made no difference at all to the results. If the right hypnotic subjects can be found, surely no more valuable work in parapsychology could be done than a number of repetitions of Vasiliev's experiments, for they appear not only to demonstrate a telepathic influence of one mind on another at a distance as did the earlier findings of Janet, Richet and Platonov, but to show that it is not a physical electro-magnetic phenomenon.

Another approach is from the study of dreams in both natural and hypnotic sleep. For a number of years a series of experiments have been carried out by Drs Stanley Krippner and Montague Ullman and their colleagues at the now famous Dream Laboratory at the Maimonides Medical Centre at Brooklyn, in which they have studied the possible telepathic production of dream-patterns in a sleeping subject by an agent concentrating on some picture in an adjacent, acoustically isolated room. The work arose when it was discovered that subjects, awakened from sleep immediately after a period of dreaming, were frequently able to recall vivid visual dream-episodes. I shall describe the typical procedure as reported in a paper of 1970.[1] Before the subject retired to sleep the agent stated, 'At various times during the night I will be concentrating on a target picture and will try, by this means, to convey my impression of the picture to you in the hope that it will appear in your dreams.' Once the subject was asleep, the agent selected at random (by a process using a random-number table) a picture in a sealed envelope from a number of others in a pool, opened it and by looking and thinking about it attempted to influence the subject's dreams. An experimenter who was with the subject recorded (on an electro-encephalograph) his or her 'rapid eye-movements' which are now well known to indicate a state of dreaming, and as soon as these were over he awoke the subject saying, 'Please tell me your dream.' (Pause) 'Is there anything else?' (Pause) 'Thank you. Please go back to sleep,' the subject's replies being recorded on tape. The subject was awakened as many times as the rapid eye-movements indicated dreaming. In the morning the experimenter had a further, post-sleep interview with the subject. Copies of all the target pictures in the pool and the transcript of the recordings were then sent to outside judges who then had to evaluate the results by deciding which, if any, of the pictures would be matched with the subject's dream-impressions. Their elaborate method of scoring hits and misses must be studied in the original account.

Here is an example of one of the dream reports from the same paper. The picture randomly selected was a colour reproduction of a painting entitled, 'Mystic Night', by Millard Sheets which (and here I quote the description given in the paper) depicts 'five female figures going through a nighttime ritual in a wooded area; a greenish-blue colour pervades the entire picture', and now I will quote what the subject said:

> *Excerpts, dream reports:* 'Being with a group of people ...
> Participating in something ... Lots of mountains and trees ...

[1] S. Krippner, 'Electrophysiological Studies of ESP in Dreams: Sex Differences in Seventy-Four Telepathic Sessions', *Journal of the American Society for Psychical Research*, vol. 64 (1970), pp. 277–85.

I kept seeing blue ... What strikes me most about the whole thing was the trees, again, and the greenery and the country ...'

Excerpts, post-sleep interview: 'The blue – this kind of sky-blue color and the foliage – I mean, there was so much greenery and country atmosphere throughout. I remember the greens and blue being terribly bright ... I have the feeling that it's some sort of – maybe like a jungle scene or something with very lush foliage. I also have this feeling that ... there's some sort of primitive aspect to whatever was in that target. I can almost see it as some sort of tribal ritual in a jungle.'

In this series there were seventy-four telepathy sessions with many different persons acting as agents and subjects and in all there were judged to be fifty-two telepathic hits and twenty-two misses. Standard statistical tests showed that the probability of such a score occurring by chance is less than one in a thousand.

My last example of the modern work I regard, in several re-spects, as the most important yet undertaken; it is that of Dr Thelma Moss, Assistant Professor of Medical Psychology, and Dr J. A. Gengerelli, Professor of Psychology, both of the Uni-versity of California, Los Angeles. They had been impressed, as have others, that such a large number of the examples of supposed spontaneous telepathy (in the anecdotal history of the subject) have been associated with some highly emotional incident such as an accident, serious illness or the death of a close relative or friend; consequently they resolved to experiment by generating emotional affective states. It had long been suggested that those who be-lieved in E.S.P. got better results in experiments than those who were sceptical. Combined with the production of emotional states, they set out to test whether those who believed in E.S.P. would in fact produce statistically more significant results, in rigidly controlled telepathy experiments, than those who were convinced that E.S.P. could not take place.[1] They worked with

[1] *Journal of Parapsychology*, vol. 32 (1968), pp. 90–100.

144 volunteers from various walks of life and arranged them in teams of two, i.e. 72 pairs which were divided into three groups of 24 pairs each: the *E.S.P. Group*, being those who believed in E.S.P. and thought they had had such experiences in the past; the *E.S.P.? Group*, who believed in E.S.P. to some extent but did not believe they had the faculty, and the *Non-E.S.P. Group* who were convinced that E.S.P. did not exist.

The essence of each experiment was this. One member of each pair, whom we may call the transmitter, was placed in a sound-proof chamber in one room and shown a series of emotional pictures — coloured lantern-slides projected on a screen — all bearing on a similar theme whilst at the same time hearing through head-phones music, voices, animal sounds, etc., appropriate to the situation presented; the other member of the pair, the receiver, sat in a comfortable reclining chair in another room which was separated by a distance of twenty feet. There was an experimenter in each room and in the receiver's room there were two screens upon which *two* lantern-slide pictures could be simultaneously projected from two lanterns electrically connected. The receiver was asked to relax and 'receive' impressions of what his partner was experiencing in the other room and then speak his impressions into the microphone of a recorder. He was then shown a pair of slides, one of which was the same as that shown to his partner and the other quite different, and he was asked to choose the one that corresponded better than the other with his impressions. Each experiment consisted of three such trials. In these first experiments the teams of the *E.S.P. Group* scored with a probability against the result being due to chance of one in three thousand, whereas the other two groups scored no more than chance expectation. Further experiments were done contrasting those who were artists or had professionally some kind of creative ability (i.e. writers, musicians, actors, painters, etc.) and those whose profession gave no hint of such qualities (i.e. those in business, trade, etc.). Here again the artistic group had a highly significant positive result, whereas the others failed to score above-chance.

More recently Dr Moss and her colleagues[1] have done perhaps the most remarkable telepathy experiment of all: they have attempted and got significant results in tests across the world. Incredible it seems, yet their experiments have beautifully designed controls; it is these which make them so noteworthy. Instead of there being many teams of just two subjects, there was a group of 22 subjects acting together as transmitters, all looking at the same picture and hearing the same sounds in a room in Los Angeles, and three other groups acting as receivers in different parts of the world: 28 in another room in Los Angeles, 15 in New York and another 14 at Sussex University in England. Now, in addition to three pairs of alternative emotional episodes or themes, as in the former experiments, there were introduced, as a control, three non-emotional 'episodes': one consisted of nine slides on each of which was a single letter of the alphabet, another nine slides each with a single short black line at a different angle, and the third a series of nine bearing numbers – all of these were shown for 10 seconds each. The order in which the experimental (i.e. the emotional) themes and the control (non-emotional) themes was presented was randomly determined. The results show that for the experimental (emotional) episodes the receivers in all three places scored better than chance-expectation, but surprisingly those in Sussex did very much better than those in New York. Taken altogether the receivers scored significantly beyond chance for the experimental (emotional) episodes: with a calculated probability of three thousand to one against it being just chance, whereas for the control (non-emotional) 'episodes' they only scored at chance-level.

Not only did the statistical tests significantly support the hypothesis of telepathic transmission, but there was some interesting qualitative evidence. As in the earlier experiments the receivers, before they were asked to choose which was the correct slide being shown, were asked to write down their impressions of what the transmitters were thinking of. In regard to a 'Space'

[1] T. Moss, A. F. Chang and M. Levitt, 'Long-Distance E.S.P.: a controlled study', *Journal of Abnormal Psychology*, vol. 76 (1970), pp. 288–94.

episode, three of the receivers at the University of Sussex wrote thus: '*War of the Worlds*, by H. G. Wells? Or the next war, involving death by the use of satellites and flying platforms'; 'I can see the world as if I were in a space ship—I'm in a cabin which is very clear and ... everything is floating'; and the third said 'Outer space with a space ship heading for the moon ... hundreds of stars'; and there were similar statements at Los Angeles and New York. The authors go on to say that it might be argued that, as space travel is so much in the minds of people today, one might well expect such phrases to occur by sheer coincidence; however, they add that 'in *no other episode* did descriptions even remotely resembling space travel appear'.

When we take together the experiments I have described—that is, those whose results have been statistically tested for significance as rigorously as those in any ordinary biological experiment—not to mention many more that I have not included, does it not begin to look as if there may, after all, be such a thing as telepathy: some form of mental communication between minds other than by ordinary sensory means? Whilst these results are not yet repeatable at will, the continuing success in obtaining significant results in *controlled* experiments must surely make its impact on the scientific world. I think we should indeed be like the proverbial ostriches with their heads in the sand if we did not admit, on the evidence now presented, that it looks at least *more likely than not* that such a faculty exists. And if it *does exist* is it not one of the most remarkable discoveries yet made? Is it not something in the universe in relation to mind which is as fundamental as gravity in relation to matter?

Again, if telepathy is true, would it not seem more likely that it is of widespread occurrence, but perhaps in the realm of the subconscious, and that only occasionally are a few unusual individuals aware of it? The philosopher Professor Broad, to whom I have already referred, certainly thought it likely. 'If paranormal cognition and paranormal causation are facts,' he wrote, '... they may be continually operating in the background of our normal lives. Our understanding of, and our misunderstandings with, our fellow men; our general emotional mood on certain occasions; ... our sudden decisions where the introspectable motives seem equally balanced; and so on; all these may be in part determined by paranormal cognition and paranormal causal influences.'[1] There is no need to labour the point further. It is becoming increasingly likely that all those psychologists who have pointed to a mental element extending beyond the physico-chemical structure of the brain have been right: eminent psychologists such as William James, William McDougall,[2] C. G. Jung, Sir Cyril Burt and others. We now learn that Freud was prepared to give a place for telepathy in his scheme of things, and was only prevented from publishing his views by the strong opposition of some of his colleagues.[3]

Telepathy, and those other queer things we have discussed, whatever they may be found to mean, are certainly concerned with life. They are as much a part of the wider biology, as I conceive it, as are the facts of bio-physics and bio-chemistry, but are so much more difficult to investigate. Their elucidation is likely to take much longer; who can doubt, however, that some of them at any rate will in time form a part of systematic knowledge? It would seem likely, I think, that it is to this side of biology that religion may be related.

For the last 350 years it has been the material side of science which has dominated the intellectual world and pushed the consideration of this other side into the background. The great success of experimental physics and chemistry captured man's attention and made him inclined to think that all else was folly. We should not forget that the great pioneer of the scientific method, Francis Bacon — whose philosophical principles had such an influence on the founders of the Royal Society — was also, as May Bell has recently reminded us,[4] a pioneer in parapsycho-

---

[1] *Philosophy*, vol. 24 (1949), pp. 291–309.

[2] He expressed his firm conviction of the reality of telepathy in his book, *Modern Materialism and Emergent Evolution* (1929), p. 97.

[3] Ernest Jones, *The Life and Work of Sigmund Freud* (1957), vol. III, p. 409.

[4] 'A Pioneer in Parapsychology', *Journal of Parapsychology*, vol. 20 (1956), pp. 257–62.

logical thought. In his *Sylva Sylvarum*, published posthumously in 1627, he proposes 'Experiments in consort, monitory, touching transmission of spirits [telepathy?] and forces of imagination', and also experiments to investigate healing by the same 'force of the imagination'; he later says 'the experiment of binding of thoughts should be diversified and tried to the full; and you are to note whether it hit for the most part though not alway'.[1] He then goes on to suggest that, from what is regarded as superstition and magical, one might be able to extract something that is 'clean and pure natural'. We may echo his sentiments nearly three and a half centuries after him.

[1] Thouless (op. cit., p. 6), who discusses the passage, *'for the most part though not alway'*, points out that it 'is, of course, a good anticipation of what has been found in [modern] E.S.P. experimentation'.

8. Back to biology and behaviour

After our excursion into that fringe subject of parapsychology, let us return to the fold of recognized biology and see how some of the more psychological features of religion may be related to what is now being discovered in that relatively new branch of the subject: the study of animal behaviour.

When we compare the period of human history with the span of time since our warm-blooded relatives the mammals first appeared, let alone the whole of evolution, does it not suggest, in spite of all the magnificent achievements in literature, art and science, that our culture must be somewhat like a veneer superimposed upon our more animal nature? F. C. Selous describes how, during an expedition in Canada, he roused a caribou stag, saw 'the dreadful terror' in its eyes and shot it; he then says, 'Did I feel sorry for what I had done? it may be asked. Well! no, I did not. Ten thousand years of superficial and unsatisfying civilization have not altered the fundamental nature of man, and the successful hunter of to-day becomes a primeval savage, remorseless, triumphant, full of a wild, exultant joy, which none but those who have lived in the wilderness, and depended on their success as hunters for their daily food, can ever know or comprehend.'[1]

We must always proceed with great caution in comparing the activities of animals to those of man; there are, however, certain patterns of behaviour which have been shown by modern experimental studies to be so widespread and deeply rooted in the animal kingdom that it seems likely that they may indeed throw light on some aspects of human life, including certain of man's religious activities. The experimental researches I am referring to are those investigations into the normal behaviour of animals

[1] *Recent Hunting Trips in British North America* (London, 1907), p. 349.

under natural conditions such as were initiated by those brilliant pioneers, Konrad Lorenz, Niko Tinbergen and Karl von Frisch, who together recently shared a Nobel Prize. I want to make sure that I am not thought to be alluding to the work of those psychologists who call themselves 'behaviourists', but in fact only deal with the reactions of animals under artificial conditions in mazes, trick-boxes and other ingenious pieces of apparatus. These latter studies no doubt tell us important things about the reflex actions of the nervous system and the physical mechanisms of behaviour, but not about the real springs of motivation.

To begin with, is there any connection between religion and sex? Many people have thought so and the idea is even becoming more widely contemplated in ecclesiastical circles. This was somewhat surprisingly emphasized by a statement under the heading 'Young people and the Church', in the 1971 example of those influential prefaces which make pronouncements upon Church of England outlook and policy at the beginning of each new issue of *Crockford's Clerical Directory*. 'It should be remembered', the statement says, 'that in the long history of mankind religion and sex have been closely intertwined as forces of human nature and that the present public preoccupation with sex may also in part be evidence for a search for God. A great problem for the church today is to discover the right response to these movements.'

The analogy between giving oneself in a union of love to a member of the opposite sex and that of entering into a complete devotion to God has long been recognized by the Roman Catholic Church in the symbolic marriage-like ceremonies which young women entering into certain closed orders may undergo when, arrayed in flowing, white wedding-garments and veils, they become what are called 'Brides in Christ'.

How the process of sex actually arose we have no idea; we do know, however, that it must have occurred very early in the history of the living world, for it is the predominant form of reproduction throughout almost the whole of both the plant and animal kingdoms. Once sex *had* appeared, however, it provided the mechanism for a greatly improved evolutionary system: the means of bringing about the maximum possible reassortment – or reshuffling – of the genes, giving us the changes in the genetic code going forward to produce the ever-varying members of the new generations for natural selection to act upon. Sexual *attraction* in bringing male and female together is therefore one of the most vital elements of behaviour in the whole process of evolution; no wonder that it plays so prominent a part in life. I have already expressed my view (p. 53) that I believe it likely that the higher animals may be conscious of their actions; whilst their coming together may be accomplished by all manner of physical signals – visual display, scents, sounds and so on – I would not be surprised to find – if only we could know it (but we cannot) – that their sexual union is accompanied by 'an ecstasy of love'.

This may no doubt be smiled upon as a romantic view, and be deprecated in any biological discussion. Yet I would defend myself by saying that the evolution of speech and the consequent development of explicit knowledge and tradition, which have so greatly enlarged our conscious view of our world, cannot really have altered the fundamental nature of the emotions; these surely belong to that deeper mental stratum of what Polanyi calls our tacit knowledge and must link with our animal ancestors. Consider the members of a hunting pack of carnivores, like hyenas or wild dogs, which under their leader execute tactical manœuvres, much as do members of a football team co-operating in a match; are we really to suppose that they do not experience the emotions of the chase? The same, I believe, can reasonably be said not only of the excitement of sexual attraction, but of that other kind of attachment which, whether we call it affection or not, has also been evolved in the course of evolution: the parental and filial attachment that plays such a vital part in the successful rearing of families in the higher vertebrates – the birds and mammals. It is this latter form of biological 'love' that has been so much more important in the development of religion than has sex.

Apart from the exceptional marriage-like act in the Brides-in-

Christ ceremonies, I doubt whether normal sex has played or is now playing such a part in relation to religious feelings as has been suggested in the quotation I have given from *Crockford's*. There is, however, another way in which sex has entered into religion, although again I do not think it has formed anything like so large a part as some psychologists have supposed; this other way is not concerned with normal sex, but a form of deviation. Whilst I would certainly agree that it has played some part, I believe that on the whole it has been mistaken for something else which also has its roots deep in animal behaviour, but was not originally concerned with sex at all. This we must examine, and try to sort out which part is likely to be related to the sexual deviation and which to quite another and much more remarkable element, evolved far back in biological history.

Just as the passions of sex may, for sheer physical satisfaction, be turned to lust instead of to real love, so religion may be twisted at times in dreadful ways that suggest a parallel, indeed in some cases more than a parallel, with lustful, sexual distortions. History tells us of the almost unspeakable cruelties that have in the past been perpetrated in the name of religion; one need only recall the ghastly horrors of the tortures carried out under the Inquisition and the burnings at the stake. Then there is the very opposite of this: the desire for self-sacrifice and self-abasement so frequently found associated with a devotion to God; it is a desire which from time to time has merged into the practice of physical self-torture – as in the flagellants of the Middle Ages who went about in processions, whipping each other into frenzies of supposed religious fervour – a practice well-known in the psychology of the abnormal to be an ecstatic sexual deviation. There are these two forms of sexual distortion – sadism and masochism – which in some curious way have become entwined into religious behaviour. Aldous Huxley, in his novel of the future, vividly portrayed the terrible masochistic passions of the adherents of the half-Christian, half-heathen religion that lingered on in the imagined 'native reserve' of his *Brave New World*; here no doubt he was drawing upon, and mixing together, accounts from medieval Christendom and the anthropology of some primitive tribes.

It may seem at first sight strange how these two forms of generating ecstatic excitement through pain—one active and the other passive—should not only have become associated with religion but also became forms of twisted sex. It is here that the study of animal behaviour can help us; before, however, making any such comparison, we must look a little more closely at the ways in which it has been *thought* that such sexual distortions have influenced man's religious behaviour, and we must see just what has to be explained. To begin with, let us be sure that we understand what it is that we are talking about. 'Sadism', writes Havelock Ellis in his *Psychology of Sex* (Heinemann, London, 1933, p. 170), 'is generally defined as sexual emotion associated with the wish to inflict pain, physical or moral, on the object of the emotion. Masochism is sexual emotion associated with the desire to be physically subjugated or morally humiliated by the person arousing the emotion.' These terms are of course derived from the names of the two authors who gave prominence to these forms of deviation in their books: the Marquis de Sade (1740–1814) and the Austrian novelist, Sacher-Masoch (1836–1895). It has been noted that in some people there is a complex mixture of the two forms of deviation.[1]

Freud believed that both these elements can be found in what he called the erotic period of very early life. In chapter 6 I have expressed my scepticism of the reality of this early eroticism largely because the direct observations by Professor Valentine on infants (referred to on p. 113) do not support Freud's contentions. Valentine points out that there is a relatively independent impulse of aggression which in its extreme form may well appear to take the form of cruelty for its own sake but which has no sexual significance whatever. 'We may recall', he says, 'that this impulse is so lively sometimes in apparently normal children that there is mere play at pugnacity and aggression. An outlet is

[1] Clifford Allen, *A Textbook of Psychosexual Disorders* (Oxford University Press, London, 1962), p. 104.

found without any external stimulus.' Apart from the validity or otherwise of Freud's views regarding infant life, he certainly believed that these two forms of deviation played an important part in the psychology of religious behaviour. We should recognize that in part this may be so without necessarily referring it back to early childhood. Whilst we are going to see that there are other biological connections which involve a different origin for much of it, it is right that we should point out what the Freudians have been saying about all this.

We saw (p. 115) how far some Christians may go in accepting Freud's teachings in relation to certain theological ideas as exemplified for instance, in the writing of the Rev. Dr Lee. I quoted a passage from his book dealing with doctrines which encouraged a sense of sin and the building-up of a feeling of guilt and unworthiness. He pointed out the terrible vicious circle that could be engendered: the more guilty the ego is made to feel, the more strongly the super-ego (i.e. the conscience) attacks it, thereby increasing further the feeling of guilt. I will now continue the same quotation from where I broke it off; here he brings in the sadistic and masochistic elements and shows them at work at the back of the mind. He says (p. 163):

> The only brake on the process is obtained through penances and mortification, even to the extent of self-inflicted pain. By accepting these the Ego is able to regain some of its self-esteem, for they are the token of its obedience to the Super-ego. Further, since in this type of character there is usually a strong masochistic (enjoyment of suffering) tendency in the unconscious, the Id gets satisfaction from the suffering and its pressure on the Ego is reduced in other directions. The masochistic tendency in the Id is matched by the aggressive sadistic component of the Super-ego, so that this severe self-discipline produces a considerable libidinal pleasure and is not simply a moral achievement ... Fasting and mortification and self-denial are often regarded as the sign of holiness. Psycho-analysis shows that they readily become

perversions of the Id and a crippling of the Ego that renders
the personality unable to cope with the problems of life. It
forces a retreat from life to a hermitage or convent. It is not
a religion for this world. It is an escape from this world, its
interests and its works, into the other world.

You may remember also that in the earlier chapter I quoted him
as complaining that such a religion was 'much more occupied
with sin than with love' and was very different from that of
Jesus as recorded in the gospels.

I have deliberately taken in the first instance, the views of a
Christian who accepts the Freudian view of the importance of
sadism and masochism in the psychology of some forms of religious life, but who, in recognizing them for what they are, has
been able to reject the doctrines of guilt and sin; he sees how these,
their product, have played such havoc in the lives of many who
might otherwise have had a very different and more healthy outlook on their world.

I must now present the views of those who actually believe that
the whole of religion may be explained away in terms of this
masochistic–sadistic complex. As an illustration of this outlook I
will take a somewhat extreme example to emphasize how strongly
it may be held. Dr David Forsyth F.R.C.P., who was Senior
Physician to the Psychological Clinic of the Ministry of Pensions,
took this subject as the theme of his Presidential Address to the
Psychiatry Section of the Royal Society of Medicine in 1934. He
expanded this into a book, *Psychology and Religion* (Watts & Co.,
London, 1935), in the preface of which he says the Society re-
fused to publish his address in their *Proceedings*. It must certainly
have shocked many. Only a quotation can convey the scope and
vigour of his presentation: on p. 149 he writes:

> The masochistic enjoyment of suffering is exhibited in the
> wide-spread habit of self-denial, including poverty, fasting,
> and sexual abstinence. The whole custom of religious penance
> comes in this category. To a more unmeasured degrée
> masochism is indulged in the innumerable kinds of self-

mortification practised by many Christian, Indian fakirs, and others, from wearing hair-shirts next to the skin to submitting to tortures and revolting degradations. To cite only a few of the many in Christian history, we have the extraordinary austerities practised by St. John of the Cross, the loathsome penance of St. Catherine of Genoa, the deliberate quest of the repulsive by St. Francis ...

Masochism comes to full flower in the spirit of the martyr, and the acme of masochism is reached in martyrdom itself, when the greatest of self-sacrifices, that of life, may be sought and enjoyed—all the more, often enough, for its added concomitants of torture and suffering ...

Just as the teaching of Mahomet is ... essentially sadistic, so is the teaching of Christ essentially masochistic. The spirit of self-sacrifice which permeates Christianity, and is so highly prized in the Christian religious life, is masochism moderately indulged. A much stronger expression of it is to be found in Christ's teaching in the Sermon on the Mount. This blesses the poor, the meek, the persecuted; exhorts us not to resist evil but to offer the second cheek to the smiter; and to do good to them that hate you and forgive men their trespasses. All this breathes masochism, and nothing about it is sadistic. While Mahomet was virile and sadistic, Christ was gentle and masochistic ...

Most people will indeed feel that this statement is outrageous, and so it is; yet I am sure that no doctor with a psychiatric training would say that *some* acts of humiliation and the self-infliction of pain could be anything other than a masochistic impulse. I think there can be no doubt that the enforcement of celibacy in the early church, with the suppression of any normal sexual outlet, helped to make acts of penance, self-mortification and severe physical discipline a general practice. A tradition had become established that this was the way to create a zealous and dedicated personality. There was then no psycho-analysis to show the hidden springs of repressed sexual impulses. These unconscious elements almost certainly accounted for *some* of this behaviour *but by no means all*. A very important piece of the puzzle had been missing. This was only discovered comparatively recently, and until it was found I do not believe that the psychologists really understood how these curious so-called deviations, both active and passive forms, ever became linked with sex at all. This new contribution to knowledge throws, I believe, a flood of light not only on the problem we have just been discussing, but on a large part of religious activity; it comes from the new researches into animal behaviour.

Before we come, however, to this biological contribution, there is something else from the psychological side which should be mentioned, something which interlocks with this hitherto missing part of the jig-saw. A deeper acquaintance with psychopathology now shows us that there are two *quite distinct* forms of so-called masochism. One of them, although showing effects very like those produced by the other, is now realized to be in fact far removed from sex. The distinction between them has been well made by Dr Clifford Allen in his *Textbook of Psychosexual Disorders*. He sharply divides the religious form, which he calls *moral masochism*, from the more usual kind which he calls *erotogenic masochism*; indeed he reminds us that Freud himself not only distinguished these two types but added a third, which he called the *feminine* kind, and had then said that the moral form 'is chiefly remarkable for having loosened its connection with what we recognize to be sexuality. To all other masochistic sufferings there still clings the condition that it should be administered by the loved person; ... in the moral type this limitation is dropped. It is the suffering itself which matters; ...'

Dr Allen then goes on to say that it is possible that numerous psychiatrists would refuse to recognize this latter as a real perversion (i.e. sexually connected) and further suggests that for some unknown reason moral masochism appears to be commoner in the East than in Europe or America. 'The Fakirs', he says, 'who lie on beds of nails, who thrust skewers through their cheeks, who hold an arm in one position until it withers, ... are all examples of moral masochism. The history of every religion is redolent of it and ... where excessive mysticism is favoured it reappears.'

Now that the psychologists tell us that we must distinguish this moral, or as I would prefer to call it, religious masochism, from the sexual type, we can better appreciate the significance of the contribution to our problem which has come from the study of animal life. It comes in the first place not from sexual behaviour at all but from two complementary kinds of reaction between members of the same species—aggression and submission —which occur again and again in the course of the evolution of the higher vertebrates: among fish, birds and mammals. Such behaviour may be seen for example between rival males competing for breeding or feeding territory, or between different members in a social hierarchy as among gregarious monkeys or in a female society as in the pecking order among hens.

Frequent conflict between rival members of the same species, *if fought out to the death*, would be harmful for the race; natural selection has consequently favoured patterns of behaviour which normally prevent this fatal outcome. In its simplest form it would amount to no more than attack and retreat. The owner, A, of a piece of territory, which he has taken possession of, at once adopts a threat posture towards the interloper, B, who retreats back into his own territory; now if A invades the territory of B, then B will threaten A who in turn retreats. Dr Tinbergen illustrated this with a very simple experiment with sticklebacks. Males A and B had built nests at opposite ends of an aquarium and defended their respective territories. He then enclosed each male in a glass tube and placed them side by side in the territory of A. At once A tries to attack B, and B in its tube turns away from A and tries to flee; he then moves the two tubes over to the other end of the aquarium into the territory of B and at once the behaviour-patterns are reversed, B tries to attack and A turns away and tries to flee.

We see just the same kind of behaviour in many species of birds in regard to the area they have claimed exclusively as theirs for the gathering of food to feed their young; the males defend their territory by driving off other males who may try to trespass on it. Actual fighting, however, rarely occurs; the attacking male usually adopts certain postures which at once have the effect of intimidating his adversary. The robin, for example, displays his red breast, which, writes Dr Lack, 'is stretched and so held that the intruding robin sees as much of it as possible'. The threat is certainly effective. 'The intruding robin usually departs almost at once, and rarely does the attacking bird have to change from posturing to direct attack to achieve this.' The exhibition of the red breast suffices. 'Just as its song is a war cry,' says Lack, 'so its red breast is war paint, both helping to prevent a fight coming to blows.' Another example is the curious forward threat-posture of the black-headed gull, described by Dr Tinbergen, in which the bird adopts a crouching position, with its neck and open beak stretched forward in a menacing attitude. The male stickleback, I should also add, has a special threat-posture, 'standing' vertically on its head in the water with its sharp spines erected.

When actual fighting between rival males does occur under natural wild conditions it rarely ends in one killing the other; generally one, before it has been too severely damaged, will decide it has had enough and will flee. Only with animals kept in captivity where flight is impossible do we get the unusual occurrence of an animal killing another of its own kind. Now, in a number of species, particularly among birds and mammals, instead of escape a curious act of appeasement has developed, the opposite of threat; it is a surrender which at once has the effect of stopping the fight. Konrad Lorenz in his charming book, *King Solomon's Ring* (Methuen, London, 1952), gives a number of examples including a dramatic account of a fight which he saw between two wolves in Whipsnade Park. The younger one is gradually being forced backwards towards a fence, strikes the wire-netting and stumbles; the older one is upon him. 'And now', says Lorenz, on p. 186, 'the incredible happens, just the opposite of what you would expect. The furious whirling of the grey bodies has come to a sudden standstill.

Shoulder to shoulder they stand … in a stiff and strained attitude, … the older wolf has his muzzle close, very close against the neck of the younger, and the latter holds away his head, offering unprotected to his enemy the bend of his neck, the most vulnerable part of his whole body!' It is a signal of submission; the fight is stopped.

Another example he gives (on p. 194) is that of the fighting of turkey-cocks, which indulge in a wild wrestling-match. The one who is losing suddenly adopts a posture of submission by lying with outstretched neck upon the ground; 'whereupon', says Lorenz, 'the victor behaves exactly as a wolf or dog in the same situation, that is to say, he evidently *wants* to peck and kick at the prostrated enemy, but simply cannot; he would if he could but he can't!'

This behaviour is certainly a remarkable product of evolution. The humbled creature, whether bird or mammal, suddenly removes all obstacles from the path of attack and at once takes up a ritualized posture of submission which, in the words of Lorenz 'raises an insurmountable inner obstruction in the central nervous system of the aggressor'. Here we see these two opposite kinds of action, aggression and submission, evolved entirely independently of sex; both are vital adaptations for the success of the species and the fact that they are so widespread in the animal kingdom shows how fundamental they are. With their painstaking researches, these same students of animal behaviour have now shown experimentally, often with the ingenious use of models, that in many species these two types of action have become *secondarily* incorporated into sexual life by becoming part of the mating ritual with the female taking the more passive role.

Whilst we must always be cautious in attempting to link human actions with those of animals, the fact that these two types of behaviour have become entwined in the sexual life of so many different species including our nearest relatives, the monkeys and apes, must surely help to explain how they have entered also into the sexual life of man. We have noted (p. 144) that the psychologists tell us that there is nearly always a mixture of these two tendencies in any individual. Only in exceptional people may they come to have a prominent part in the sexual life of a married pair as in the horrifying cases of a wife-beating husband or, on a lighter note, the wife who yearns romantically for her 'caveman' and is disappointed at the mildness of her husband. It is only in cases where the development of a person's sexual life has been disturbed that we may find erotic pleasure being sought either in sadism or masochism.

Just as the study of animal behaviour helps to explain how aggression and submission entered sex in human life, so also does it show that what we call moral or religious masochism is most likely linked, *not* with sex, but with that earlier, more fundamental submissive act. Lorenz, whilst not discussing any such relationship with religion, certainly connected examples of man's non-sexual behaviour with that of animals. After discussing the examples of the wolves and the turkeys, he asks,

> And what is the human appeal for mercy after all? Is it so very different from what we have just described? The Homeric warrior who wishes to yield and plead mercy, discards helmet and shield, falls on his knees and inclines his head, a set of actions which should make it easier for the enemy to kill, but, in reality, hinders him from doing so. As Shakespeare makes Nestor say of Hector:
>
>> Thou hast hung thy advanced sword i' the air,
>> Not letting it decline on the declined.
>
> Even today, we have retained many symbols of such submissive attitudes in a number of our gestures of courtesy; bowing, removal of the hat, and presenting arms in military ceremonial.[1]

As a religious feeling in man — that of being in contact with some power which appears to be greater than the self — developed and gave rise to various rites of worship, it would be natural for the submissive act, originally one of appeasement to a superior

[1] *King Solomon's Ring*, p. 196.

person, to be incorporated. It would become an act of paying homage to this element which had now become personified through the transfer to it of the emotional feelings of the child–parent, love–fear, relationship. This mystery, for me, is as much a part of the natural world as is that of the conscious mental side of animal life; it is a part of the biological system and, as I have said before, as important as sex. On the opposite, the sadistic, side, Anthony Storr has recently argued powerfully that 'Cruelty is more closely linked with the pleasure of power than with the pleasure of sex; and those to whom it has most appeal are those who have most felt themselves to be insulted and injured.'[1]

In the following chapter we shall see something else from the field of animal behaviour which I believe adds strong support to this view of religious behaviour. In passing, let me say that I hope it will not be thought from my argument in this chapter or the next that I am intending in any way to belittle the concept of Divinity—quite the reverse; what I intend to imply is that those who feel that they can best approach what they call God by making a physical act of obeisance—as on their knees—need not feel it to be either a childish or a superstitious act, as if it were something to be ashamed of, but can recognize it as one having a deep and significant root in our biological history.

[1] *Human Destructiveness* (Basic Books, New York, 1972), p. 108.

9. Dog and man: man and God —is there a parallel?

There is a very remarkable, in fact unique, happening which has taken place within the biological system and yet is very like the relation that so many men and women have to what they feel to be a reality and which they call God. It is the dog's devotion to man. Here is an animal that has transferred his loyalty and obedience from his former pack-leader to a new master: moreover, an animal which is not only a faithful follower, but one that can have a devotional child-like love-relationship with this new master. You have only to look into the eyes of a dog to see the truth of this. Are they not like the eyes of the devout kneeling at the altar rail? I do not say this in any sense of mockery.

I had tentatively and briefly mentioned this similarity in my book *The Divine Flame* (1966), p. 172, when I said, 'it may possibly help us to appreciate the nature of man's religious behaviour in more biological terms'. Having thought more about it, and indeed having found that there is much more evidence available to support such an idea than I had originally supposed, I now come to think that it indeed begins to look as if it should be regarded not just as an imaginative analogy, but as a close parallel involving very similar biological elements.

Since I put this suggestion forward, my attention has been drawn to two much earlier references to the idea of man being like a god to a dog, although these are not presented in a biological context. The first comes from the great Francis Bacon in his essay, 'Of atheism':[1]

---

[1] *The Works of Francis Bacon*, vol. II, *Essays Civil and Moral*, No. 16, (W. Baynes and Son, London, 1824), p. 291.

They that deny a God destroy man's nobility; for certainly man is of kin to the beasts by his body; and, if he be not of kin to God by his spirit, he is a base and ignoble creature. It destroys likewise magnanimity, and the raising of human nature; for take an example of a dog, and mark what a generosity and courage he will put on when he finds himself maintained by a man, who to him is instead of a God, or *melior natura*; which courage is manifestly such as that creature, without that confidence of a better nature than his own, could never attain. So man, when he resteth and assureth himself upon divine protection and favour, gathereth a force and faith which human nature in itself could not obtain; therefore, as atheism is in all respects hateful, so in this, that it depriveth human nature of the means to exalt itself above human frailty.

The second reference comes from *Essays and Addresses*[1] by Baron F. von Hugel:

... Our dogs know us and love us, human individuals, from amongst millions of fairly similar other individuals. Our dogs know us, and love us thus most really, yet they doubtless know us only vividly, not clearly; we evidently strain their minds after a while – they then like to get away amongst servants and children; and, indeed, they love altogether to escape from human company, the rich and dim, or (at best) the vivid experiences – the company that is above them, to the company of their fellow-creatures, the company that affords so much poorer but so much clearer impressions – the level company of their brother-dogs. And yet, how wonderful! dogs thus require their fellow-dogs, the shallow and clear, but they also require us, the deep and dim; they require indeed what they can grasp; but they as really require what they can but reach out to, more or less – what exceeds, protects, envelopes, directs them. And, after a short

[1] Vol. I (Dent and Sons, London, 1921), pp. 102–3.

relaxation in the dog-world, they return to the bracing of the man-world.

Now pray note how if religion is right—if what it proclaims as its source and object, if God be real, then this Reality, as superhuman, *cannot possibly* be clearer to us than are the realities, and the real qualities of these realities, which we have been considering. The source and object of religion, if religion be true and its object be real, *cannot*, indeed, *by any possibility, be as clear to me even as I am to my dog.*

It has often been pointed out, of course, how alike are dog and man in certain aspects of their behaviour. This was well expressed by Francis Galton in his *Inquiries into Human Faculty* (1883), when, in discussing man's domestication of animals, he comes to the dog as a companion to man.

We observe how readily their proceedings are intelligible to each other. Every whine or bark of the dog, each of his fawning, savage, or timorous movements is the exact counterpart of what would have been the man's behaviour, had he felt similar emotions. As the man understands the thoughts of the dog, so the dog understands the thoughts of the man, by attending to his natural voice, his countenance, and his actions. A man irritates a dog by an ordinary laugh, he frightens him by an angry look, or he calms him by a kindly bearing ...[1]

My attention was drawn to this passage from Galton by reading Professor Carveth Read's *The Origin of Man and his Superstitions* (Cambridge University Press, Cambridge, 1920). After giving this quotation, he goes on to say, 'No more, if as much, could be said of the terms upon which we stand with the tame chimpanzee in spite of greater physical and facial resemblance and nearer kinship.' He then asks what is it that 'can connect us so closely in mind with an animal so remote from us in lineage and anatomy as the dog is?' His answer is that we have both come

[1] p. 262.

to be adapted to 'the same social conditions: the life of the hunting pack'. The main thesis of Carveth Read's book, which I believe has been unjustly neglected, is that man's social life and the basis of his religious beliefs (which Read calls his superstitions) have both come about through his having passed through a hunting phase; breaking away from the rest of the primates in becoming largely a carnivore, he became more than an ordinary hunter, for he hunted in packs in a manner more like that practised by the wild dogs than that of any other animal. Whilst he admits that it is possible that our ape-like ancestor may have been more sociable than any of the other apes, 'sociability', he says, 'in ape-life would in no way account for our present character as men: nothing accounts for it except the early formation of the hunting pack.' At this point I should perhaps mention what will be stressed later on (p. 160) — that it is indeed the *combination* of certain ape-characters with the new, carnivorous hunting behaviour that led to man's advance; he left the hunting, dog-like animals behind because he had additional features that they have never had. What can this theory have to do with religion? We shall see.

At the time he wrote, Read was obviously much influenced both by the writings of Sir Edward Tylor, deriving religion from animism (the belief in spirits), and by those of Sir James Frazer deriving it from magic. He hardly refers to Marett and gives little attention to Durkheim, so that his ideas of primitive religion are coloured by those of the earlier writers; hence his emphasis on the origin of man's 'superstitions'.[1] It was, I think, because he related man's primitive religion — 'his superstitions' — back to the life of the hunting pack that most people thought his speculations too far-fetched to be worth considering.[2] Recent studies, however, particularly those of Schaller and Lowther

[1] See discussion on p. 74.
[2] He evidently realized this, because subsequently he split his book into two and in 1925 published revised editions of the two parts: *The Origin of Man*, which deals with his hunting-pack theory, and *Man and his Superstitions*, as a separate discussion.

(1969) which I shall presently discuss, have now most convincingly shown how important was the carnivorous hunting stage in man's early development. This new work should have revived interest in and given new importance to Read's earlier thesis; the gap, however, has apparently been too long, for the new authors seem not to have heard of him. I shall just summarize Read's theory of man's origin via the hunting pack, next briefly review the modern animal-behaviour research which now confirms it and then come back to his discussion of the origin of man's 'superstitions'. This, in turn, will lead up to the object of my exercise: a reconsideration of the dog–man, man–God parallel in the light of these discussions.

Read opens his argument by pointing out that there was one major factor which, before the coming of speech, first distinguished man from all his ape and monkey relatives; quite early in his lineage his distant ancestors must have changed from being largely fruit-eaters to become hunting carnivores. Whilst apes may occasionally take birds' eggs, young birds and even small mammals, and some monkeys may at times eat insects, worms, frogs and lizards, all the primates other than man are essentially vegetarians, except the crab-eating macaque monkey which feeds along the sea-edge of south-east Asia.[1] The earliest known men were hunters, and weapons are among the oldest known artifacts; agriculture is a comparatively recent discovery. 'With-

[1] This indeed is how I believe man first became a hunter. Having learnt to use stones as tools on the sea-shore to crack open shellfish, as the Californian sea-otter does, he then fashioned stones *into* tools and came to make flint spearheads for attacking larger fish and eventually seals and sea-cows (dugongs and manatees); next I imagine him, with improved upright posture gained in the shallow sea, spreading inland to hunt the deer and antelopes in packs, as natural selection gave him better legs for speed in the chase. Desmond Morris, in discussing my hypothesis in *The Naked Ape*, says (p. 45), 'Even if eventually it does turn out to be true, it will not clash seriously with the general picture of the hunting ape's evolution out of a ground ape. It will simply mean that the ground ape went through a rather salutary "christening" ceremony!' I certainly agree that it does not clash, but, if true, I think it was rather more than a mere christening—it was the all-important weaning from the fruits of the trees to flesh by way of succulent bivalves and other tender 'fruits of the sea'. All this, however, is another and earlier story: see the brief footnote on p. 61.

out the adoption of a flesh diet,' he says,[1] 'there could have been no hunting; but a flesh diet obtained without hunting (supposing it possible) could have done nothing for the evolution of our family. The adoption of the hunting life, therefore, was the essential change upon which everything else depended.' He pictures our early ancestors 'cooperating in the chase, forming a hunting pack, as a sort of wolf-ape'. A little later he continues, 'The new pursuit was of a nature to engross the animal's whole attention and coordinate all his faculties; and to maintain and reinforce it, his structure in body and mind may reasonably be supposed to have undergone rapid modification by natural selection.' Here in a footnote he refers to the passage from Alfred Russel Wallace's *Darwinism* which I have quoted on p. 65.

He now goes on to emphasize that man may have been incapable of killing enough prey single-handed, but would greatly profit 'by becoming both social and co-operative as a hunter, like the wolves and dogs'.[2] This indeed is what the modern behaviour-work is confirming, by giving us detailed statistics to show that all the different species of hunting dogs and dog-like animals are much less successful in obtaining their prey when the pack size is reduced below a certain efficient level. 'The pack', says Read, 'was a means of increasing the supply of food per unit; and gregariousness increased by natural selection up to the limit set by utility. Hence man is in character more like a dog or a wolf than he is like any other animal.'

Read goes on to stress that the society thus formed has done more than anything else to promote human life; it could have done little for us if it had been a mere flocking together for mutual safety without any *active* purpose. This element is I believe of paramount importance. 'It is everywhere purposeful,' he says, and then he proceeds (also on p. 32) to suggest that 'some development of the rudiments of speech may be confidently traced to social co-operation.' Now let us see how the modern behaviour-studies have brought strong confirmation of Read's initial ideas.

[1] This and other quotations in this paragraph are taken from his *The Origin of Man* (2nd edn, 1925), pp. 2–6.   [2] Op. cit., p. 32.

Desmond Morris in *The Naked Ape* (1967), to which I have briefly referred in the footnote on p. 158, gives great prominence to the hunting phase in man's evolution; he is a bridge between Read and the modern research. He mentions no names of authors in his text, but refers the reader to the bibliography for each chapter at the end of the book; here Read's book figures as the earliest of his references, so that his discussion is based upon both sources, although the behaviour-work on the hunting carnivores in Africa was only just beginning when he wrote. He now adds to the discussion a number of very important points: the nose of the new hunting ape was too weak, his ears not sharp enough, and his physique inadequate for the arduous chase. And 'In personality,' Morris says, 'he was more competitive than co-operative and no doubt poor on planning and concentration. But fortunately he had an excellent brain, already better in terms of general intelligence than that of his carnivore rivals. By bringing his body up into a vertical position, modifying his hands in one way and his feet in another, and by improving his brain still further and using it as hard as he could, he stood a chance.' Morris then goes on to discuss a most interesting feature of human evolution which I shall refer to later in the chapter because it relates in an important way to my suggested 'dog–man: man–God' parallel. I believe it is a key which may unlock more than Morris supposed, but more of this later.

In 1968, in a chapter on 'The Evolution of Hunting' in the book, *Man the Hunter*,[1] Washburn and Lancaster point out that hunting

> is a way of life, and the success of this adaptation has dominated the course of human evolution for hundreds of thousands of years. In a very real sense our intellect, interests, emotions, and basic social life – all are evolutionary products of the success of the hunting adaptation.

In the following year came the illuminating paper by George B. Schaller and Gordon R. Lowther, which brings such strong confirmation to Read's views and bears the title, 'The Relevance of

[1] Edited by R. Lee and I. DeVore, Chicago, 1968.

Carnivore Behaviour to the study of early Hominids';[1] it is based upon their own observations, together with those of a number of others, made upon the behaviour of the hunting carnivores in the Serengeti National Park of Tanzania and upon a comparison they make between such behaviour and what is inferred regarding that of early man. They begin by drawing attention to recent research on the social systems of apes and monkeys, research which shows that they are so strongly influenced by the ecological conditions under which they live that such systems are very poor indications of evolutionary relationship. Closely related species may differ greatly in their social behaviour, whereas those more distantly related may have come to have closely similar behaviour-patterns. Whilst anthropologists have characteristically looked for clues as to the possible social systems used by early man from the behaviour of other primates, 'there is little basis', they say (p. 308), 'for drawing comparisons ecologically. All monkeys and apes are basically vegetarians ... Man on the other hand has been a hunter and a scavenger for over one million years.' The wolf, the African wild dog, the spotted hyena and the lion 'possibly resemble the early hominids', they say, 'more closely in their social systems than any living non-human primate'. These words might almost have been taken straight from Carveth Read writing over fifty years ago, yet I am sure they were not; they are independently drawn from those painstaking studies in animal behaviour, done both by Schaller and Lowther themselves as well as others, all of whom are, without realizing it, splendidly vindicating that far-sighted philosopher.

The famous Serengeti region lies in that part of East Africa which has yielded so many specimens of early man, and the habitat, whilst somewhat drier, appears to have changed little since he lived there; whilst some of the larger mammal species have become extinct, the actual quantities of game in terms of flesh was probably, they think, much the same as it is today. The object of their study, they say, is not an attempt to reconstruct the social life of early man but to describe 'some aspects of carnivore

[1] *Southwestern Journal of Anthropology*, vol. 25 (1969), pp. 307–41.

behaviour which seem to have particular relevance to the study of the early hominids when they were at a stage of cultural development in which they lacked fire and sophisticated projectile weapons, but probably used some simple generalized tools'. This they proceed to do, making studies of the hunting behaviour of the various carnivorous species and comparing them with certain historic and contemporary human hunting–gathering groups such as Bushmen, the Hadza and the Mbuti pigmies. It is not my intention to go deeply into the details of this modern work; let me use a small part of the summary which Schaller himself gives in a later work to indicate something of its scope:

> A non-human primate derives several advantages from living in a group, including the learning of traditions and protection from predators. While a carnivorous or omnivorous hominid might benefit in the same way, additional selective forces favored its group existence ... The descriptions of cooperative hunting in lion and wild dog show that hominids at whatever stage of mental evolution could have employed relay races, encircling of prey, and other techniques without recourse to an advanced system of communication such as language. Group life also makes a division of labor possible, with, for instance, several adults protecting young at the home site while the rest hunt and bring back the spoils to share with the others — a system used by wild dogs but not by nonhuman primates. Before setting out on a hunt, hominids probably indulged in some activity analogous to the greeting ceremony in wild dogs which strengthened social bonds and synchronized behavior. The size of the hunting group was most likely flexible and depended on the prey that was to be pursued, as is the case with hyenas ...[1]

My reason for introducing this work is, as I have said, to show how completely the modern field-studies in animal behaviour support the first stage of the original thesis of Carveth Read. Let

[1] *The Serengeti Lion: a Study in Predator–Prey Relations* (University of Chicago Press, Chicago, 1972), p. 379.

us now turn to those other thoughts to which he was led by these ideas. I can best do so by quoting a few passages from his work of fifty years ago.

> The general structure of any human society, however, whether of the tribe or nation or of some subordinate group —a trades union or a music society—retains the original character of the pack—a common object of pursuit and an organization of leaders and followers.[1]

Now let us see how he supposed religion arose through the development of superstitions as hunting gave way to agriculture, but we must remember that, as I have already remarked, he was writing under the influence of Edward Tylor and James Frazer.

> The adoption of even a primitive agricultural or pastoral life may make hunting a secondary interest. In such cases the natural leaders of a clan are no longer (as in the old pack) plainly indicated; and if society is to be saved from anarchy some new control must establish itself for the preservation of tradition and custom. Conceivably this happened in several ways; but in fact (I believe) we know of only one, namely: First, the rule of wizards, who are chiefly old men credited with mysterious power that makes the boldest tribesman quail, such as the headman or elders of an Australian tribe ...
> ... and to Religion itself, magical beliefs contribute their support. The inevitable development of illusory imaginations along with common sense, then, assisted early and also later culture, because they preserved order and cohesion by re-awakening the ancient submission and loyalty of the pack ... Excessively imaginative and superstitious tribes may sometimes have been eliminated; for common sense also has biological utility. But ... imaginations utterly false have had their share in promoting 'progress'; cooperating with agriculture and trade, magic, religions and the fine arts have, by

[1] *The Origin of Man* (2nd edn, 1925), p. 53.

supporting government and civic order, helped in accommodating us, even in some measure adapting us to our present condition such as it is.[1]

This must suffice as an indication of Carveth Read's lines of thought, in stressing the behavioural closeness of man and dog during the original development of their social life from that of the hunting pack. His discussion of superstitions in this context may be more of a digression; whilst no one can doubt that superstition has played its part in religion and does so even today, the idea of God, I believe, arose in a very different way – one which lies at the heart of this 'dog–man: man–God' parallel. To this we must now turn.

How did the dog become attached to man in the first place? Why did it transfer its loyalty from its own pack-leader to a new master? There are several suggestions. Konrad Lorenz in his book, *Man meets Dog*, makes one which certainly appears plausible. The wild, jackal-like[2] dogs from which our domestic breeds are derived he imagines to have followed the early hunting, human tribes much as jackals may follow man today; they were, he thinks, encouraged to do so by being thrown scraps of food because they were useful in surrounding the camp settlements at night and, by their barking, giving an alarm warning of any approaching large beast of prey. So, by being encouraged, they followed man on his hunting expeditions and before long, by being given rewards of food, they actually came to help in the chase, gradually becoming subservient to man the hunter instead of to their own original pack-leader. Thus now, according to Lorenz, instead of following behind, they went ahead like hunting hounds. (We may note that Read at one point traces man's delight in blood-sports – even pheasant shooting – back to the days of the hunting pack; I have

[1] *The Origin of Man and his Superstitions* (Cambridge University Press, Cambridge, 1920), p. 69.

[2] Opinion appears to be divided as to whether the domestic dog is derived from the jackal or the wolf or again (as Lorenz himself believes) that some breeds came from one source and some from the other with many kinds being a varying mixture of the two.

never followed hounds myself, but I have been told, by those who do, that in the chase there is aroused a deep, passionate excitement that no other human activity can give.) So gradually the once-wild dogs became hunting hounds, submissive to their new masters.

Another version is given by the late F. E. Zeuner in his *A History of Domesticated Animals* (London, Hutchinson, 1963). In a chapter on the origins of domestication, he says that pet-keeping is particularly likely to have played its part in the case of the dog, since the scavenging habits of the species will often have brought them in contact with man, so that pups may occasionally have been adopted. He relates (p. 39) that there is according to Yoti Lane (*African Folk Tales*, London, 1946) a camp-fire story from the Calabar Africans of Southern Nigeria, which tells just this: 'a boy adopted a wild dog's pup, grew fond of it and brought it up in the village in spite of the attempts of the pup's mother to rescue her child. When fully grown, the dog induced a bitch to join him, and their litter became used to camp conditions immediately. They went out on hunting expeditions with their hunter friends. Subsequently the inhabitants of other villages imitated the practice.' Most likely this and Lorenz's explanation may both have been true, and perhaps these processes combined in different degrees in different areas; in fact Lorenz himself includes the puppy-rearing version in the origin of house-dogs. Later in his book, Zeuner states that the earliest archaeological dated evidence for the presence of domesticated dogs comes from various Mesolithic sites, ranging from North Europe to Palestine.

The idea of comparing the dog-and-man situation with the devotional relationship of man to the element he personifies as God first came to me after reading Lorenz's account of the dog-and-man relationship in his *King Solomon's Ring*. He points out that the single-hearted devotion of the dog to its master has two distinct sources which have become combined. First of all there is the submissive attachment which every wild dog shows towards its pack-leader, which becomes transferred on to the new master. This is straightforward and easily understood. On to this, however, something has been added which is really most extra-ordinary. It is something which has *in itself* a curious biological parallel between dog and man; and in the dog, moreover, it is one that has been produced by man himself. To explain this, and I think it is important that we should fully understand it, I must make a somewhat technical digression.[1]

It has been known for nearly fifty years that the Mendelian genes which govern heredity (or, as some might prefer to say to-day, the elements of the genetic code of the DNA) affect not only the form, i.e. the colour, shape, size, etc., of different parts of the bodies of animals and plants but the relative rate at which they develop. In other words, under the influence of such genes some parts of the body may be more precocious in development than others or again some parts may be relatively retarded. This may give rise to the interesting condition known as neoteny. Perhaps the best-known example is that of the North American Sala-mander, *Amblystoma tigrinum*, which in its fully developed con-dition, as found in the United States, has lost its gills, breathes by lungs and spends most of its time on land; in Mexico, however, this same species usually becomes sexually mature and breeds in a condition of body which is really larval: this is the Axolotl, which keeps its external gills and remains in the water. This condition of neoteny is brought about in some cases, as here, by a relative retardation in the rate of development of the rest of the body as compared with that of the reproductive organs, or in others by the reverse process of an acceleration in the development of the latter; the result is the same. In the Axolotl we see a species which is only partially neotenous, for it may be converted, either in nature or experiment, into the fully adult *Amblystoma*. Some other newt-like forms such as *Necturus* and *Proteus* are permanently in the neotenous condition; here we see an evolutionary step brought about by fixing this change in the relative rate of development of body and reproductive organs. Now a similar kind of change,

[1] For a full discussion of the earlier biological background to this question see my essay, 'Escape for Specialization', in *Evolution as a Process*, ed. Huxley, Hardy and Ford (Allen & Unwin, London, 1954).

although not quite for the same reason, has happened to man; and then, and this is what is so extraordinary, man, in a curious way, made something like it happen to the dog. But we must not go quite so fast; there is more yet to explain before we come to that.

It was the Dutch anatomist, L. Bolk, who first drew attention to man's neotenous condition, although, curiously, he did not seem to be aware of the general phenomenon in the animal kingdom at large and called the process not neoteny but foetalization.[1] He showed that there were many characters of the adult structure of man which were very similar to those of very young, even foetal, stages of the apes. There are, among many other features, the relatively high brain-weight compared to the size of the body, and what is called the cranial flexure which is the downward, right-angle bend of the head in relation to the line of the spinal column. This is present in all embryos, but in all other mammals it becomes straightened out before birth so that the head of the adult looks forwards in direct line with the backbone, which is more or less horizontal in an animal going on all fours. In man, who has adopted the erect posture, this foetal flexure is retained so that, with the backbone now *vertical*, the head and eyes will nevertheless point and look forward, essential for the hunt. There are other features too which are embryonic in man's ape relations but are retained by adult man; I will only mention some of them. Most important is the retarded closure of the sutures between the bones of the skull, allowing a great development of the brain during a long period of its growth after birth, which also gives a long period of education—learning by experience; then there is the flatness of the face helping in stereoscopic vision, and there is the hairlessness of the body.[2]

At this point let me remind you of the quotation I gave from Desmond Morris's *The Naked Ape;* we left him (on p. 160) saying that man's hunting-ape ancestors could only stand a chance of competing with his carnivore rivals 'by improving his brain still

[1] L. Bolk, *Das Problem der Menschwerdung* (Jena, 1926).
[2] This I believe may also relate to his semi-aquatic phase which I suppose predated the hunting period; see footnote on p. 61.

further and using it as hard as he could', and then he went on to show that the hunting ape was only able to increase his brain-capacity in just such a way that Bolk had pointed out—or to use his own words, 'by becoming an infantile ape'. This is the important key I mentioned, suggesting that it might unlock more than appeared at first sight.

To explain what I mean, let me put another piece of the puzzle together by returning to the dog and taking up that second factor which, as Lorenz pointed out, went to the making of the single-hearted devotion of the dog to his master. Firstly, as we saw, there is the submissive attachment which every wild dog shows towards his pack-leader and which is transferred by the domestic dog to a human being. I will now quote Lorenz direct:

> To this is added, in the more highly domesticated dogs, quite another form of affection. Many of the characteristics in which domestic animals differ from their wild ancestral form arise by virtue of the fact that properties of body structure and behaviour, which in the wild prototype are only marked by some transient stages of youth, are kept permanently by the domestic form. In dogs, short hair, curly tail, hanging ears domed skulls and the short muzzle of many domestic breeds are features of this type. In behaviour, one of these juvenile characters which has become permanent in the domestic dog, expresses itself in the peculiar form of its attachment. The ardent affection which wild canine youngsters show for their mother and which in these disappears completely after they have reached maturity, is preserved as a permanent mental trait of all highly domesticated dogs. What originally was love for the mother is transformed into love for the human master.

Just as *natural selection* produced infantile characters in man himself—characters that meant so much to him in his own evolution as a hunter—so man in turn, by *his own powers of selection*, but for quite other (partly aesthetic) reasons, has by breeding done the same thing to his dog. He has now not only a faithful, loyal follower, but a companion who feels for him a wholehearted loving devotion. It is not a sexual loving, but a filial loving; it is a deep affection for a *particular* master or mistress, the one to whom the young dog has given his attachment. The master, or more usually the mistress, may give a deep parent-like love in return. Here I cannot resist recalling that Niko Tinbergen has pointed out that it is the little lap-dogs with their infantile characters – their round baby-like faces – that childless women select as their pets.[1]

Now Lorenz makes a very interesting observation about the attachment of a dog to his master:

> The 'sealing of the bond', the final attachment of the dog to one master, is quite enigmatical. It takes place quite suddenly within a few days, particularly in the case of puppies that come from a breeding kennel. The 'susceptible period' for this most important occurrence in the whole of a dog's life is, in Aureus dogs, between eight and eighteen months, and in Lupus dogs round about the sixth month.[2]

One must not attempt to press an analogy or parallel too far; but it should be observed, I think, that here, in an animal, we see something occurring at a phase in development which is not altogether unlike the almost sudden 'conversion' that occurs in the religious life of many human adolescents. Be that as it may, the faithfulness, love and devotion of a dog for his master or mistress shows us, I believe, the same elements that make up the essentials of man's attitude to his personal God.

Does not all this point, some may say, to the final destruction of theistic religion? Not at all, I would say. What it *does* show is that the relationship of man to what he calls God is a biological one, in just the same sense that the association of the dog with man is a biological one. This is what I mean when I speak of the biology of

---

[1] *The Study of Instinctive Behaviour* (Clarendon Press, Oxford, 1951), p. 209.

[2] *King Solomon's Ring* (Methuen, London, 1952), p. 118. The terms Aureus and Lupus refer to two main types of dogs: the former, according to some authorities, having more jackal 'blood' and the latter more wolf 'blood' in their ancestors (see footnote on p. 164).

God; *this* is what my book is about. What we call God must be related to man who, in turn, is very much a part of the organic system. That is why, to my way of thinking, the behavioural relation of the dog to man is not just an illustrative analogy; it is a clear demonstration that the same biological factors, resulting from the same kind of social development (that of the pack), have become involved in the formation of man's images of God.

I say images of God, and not image, because the concepts of Deity are different among different peoples and, indeed, we see a change in the image of God taking place in the course of human history. That surely is a good deal of what the Bible is about – the changes taking place in the image of God as recorded in the literature of a single people: the change from the stern image of a wrathful, jealous God demanding that lambs shall be sacrificed as an appeasement for the people's sins, shown to us in the Old Testament, to that of the loving Father of the New Testament. Is not this involving the same principles as those in the change of emphasis from a strict obedience to an undisputed pack-leader to that of the more filial-like devotional relationship of the domestic dog to man? Of course I am not trying to suggest that there is any direct relationship between dog and man in any genetic evolutionary sense; they are members of two quite different orders of mammals whose distinct ancestral stocks go back at least to the beginning of the Paleocene period of nearly a hundred million years ago. What I am suggesting is that the principles operating in these two widely separated species are in fact the *same biological principles;* and they are the same just because primitive man, the hunting hominid, is *closer* in *social behaviour* to the hunting dog than he is to any other member of the animal kingdom. It is almost superfluous to add that religion, of course, is a manifestation of social behaviour.

As I write, I can at this point imagine gasps of horror from two different classes of reader. Some gasps will come from those believers in God who, in spite of what I said two paragraphs ago, will imagine that this surely *must* destroy the validity of a theistic religion. The other will come from those who are vegetarians as a matter of principle; the very idea that our religious feelings have sprung from the social behaviour of hunting *carnivores* may make them, at first, recoil with intense displeasure and disbelief. In reply to both of these cries of objection I would say, look a little closer and both horrors will dissolve.

My answer to the first problem is this. Whilst the emotional principles have the same biological basis in both dog and man, those of man in forming a religious outlook present us with something quite new in the course of evolution. In one sense, something has occurred as new as the coming of speech and language, and indeed related to it as we shall see, but in another and perhaps better sense, as new as the discovery of the making of fire; the phenomenon of fire, unlike that of speech, has always existed in the world, but of all the animals man alone has learnt how to *make it*. What we may call the Divine, or in human terms God, has I believe always been a part of the living system, a part related to that which is still a mystery, the mystery of consciousness; here, of course, I am at present a heretic in biology, and the justification of my views I must leave (in order to avoid a lengthy digression) to a later chapter (p. 204), where I shall be discussing process theology in relation to Whitehead's philosophy. My views have, I believe, as I shall hope to show, a sound intellectual foundation. What I am trying to say here, and what I shall now go on to amplify, is that man discovered something in the universe which may have been felt before by animals (who knows?) but which could never have become a conception without the coming of speech. When men were able to communicate their ideas to one another they must have begun to discuss some strange feelings they experienced from time to time, feelings of some power which appeared to them to lie outside themselves; such feelings have come to man again and again in all parts of the world and in all kinds of societies, from those of primitive tribes to those of the most sophisticated and civilized cultures. As hunting gave way to the herding of domestic animals for food, and agriculture began with the planting of crops, man I believe began to direct towards this imagined 'something other' the emotions that had developed originally as part of the hunting-pack system. This 'something other' I believe to be very real.

Does not such a consideration also answer the second objection? What began as a part of that social behaviour which was developed in the quest for flesh, became in part turned into something quite different; at first no doubt it was mainly a conversion of the obedience to a pack-leader into a sense of combined fear and loyalty to a new invisible 'leader' which had developed in man's imagination through his discussion with his fellows of the strange something he came to *experience*. Later, as the emotions of the child–parent relationship became incorporated, the feelings of a devotional love were added to those of fear and loyalty. What man calls God is only known to him *through* experience, either through his own personal experience or by hearing (or reading) of the experience of others – the prophets, saints and mystics. Surely, as we think about it, we shall realize that there is no need to be any more shocked, by finding that the emotions originally developed in the hunting life should be turned to higher things, than there is for us to be dismayed by knowing that in every history of man's religion itself (and in fact, for us in the West, in our own Judao-Christian strand of it) blood sacrifices have played their part, before being converted into less barbaric sacraments. Let me remind you of the quotation I gave from Marett on p. 80 which began, 'Thanks to the grosser forms of the sacrificial rite, the middle religions – not those of savages so much as those of half-civilized peoples – reek of blood like a shambles.'[1] One might almost be tempted to suggest that the prominence of blood sacrifices in the development of religion may have been not unrelated to the carnivorous nature of man's early life; that, however, may be just a fanciful aside.

Whilst Read may in part have been right in believing that the 'superstitions of man', as he calls religion, were invented as wizardry to maintain discipline in the tribe when hunting gave way to agriculture, I am convinced by experience, as are countless others, that the basis of religion is not just superstition. Magic,

[1] *Faith, Hope and Charity in Primitive Religions* (1932), p. 90.

wizardry and animism have all come into religion at different times, but they have, I believe, only become attached to a very different something which is a real part of human experience. This, according to some, may be no more than an experience of an element within the subconscious mind of the individual, or it may, as Jung has believed, be an element within a greater collective unconscious of mankind, or yet again, as I in fact think likely, for reasons to be discussed in subsequent chapters, something much more profound. Whatever view we take does not affect the subject of this particular chapter which is a discussion of the parallel, and the reasons behind it, between the relation of dog to man and that of man to the element he calls God. Any discussion of the actual nature of the experience of God must come later. I will only say now that I do not believe that the curious things we discussed in the earlier chapter on parapsychology can any longer be entirely dismissed as nonsense; there is too much experimental evidence of something which appears to link one individual consciousness with another, and so to suggest a transcendent world which man at times can experience in an extra-sensory way.

Primitive man felt something, whether he called it Mana, Waken or by any other name, something which gave him power, strength and encouragement to overcome difficulties and achieve aspirations; and this, as we have seen in chapter 5, is at the heart of all religion. It is this that man personified as an invisible Presence and it is this that appears to respond to man's approach.

Finally, before leaving man's social behaviour related to the earlier days of his life in the hunting pack, there is yet one other aspect of it which may bear on his later religious life. It can hardly be said to relate to the social life of the hunting dogs; or does it? There are some who might perhaps say yes to this; be that as it may, it relates particularly to man's hunting days and so may well come into this chapter, especially as it certainly relates again to the earlier writings of Carveth Read. We recall how he emphasizes that life in the hunting pack was essentially purposeful. The members of the pack are held together as a team, collaborating in the common quest. The rudiments of speech he believes may confidently be traced to such co-operation. I will give a direct quotation from his chapter on the 'moralization of the hunters' (here he is dealing with man the hunter, not the dog):

> No doubt the affections of family life continued from the anthropoid condition, in which the protracted youth of children had developed them even beyond the warm attachment which prevails among the lower Primates; and with the still more protracted youth of the stock, advancing toward the status of Man, the family affections became more enduring. The extension of goodwill beyond the family depends (*a*) upon occasions of co-operation and (*b*) upon the absence of occasions of rivalry and antagonism with those outside. The first of these conditions was daily supplied by the hunting life; but the second not until customs had been established of sharing the prey. Friendliness and the disposition to mutual aid must be so useful to a hunting-pack that is not merely seasonal but permanent (as I take ours to have been), both to individuals and to the pack as a whole, within certain limits (as that the wounded, sick or aged must not amount to an encumbrance), that we may suppose natural selection to have favoured the growth of effective sympathy, not merely in giving warning of danger or in mutual defence, but so far as it is actually found at present in backward tribes. It nowhere seems to be excessive; and its fuller manifestation in some civilized countries seems to depend less upon a positive increase of benevolence in the generality than on the breaking down here and there of conditions that elsewhere oppose and inhibit it.[1]

Here is the beginning of comradeship and brotherly love. As I stressed in my book, *The Divine Flame*, may not all forms of love be biologically related? We have already been discussing two kinds of love developed in the course of evolution (p. 142), that related to sex and that of the offspring–parent relationship; here,

---

[1] *The Origin of Man* (2nd edn, 1925), pp. 81–2.

in the bonding together of members of a species for a common purpose, the evolutionary process may have developed yet another variety of the same all-important emotional force which I believe to be a reality in the living system. In that great mine of evidence of man's evolving religious experience, the Bible, we see striking and significant changes in the meanings and use of the words for love; if what I have just been saying may shock some biologists, I do not think it should upset the theologians. We see, for example, in the Old Testament, a change in the way in which one Hebrew word, *ahebh*, may be used: from meaning sexual love to the love of righteousness; or again in pre-Biblical Greek we see the same transition but with the use of different words: from the sensuous *eros*, through the friendly love of *philia* to the *agape*, the predominant love in the New Testament.[1]

'God is Love', said St John. Brotherly love – the *agape* of the New Testament – is certainly at the heart of Christianity. Comradeship in striving for a common purpose may convert a secular movement into a fervour that is almost religious. I am far from being a Communist, yet I must admit that those so-called 'Anti-God' posters that came out of Russia in the 1930s struck me as being the most passionately religious pictures that have appeared in the present century. Again, looking at the banners carried in the development of the British Trades Union movement in the nineteenth century, reproduced in colour in that splendid book, *Banner Bright*,[2] we see again religious themes, usually taken from the Bible, exemplifying the spirit of unity (often also with the symbol of clasped hands of friendship) among the working men in their cause against oppression.

There was also an almost religious spirit, but perhaps never called so, in the rank and file of the soldiers in the early years of the First World War; it was the spirit of comradeship of those striving with a common purpose – the overthrow of the danger of

---

[1] See the volume on *Love* by Quell and Stauffer, 1933 (translated by J. R. Coates, 1949) in the series on 'Bible Key Words' from G. Kittel's *Theologisches Wörterbuch zum Neuen Testament* (A. & C. Black, London, 1949).

[2] John Gorman, *Banner Bright* (Allen Lane, London, 1973).

a domination by the Kaiser's Germany. This was the case again in the Second World War against Hitler. There are many who have said that in spite of all the dangers and horrors of war, and the imminence of death, at no time in their lives have they felt such satisfaction as in the war, when banded together with others for the same cause which they felt to be just. It was that spirit which was immortalized in Donatello's early fifteenth-century statue of St George in Florence; I remember how moved I was when I first saw it in 1921 – there indeed was the spirit of the 1914 soldier – and, no doubt, of 1940 too.

Man feels that, for the satisfaction of his soul, he must be living for a purpose; this no doubt also originated far back in his history, in the life of the hunting pack, but no matter. It is our great task today, before it is too late, to make a social purpose which will satisfy this urge; I believe that, if we don't, our society will break up into warlike bands. The task of finding such a common quest is surely far more important for the future of mankind than further extensions of physical and chemical technology. Perhaps at this point one might be excused for wondering whether the feeling that so many have, that there surely must be a purpose in the universe itself, may possibly stem from the same origin. This question, however, we must reserve for our later discussion of a more natural theology.

But to return for a moment to the spirit of war. We must remember that in a conflict, whether on religious grounds or one of different ideologies, those taking part on each of the opposing sides may well be driven forward by a uniting sense of purpose which they deem to be right. I have little doubt that the fervour of the Hitler movement, the spirit that brought the Nazi party to power, was generated among its supporters as a feeling for a just cause: the revolt of a great section of humanity against the terms of the Treaty of Versailles. Hitler himself felt he was a man of destiny – a man who could change the world; and in his ascendant days it certainly seemed as if he felt a superhuman power behind him. Let us remember what Marett wrote in a continuation of the same passage that I quoted a few pages back (p. 172):

If religion is liable to unloose the beast in us even while seeking to free the man, we must learn how this deviation occurs, so that religion may be kept to the true direction. As psychologists, then, we must not be content to speak together in whispers about the lust or the cruelty that found their way into the religious complex together with the noblest of the human tendencies. Let us honestly proclaim that religious emotion is ambivalent, exciting the mind at once for better and for worse. At times, then, man is apt to think that he has reached the heights when he has merely touched the lowest depths of his spiritual nature.

Science is the same in any country of the world, and its theories are constantly changing as new facts are brought to light by observation and the advance of experimental research. Until we have a similar universal outlook in regard to religion, and the part it may play in the lives of men, we shall always be in danger of the outbreak of bitter wars fought by those who either have different images of what they call God, or different ideologies they feel with an equal passion. Whilst we can never hope to mould all humanity into a single religious pattern, could we not move towards a new kind of theology which would recognize that the expressions of religion are likely to be as various as are the characteristics of different nationalities, and indeed as various as the ways in which members of the same peoples may experience what they call God or the sense of transcendence? Such a new theology would be as progressive as science; it would be prepared to change its theories as new facts are provided by the discoveries in biology, psychology, and perhaps in that infant half-science of parapsychology; it would incorporate, as well, those from the researches into the nature of religious experience itself. It must also recognize that the experience of what a man may call God, or an ecstatic mystery, can be just as real and as moving to the person concerned whatever his particular faith may be: whether he calls himself a Buddhist, a Christian, a Hindu, a Jew, a Muslim or an open-minded agnostic.

What man calls God can only be known to him through his experience; psychologists no doubt will continue to debate the nature of this feeling, and this is all the more reason for studying the records of it in a systematic way.

10. *God as experience*

We saw in chapter 5 that there appears to be an outstanding common factor in religion in its simplest form, wherever it may occur, among both primitive and sophisticated peoples. Let me recapitulate.

Marett presented the evidence that primitive man enjoys an 'assurance that he is in touch with powers of grace that can make him rise superior to the circumstances of this mortal life' (p. 75), and Durkheim that 'the believer who has communicated with his God ... is a man who is *stronger*. He feels within him more force, either to endure the trials of existence, or to conquer them. It is as though he were raised above the miseries of the world' (p. 76). Or again, as Malinowski said, 'belief is not the alpha and omega of religion: it is important to realize that man translates his confidence in spiritual powers into action' (p. 85). We compared such statements by anthropologists with some made by eminent psychologists concerning the effect of religion upon more sophisticated people: William James had said that prayerful communion 'produces regenerative effects unattainable in other ways ... as though transmundane energies, God, if you will, produced immediate effects within the natural world' (p. 86). Sir Frederic Bartlett (also p. 86) said that many humble people he had met and respected had done 'many things which all ordinary sources of evidence seem to set outside the range of unassisted humanity. When they say "It is God working through me" I cannot see that I have either the right or the knowledge to reject their testimony.' Then, looking at the great religions of the world, we saw the striking universality of this sense of dependence upon a spiritual power.

Perhaps it may be thought by some that the humble people respected by Sir Frederic, and indeed that the majority of those of different religions, who experience the feeling of Divine help, were all relatively simple souls who might imagine anything suggested to them by the tenets of their faith. For those who might think this, let me take two examples from the intellectual world. The first is taken from an address which Baroness Mary Stocks gave to the World Congress of Faiths, entitled 'The Religion of a Heretic'.[1] She says,

> ... Is there something that comes to meet us? Beatrice Webb's answer as recorded in her autobiography carries us straight into the realm of religious faith. 'For my own part', she writes, 'I find it best to live as if the soul of man were in communion with a superhuman force which makes for righteousness.' Beatrice Webb was conscious of experiencing a sense of reverence or awe—an apprehension of a power and purpose outside herself—which she called 'feeling' and which was sometimes induced by appreciation of great music or corporate worship. But her experience went further than this nebulous fleeting 'feeling'—because as a result of it she achieved a religious interpretation of the universe which satisfied and upheld her and enabled her to seek continuous guidance in prayer—and this without compromising her intellectual integrity ... Now *that* is a big step forward from rationalism, and once it is taken (as I take it in company with Beatrice Webb) it opens up a great expanse of undiscovered country—the territory that lies beyond reason—and includes what those who have explored it have discovered, or thought they had discovered, by extra-sensory perception.

It is clear that Mary Stocks and Beatrice Webb have the same feeling of being in touch with some Power outside themselves. Next I give a passage from Dr L. P. Jacks's Hibbert Lectures of 1922 published under the title of *Religious Perplexities*.

> All religious testimony, so far as I can interpret its meaning, converges towards a single point, namely this. There is that in

[1] *World Faiths* (Journal of World Congress of Faiths), no. 60 (London, July 1964), p. 2.

the world, call it what you will, which responds to the confidence of those who trust it, declaring itself, to them, as a
fellow-worker in the pursuit of the Eternal Values, meeting
their loyalty to it with reciprocal loyalty to them, and coming
in at critical moments when the need of its sympathy is
greatest; the conclusion being, that wherever there is a soul
in darkness, obstruction or misery, there also is a Power
which can help, deliver, illuminate and gladden that soul.
This is the Helper of men, sharing their business as Creators
of Value, nearest at hand when the worst has to be encoun-
tered: the companion of the brave, the upholder of the loyal,
the friend of the lover, the healer of the broken, the joy of the
victorious – the God who is spirit, the God who is love.

And later in the same book he speaks of the power that can be
received:

Religion is a power which develops the hero in the man at
the expense of the coward in the man. As the change proceeds there comes a moment when the cowardly method of
reasoning, with its eye on safety, ceases to dominate the soul.
At the same moment the heroic element awakes and looks
with longing towards the dangerous mountain-tops.

This second quotation from Jacks reminds me that as a young
man I was much struck by a passage in H. G. Wells's *God the
Invisible King* (1917) in which (on pp. 43–7) he contrasts this
Divine power with the quite different notion of a Providence
which interferes with the laws of nature. He recalls how Daudet
travesties the latter in his *Tartarin sur les Alpes* (1885) by likening
it to a net which Tartarin had been told was stretched beneath
him as he made dangerous ascents; the feeling that the net was
there to save him gave him confidence to be more daring and so
to attempt and achieve goals impossible without it. The supposed
net, of course, was but a device to increase his bravery, and all
ideas of Providence, implied Daudet, were a similar invention.
Then two pages later, after discussing such thoughts of

benevolent intervention, Wells says this—which many who are
not familiar with this book may find remarkable as coming from
him:

> Nothing of such things will God do; it is an idle dream. But
> God will be with you nevertheless. In the reeling aeroplane or
> the dark ice-cave God will be your courage. Though you
> suffer or are killed, it is not an end. He will be with you as
> you face death; he will die with you as he has died already
> countless myriads of brave deaths. He will come so close to
> you that at the last you will not know whether it is you or he
> who dies, and the present death will be swallowed up in his
> victory.

A year later came his novel, *The Undying Fire*, in which he presented a modern version of the Book of Job. Listen to his hero,
the schoolmaster Job Huss, afflicted on all sides, proclaim, 'There
burns an undying fire in the hearts of men. By that fire I live. By
that I know the God of my salvation ... Though the universe
torment and slay me, yet will I trust in Him ...'[1] It was a side of
Wells that showed itself, at any rate in print, for only a short
period.

But to return to those who look 'with longing towards the
dangerous [symbolic] mountain-tops', it is indeed strongly suggested, from the experience of all those we have been considering,
that there is within the 'climber' a means of drawing upon a
strength and courage that has a reality and is, as Wells has said,
nothing to do with being saved if he should fall. It is, indeed,
especially so in tasks which are idealistic rather than those of
physical achievement. The strength that is gained from religion
for the fulfilment of some worth while aspiration—according to
those who are moved by spirituality—is not that of feeling that
there is comfort and support if one should fail; it is a force that
drives one on without any thought of failure.

That great scientist, Louis Pasteur, who was a Roman Catholic

[1] Op. cit., p. 144.

all his life, said when replying to the speech of welcome made to him on his election to the Académie Francaise,

> So long as the mystery of the infinite weighs on the human mind, so long will temples be raised to the cult of the infinite, whether God be called Brahmah, Allah, Jehovah or Jesus ... The Greeks understood the mysterious power of the hidden side of things. They bequeathed to us one of the most beautiful words in our language – the word 'enthusiasm' – *en theos* – a god within. The grandeur of human actions is measured by the inspiration from which they spring. Happy is he who bears a god within – an ideal of beauty and who obeys it, an ideal of art, of science. All are lighted by reflection from the infinite.[1]

How splendidly expressed: the God within that reflects the mystery of the infinite beyond – that which may be called God by as many different names as there are different faiths. As Aldous Huxley said in his *Perennial Philosophy*, this is the inexhaustible theme that 'has been treated again and again from the standpoint of every religious tradition and in all the principal languages of Asia and Europe'.

What we call God is a human *experience*. Any authority declaring the nature of God in the sacred writings of the various religions of the world is derived from the experience of the holy men of each of these particular faiths. All such authority is based upon original experience. If we are to extend the idea of a biology of God towards a more scientific natural theology, it must I believe be through a more systematic study of man's experience of what appears to him to be the Divine or the transcendental element in the world. In the introductory chapter, where I was discussing the possibility of this biological approach, I briefly mentioned (p. 17) the founding of the Religious Experience Research Unit at Manchester College, Oxford, where my colleagues and I are making just such an attempt. We are setting out to study

---

[1] The translation given by Arthur Koestler in his *The Act of Creation* (Hutchinson, London, 1964), p. 261.

the nature of this experience. How good is the evidence for the existence of that element which the examples we have been considering seem to suggest—that there is something far more fundamental to religion than fear and superstition? This is what I believe is so important to investigate. The collection and study of examples of this evidence is what we are engaged upon.

Whilst the series of volumes, which I hope will soon follow from the unit, will be describing our methods in detail and the full results from the different sides of the work, I propose here to give an outline sketch of the way we are proceeding, and something of the nature of the experiences being revealed. It is intended only to show the beginnings of such a science, or rather an incipient science I should say, for it is clear that like many another science, it must pass through a long phase of observational natural history before it can pretend to have reached full scientific status. Our first volume, to be entitled *Exploration into Religious Experience*, will I hope be published before very long.

We are essentially concerned with the study of the experiences of those living at the present day: people we can go back to for further information concerning the experiences of which they have written to us in response to our requests. I sometimes get almost abusive letters saying, 'Are you not ashamed of yourself doing what you are doing? Are you not *satisfied* with what is given us in holy writ? Why need you be seeking for more evidence?' I write back to say that, of course, the scriptures and the writings of the mystics contain some of the most profound examples of such experience, but is it not also important to demonstrate that these experiences appear to be just as real and vital to modern man as they were in the lives of those of long ago? I like the saying of Dean Inge: 'Religion is concerned with that which is and not with that which was.'

Our first attempt at the collection of accounts of personal experience and feelings was to seek the help of the editors of every religious journal published in Great Britain; we asked them if they would kindly co-operate by publishing an article giving examples of the kind of experience in which we were interested, and appealing for personal records to be sent in, together with relevant information concerning the age, sex, religious upbringing, etc., of the writers. We also promised that all such material would be treated as strictly confidential, with names suppressed in any published reports on the research. Some thirty journals accepted these appeals either in full or sometimes in shortened form; the result, however, was disappointing in that we received barely 200 replies, and these gave by no means a good coverage of age range or of sex, there being a high proportion of the elderly, and far more female than male respondents. It was clear that we had to enter the more general journals of wider circulation.

Our change of fortune in this direction began when the editor of the *Guardian* asked if I would give an interview to their then chief feature-writer, Mr Geoffrey Moorhouse, for an article on our work; I readily accepted, but stipulated that I should be able to check the article for factual statements before publication and that it would also include our appeal for records of experience. This excellent article, in spite of, or perhaps because of, a somewhat sensational editorial heading ('Sir Alister's "trip" to Heaven') which neither Mr Moorhouse nor I had expected, attracted a great deal of attention and brought in a very good crop of records covering a wide age-range from sixth-form boys and girls upwards. This led to a similar request by the editor of the *Observer* colour-supplement for a longer article, to be written by Mr Peter Lewis; again I made the same conditions and the appeal was put in a special panel to catch attention; again the response was splendid, with a good age-range of both sexes. Following a lecture I gave at the Royal Institution, entitled 'A Scientist looks at Religion', the feature-editor of *The Times* asked me for two articles on our work, and a year later Mr Lewis wrote two articles, with appeals for accounts, for the *Daily Mail*. Mainly as a result of these articles, but also because of some appeals made through the B.B.C., and other articles in journals in the U.S.A., Australia and New Zealand, we have now received close on 4,000 personal records.

Some psychologists have suggested that at the very outset we should have started with a definite questionnaire. With this I disagree. Quite apart from the likelihood that many may be put off by such an approach, the very manner of asking the questions would be apt, I believe, to give a slant to the content of the replies. The specimens we are hunting are shy and delicate ones which we want to secure in as natural a condition as possible; we must at all costs avoid damaging or distorting them by trying to trap them within an artificial framework. In the first instance we want a brief description set down in the words and manner thought most fitting by those who have had the experience.

There are two difficulties that I should here mention and discuss. The first of them I have already briefly mentioned in the introductory chapter, but I must now say a little more about it, for it touches the very nature of our method. It is certainly true that the real essence of any deeply-felt religious experience cannot adequately be described in words; it is ineffable. Whilst we recognize this, we also realize that we can only make a systematic *objective* study of people's *written attempts* at describing what their subjective feelings were at the time of their communion with the transcendental. No one can describe the essence of love in words (poetry perhaps, but not in prose), but people can give some account of the intensity of the emotion aroused and its effect upon their lives; it is the same with experience of the Divine. Only by studying a large number of *attempts* at such descriptions can we begin to have some knowledge of their nature, and also of the effect of such experience on the lives of those concerned. The very fact that a large number of people say very much the same kind of thing — that they have had an *indescribable feeling* of joy, of a sense of the Divine Presence, of spiritual union with the transcendental and so on, and that it has a marked effect upon them — *this* is what is important to record; it is possible to collect the objective evidence that many people *say* they have had remarkable, *ineffable* experiences that are of the highest value to them in their lives. This is what our research is about.

The other difficulty concerns what is meant by the term 're-ligious experience'. Because it may lead to misunderstanding I have sometimes regretted using it in the name of our unit; I did so partly because it was used by William James in the title of his famous book and, as I have already said, I felt we were humbly following his lead. There can be no doubt that for some the phrase makes them think that it can only refer to the more dramatic isolated experiences. Perhaps it would have been better to have termed the aims of the unit research into spiritual awareness, for we are just as interested in those who experience such a continuing feeling of the transcendental as we are in those who have these more exceptional and occasional ecstatic moments. In our appeals for written accounts we now try to emphasize that we are equally interested in both types of experience. I mainly decided, however, on the unit's title because we are essentially dealing with the *experiential* side of religion in *all* its aspects. There is, as Professor C. C. J. Webb said, 'a serious danger of overlooking the existence of a genuine religious experience which, although taking forms perhaps less strange and striking is not therefore less real and significant, in a vast number of persons who, though innocent of mystical raptures, or of crises of conversion, yet pass their lives against the background of a constant consciousness of being in the presence of a Power behind appearance ...'[1]

It is later in our work, after the sorting and classifying of the material, that we do indeed use questionnaires, but first a few words about classification. Originally I had thought it might be somewhat like a biological taxonomy: those kinds most like one another being grouped together in *genera*, and those genera appearing to have points in common would be classed in *families* and so on. In reality however it is much more complex. We had begun by thinking we could distinguish two main kinds of experience: those of people who felt a general sense of spiritual awareness and those of a more ecstatic or mystical kind. We soon found, however, that many accounts combine a number of quite different elements, and some indeed are a combination of the two main types just mentioned: for example a person who has hitherto been agnostic may quite unexpectedly have an ecstatic experience which convinces him that the world is not the kind of place he thought it was, and

[1] *Religious Experience* (Oxford University Press, London, 1945), p. 37.

he now adopts an attitude of general spiritual awareness. Our classification now consists in recognizing a number of distinct main elements which may be present either singly or as a combination of two or more of them in any one particular account; we recognize fourteen such different elements including, for example, what we call sensory or quasi-sensory experiences (the seeing of lights, visions, hearing voices, etc.), behavioural experiences, cognitive experiences, affective experiences, impressions of 'Providence', etc. Each of these is then divided into a number of sub-categories.

It is in the next stage that we use a questionnaire technique of eliciting further information from those respondents in the groups of experiences in which different members of staff are particularly interested. In this way we are better able to compare and contrast the original records sent in and indeed to amplify them. Edward Robinson, my senior colleague, who is specially interested in the development of religious experience in the individual, has had a very good response to his questionnaire from those who in adult life have looked back to experiences in their childhood. He has now prepared a monograph on this aspect of the work which will form the second volume in our forthcoming series of results. Similarly Timothy Beardsworth, who is studying the quasi-sensory experiences, has asked the respondents concerned to do certain psychological visual-perception tests; his work will form another volume in our series of results. Then Michael Walker and latterly Miss Joan Crewdson, who have both been concerned with those people who have described a continuing awareness of a power that appears to be beyond the self, giving them strength and encouragement in their lives, have also used the questionnaire method with very good results.

What steps are we taking, I am frequently asked, to test the honesty or validity of the accounts sent in? Apart from a small proportion from those who clearly are mentally ill, some are perhaps emotionally exaggerated and others may be written to give a swollen importance to the self, but no one with an unbiased mind, I believe, can read the majority of the accounts without being impressed by a feeling of their sincerity. Our stressing the confidential treatment of the material has I am sure been an important factor; we have received many very moving and intimate personal accounts, sometimes describing experiences related to tragic bereavement or broken lives, and others of religious feelings that the writers say they have never spoken of to any other person. I am convinced that the vast majority of these are indeed sincere and important human documents. The false records are, I believe, a small minority which, among the large number of records we are dealing with, can have no real bearing on the results.

It is not my intention in just one chapter to embark upon any detailed discussion of these results. An adequate consideration of the examples of each particular type must take a whole book to itself; these are the studies which will follow in the series of volumes now in preparation. I merely wish here to give a general impression of the variety of the experiences which our respondents feel to be of religious significance. I am only giving short extracts from a small selection taken from the first thousand records received to give some idea of their range. They do not all refer to God by name, but sometimes to a 'spiritual power', a 'superhuman force', 'something more powerful than myself' and other such phrases. I include an example of a person who says, 'I find it best to live as if one were in communion with some point outside onself', but who then goes on to say 'this does not lead me to think that there is such a point—a force or power acting independently of belief or reliance on it.' Or again in another instance a person referring to a power says, 'I think of it as faith; not faith in God, but faith which is God.' We see indeed how the experiences vary, but they all point to something felt to have a deep significance. Here then is merely a short selection of extracts, each paragraph from a different person, to be looked at like a collection of specimens gathered by a naturalist.

One day as I was walking along Marylebone Road I was suddenly seized with an extraordinary sense of great joy and exaltation, as though a marvellous beam of spiritual power had shot through me linking me in rapture with the world, the Universe, Life with a capital L, and all the beings around me. All delight and power, all things living, all time fused in a brief second.

There was a mysterious presence in nature and sometimes met with in the communion and in praying by oneself, which was my greatest delight, expecially when as happened from time to time, *nature became lit up from inside* with something that came from beyond itself (or so it seemed to me).

It seemed to me that, in some way, I was extending into my surroundings and was becoming one with them. At the same time I felt a sense of lightness, exhilaration and power as if I was beginning to understand the true meaning of the whole Universe ...

... In this way also I once experienced a type of ecstasy—a deep joy which was almost more than one could bear yet one felt one longed to prolong the experience to its uttermost. Normally though, this feeling of 'the Peace of God' comes at unlikely times. It is a moment when one realizes one's place in the universe, the deep and loving power which holds one, a complete absence of fear and worry and a great sense of joy. Nothing on earth can ever compare with this feeling.

This power is more or less constant, but there are times when it is replaced by a vague feeling of uneasiness, a tendency to worry unnecessarily, or a failure to look for priorities. I think of it as faith; not faith in God, but faith which is God.

As far back as I can remember I have never had a sense of separation from the spiritual force I now choose to call God ... From the age of about 6 to 12 in places of quiet and desolation this feeling of 'oneness' often passed to a state of 'listening'. I mean by 'listening' that I was suddenly alerted to something that was going to happen. What followed was a feeling of tremendous exaltation in which time stood still.

From quite an early age (probably about 12) I have been conscious of religious awareness, I can remember feeling so strongly about it that I wrote it down at about 12 years of age, but then tore it up later when I thought it a bit soft! Since then this feeling of being really one with God's creation has come to me increasingly, particularly since really committing myself to His service in the Church. I can only describe it as being like the feeling you get when listening to marvellous music – only more so and embracing all creation.

I heard nothing, yet it was as if I were *surrounded by golden light* and as if I only had to reach out my hand to touch God himself who was so surrounding me with his compassion.

I think from my childhood I have always had the feeling that the true reality is not to be found in the world as the average person sees it. There seems to be a constant force at work from the inside trying to push its way to the surface of consciousness. The mind is continually trying to create a symbol sufficiently comprehensive to contain it, but this always ends in failure. There are moments of pure joy with a heightened awareness of one's surroundings, as if a great truth had been passed across.

I went into the sittingroom and got on my knees in the dark atmosphere and cried 'Oh God. Oh God. Please help,' then burst into tears: something I had not done for several years. From that night onwards, a strange calm came over me as I felt the tug of an unseen hand guiding me and leading me to do things I would not otherwise have done.

I find it best to live as if one were in communion with some point outside oneself which can put one's affairs in proportion – between 'le zéro and l'infini' – and saves one from narrow self-absorption. This does not lead me to think that there is such a point – a force or power acting independently of belief in or reliance on it. Nevertheless, one sees the need for it operative in many other people.

About ten years later I began to pray for my children's safety, and this became a habit which I have never lost, and often the answer to such prayer is spectacular. Now I've evolved a belief which is identical with Beatrice Webb's: 'I find it best to live as if the soul of man were in communion with a superhuman force which makes for righteousness' ... May I add that since this belief grew in me I feel as if I had grown, as if my mind had stretched to take in the vast universe and be a part of it.

... It is, as well, not a 'happening', or a collection of 'happenings', but according to my own 'openness or receptiveness' of soul, a greater or lesser continually sustained awareness ... I see no lights, hear no voices, but I have gradually been given far greater personal power to ...

I have had no dramatic experiences ... But I have this continual awareness of this presence and this power through the Holy Spirit who dwells in me. I do things which humanly I know I cannot do and cope with crises and situations, especially at work where others go to pieces. Sometimes his joy and peace just floods over me. Sometimes his power fills me so I feel able to do almost anything.

... am continuously dependent on the loving guidance of God, who has supported me through many troubles.

I find it difficult to describe my experience, only to say that it seems to be outside of me and enormous and yet at the same time I am part of it, everything is. It is purely personal and helps me to live and to love others. It is difficult to describe, but in some way because of this feeling I feel united to all people, to all living things. Of recent years the feeling has become so strong that I am now training to become a social worker because I find that I must help people: in some way I feel their unhappiness as my own.

It seemed to me that, in some way, I was extending into my surroundings and was becoming one with them. At the same time I felt a sense of lightness, exhilaration and power as if I was beginning to understand the true meaning of the whole Universe.

When I was on holiday, aged about 17, I glanced down and watched an ant striving to drag a bit of twig through a patch of sun on a brick wall in the graveyard of a Greek church, while chanting came from within the white building. The feeling aroused in me was quite unanticipated, welling up from some great depth, and essentially timeless. The concentration of simplicity and innocence was intensely of some vital present. I've had similar experiences on buses, suddenly watching people and being aware how *right* everything essentially is.

I have a growing sense of reality, and personal identity, which comes from being united to something more powerful than myself, something that is helping me to be what I want to be.

... since the age of fifteen I have had an ever-recurring sense of a voice saying 'This is the way, walk yet in it.'

I have presented these examples, I have said, like a collection of naturalist's specimens. Can we go further with them? I have spoken of our classification and our studies of the different main types. All this we realize is indeed in the natural-history phase. Are some of them commoner than others? How do they compare in distribution one with another? To answer such questions we must give the work a more quantitative ecological type of approach. This would clearly be a logical step to take, but a very difficult one. Difficult, but not I believe impossible, given sufficient funds to support it — and it will certainly be expensive. We hope, if we get such support, to make a detailed study of the religious feelings of large random samples of the population, to enable us to answer many questions. For example do the experiences of those in a city tend to differ from those brought up in the country? Are there differences between those from the South of

England and from the Highlands of Scotland? What proportion of any population will say that they have never had any experience which they could call at all religious? Such a survey has now been planned; each person approached in the survey will be given a set of examples of different types of experience drawn from our records, and will be asked if he or she has at any time had any such feeling, or any other religious experience or none at all.

In the meantime, quite independently, Mr David Hay, Lecturer in Biology in the Department of Education at the University of Nottingham, developed a keen interest in a similar line of research. I was delighted when he wrote expressing the hope that his work could be done in co-operation with ours. He has now completed a pilot study among University students in preparation for a larger one to follow. Whilst it is based upon the responses of a random sample of only a hundred subjects (50 male and 50 female), it nevertheless provides information of exceptional interest, showing that such experience is far more frequent than might have been supposed.[1] Since this was written I have news of another important survey of religious experience made in America by Drs Andrew M. Greeley and William C. McCready of Chicago University. In the first published account they say that 'four out of ten Americans report the experience of a powerful spiritual force which seemed to lift them out of themselves'.[2]

Whilst the study of the distribution of the different types of experience among the population at large is indeed valuable information to have, it is not I believe the most important goal for our researches. From the detailed study of the different types of experience we must surely learn much more about the basic nature of this element in human behaviour. What could be more important—since the development of our civilization in the past has been so much affected by it—than a better understanding of this

[1] He gives a general account of his work in the December 1974 issue of *The Month*.

[2] *New York Times Magazine*, 16 Jan. 1975. A full monograph on the work is to be published later this year by Sage Publications, Beverly Hills, California.

remarkable side of our nature: the experience of what so many have thought of as relating to what they call God? Such studies I venture to believe may lead in time to two new developments which I shall briefly discuss in the remaining two chapters: firstly to a more rational theology in harmony with the scientific outlook, and secondly to what I like to think of as an experimental faith using the word 'experimental' in its original rather than its more confined laboratory sense: i.e. 'based on experience, not authority or conjecture'.[1]

The work we have started, I like to think, is just a beginning. There is no end to the possibilities ahead. Just as physical science has developed and its boundaries are ever expanding so this newer field of a systematic study of man's spiritual nature and potentials may be an equally productive and enlarging venture. Is it not surprising that so little is spent upon such work compared with the vast sums expended on research concerning man's bodily comfort and health? Dotted about the country are the great institutes dealing with physical and biological problems, medical, agricultural and fisheries research, and so on. Annual Government expenditure on such work in Britain, quite apart from that concerned with the defence services, runs to hundreds of millions of pounds. Even if the cracking of civilization, through the suppression of the religious forces which have built it up and sustained it, may appear to be only a remote possibility, is it not worth finding out a little more about the nature of these spiritual elements in the behaviour of mankind before it may be too late. Such research urgently requires funds if it is to continue on an adequate scale, yet perhaps no Government can be expected to provide them. Are there not some wealthy patrons who may consider endowing such research in terms equal to the benefactions given to the founding of so many university laboratories and senior research fellowships? It is my hope that their interest may have been aroused.

[1] *Concise Oxford Dictionary.*

11.   Towards a new natural theology

The philosophies behind the doctrines of religion and their acceptance by the public are, as in so many other fields, in a state of flux. At the beginning of this decade, the *Radio Times*[1] announced a new Radio 3 series, 'Is there a future for religious belief?' under the heading, 'Can Christianity survive the 70's?' On the same day *The Times* published a review of Dr John Robinson's latest book with these words: 'Religion has so completely lost its hold on the imagination of our society that it is possible that more people in this pagan land turn for comfort to Jimmy Young than to Jesus Christ.' I write this chapter as we approach the middle of the decade, and it is clear that the crisis is indeed deepening.

Recently there appeared an article[2] by Mervyn Stockwood, the Bishop of Southwark, pointing out some very significant figures. He refers to the speculation regarding the successor to Michael Ramsay as Archbishop of Canterbury, but then says the attention of churchmen might more deservedly be directed to the religious situation with which he will be faced. 'Three facts', he says, 'indicate its seriousness: the decline in regular church attendance between 1960 and 1970 was 19 per cent; in 1963 632 men were ordained to the ministry, ten years later the figure had dropped to 373; as 40 per cent of the clergy are aged 55 or over it is estimated that 6,000 will have retired by the end of the decade to be replaced by about 3,000.' He goes on to say that these figures can be matched by most denominations in Western Europe. Confirmation of this trend comes from the Scottish Episcopal Church, in a statement[3] made by Dr Lewis Robinson in Edinburgh: in the 10 years up to 1973, membership had fallen from 55,000 to 46,000,

[1] 28 Feb. 1970.
[2] *The Times*, 22 Apr. 1974.
[3] *The Times*, 29th May 1974.

baptisms from 2,700 to 1,500 and confirmations from 2,500 to 1,220.

Whilst there is this continuing decline in concern for the doctrines and the practices of the Christian churches, there is at the same time an increasing interest being shown by the general public in the philosophy behind religion, as is witnessed by the multiplication and flourishing sales of paperback books on this subject, that have flooded the bookshops since the appearance of *Honest to God*. In the Church itself there are now signs of change. The late Dr Ian Ramsay, Bishop of Durham, writing on the future outlook for religion shortly before his untimely death, expressed his view that there would come profound changes in both our theological and scientific outlooks; and Bishop F. R. Barry ended an article[1] on 'Rebuilding the house of Christian Faith' with these words: 'We need a new natural theology to supply the supporting scaffold for faith. But we cannot now build it by *a priori* argument; only by patient assembly, brick by brick, of what we know, through enquiry and experience, about the world and about the life of man.'

It is indeed encouraging to see this revival of interest in a natural theology in ecclesiastical circles, and particularly encouraging is the recognition that it must be built up by patient inquiry, in fact by the scientific method applied to the study of experience. Theology itself is still defined in the *Concise Oxford Dictionary* as the 'science of (esp. Christian) religion', but this is using the term science in the old sense simply of knowledge; few today would admit that it forms a branch of what we now call science. *Natural theology*, however, may eventually win back its place therein; it is described in the same dictionary as 'dealing with knowledge of God as gained from his works by light of nature and reason'.

I am sometimes asked, 'Why, if religion is dying out, do we need a new natural theology?' My answer is that it is not the deep-felt experience of religious feelings that is dying out, but the institutional religion of the churches that is in such a sharp decline; and this decline, I suggest, is largely to be explained by the obvious

[1] *The Times*, 18 Sept. 1971.

gulf between the doctrines of orthodox theology and the findings of both scientific and historical research. For a sound and stable society, I believe, we must have a religious philosophy that can satisfy both the heart and the mind.

Natural theology has never really recovered from the shock it received when the Darwinian doctrine of natural selection cut away its supposed strongest support: Paley's argument from design (p. 28). All the attempts that have been made to rebuild the ruins have so far failed to find general acceptance in the intellectual world; being based upon no more than speculation and *a priori* arguments, they cannot stand up against scientific reasoning. There had been a hope in the early days of the century that such a new natural theology might have been based upon the psychology of William James. Archbishop Frederick Temple as long ago as 1857 had declared, 'Our theology has been cast in a scholastic mould, i.e. all based on Logic. We are in need of and we are being gradually forced into a theology based on psychology.'[1] This hope, however, was soon dashed, as we saw in chapter 6 (p. 107), by the coming of Freud's 'new psychology', as it was then called, and the shattering experience of the First World War. So many theologians, as we also noted, turned away from reason to the neo-Calvinism of Karl Barth, back to the Reformation concept of a dogmatic trust in the Scriptures as truly the written word of God. 'What is God,' asks Barth, and goes on to reply:

> Reformed teaching in principle does not answer this question by any free thought, i.e. as if the question had been raised and had to be answered by man himself. On the contrary, it answers it on the basis of God's own revelation. That is, it answers it from the standpoint of man who has been told by God himself, in the Person of Jesus Christ, who God is.[2]

There were, of course, notable exceptions amongst the academic theologians who stood against the Barthian flood. The late

[1] Quoted by H. D. A. Major in his *Basic Christianity* (Blackwell, Oxford, 1945), p. 54.
[2] Quoted by F. W. Camfield, *Reformation Old and New* (1948).

Dean Lowe of Christ Church wrote as follows concerning the interpretation of the Scriptures:

> Nor can I feel that there is much hope for us in the dialectical neo-Calvinism which exalts the Word of God into a slogan at the cost of completely obscuring what the Word of God is ... No doubt Karl Barth's interpretation of the Bible is thoroughly theological ... But ... the theology seems to me both obscure and defective. We must remind ourselves that a theological interpretation is no advantage if it means the arbitrary foisting of our own inadequate theology into the text. That is one of the things from which the historical critics were rightly trying to escape.[1]

The more prominent natural theologians, however, between the wars, F. R. Tennant with his *Philosophical Theology* (Cambridge University Press, Cambridge, 1928), William Temple in his Gifford Lectures, *Nature, Man and God* (1934), and John Oman in his *Natural and the Supernatural* (1931) had unfortunately made little impact. The situation was well summed up by H. E. Root in an essay in the volume, *Soundings* (ed. A. R. Vidler, 1962). In his opening paragraph he says (p. 3), 'Most people who think about these things at all agree that natural theology is in a poor state. Ninian Smart has aptly called it "the sick man of Europe".' And at the end (p. 19), he says, 'Academic theology has lived on its own fat. The supply of fat is running out ... It will take decades or generations before we know whether natural theology still has enough life in it to seek new kinds of nourishment ...'

It is not my intention to discuss all the twists and turns of modern theological discussion, nor am I competent to do so. However, before coming to a relatively new development which may have a distinct bearing upon a future natural theology, I must make some mention of the so-called 'Death of God' arguments which have been shaking the ecclesiastical world and spilling over to excite the general public. It was the book, *Honest*

---

[1] *The Interpretation of the Bible: the Edward Alleyn Lectures, 1943,* Edited by C. W. Dugmore, p. 119.

to God, by Dr John Robinson, formerly Bishop of Woolwich, that made the great stir when a pre-publication instalment appeared in the *Observer* with the banner headlines, 'Our Image of God must Go', to be echoed in a hundred other less restrained newspapers under such titles as 'God not a Daddy in the Sky' (*Daily Herald*). But Robinson was going further than the *Herald* supposed. Of course in sophisticated circles the idea of God 'up there' in any astronomical sense had long been abandoned; what Robinson was doing – and what was hardly grasped by the man-in-the-street – was no less than beginning to doubt the validity of even considering God 'out there', meaning outside the actual spatial systems in a kind of spiritual or metaphysical transcendence. Robinson expresses the gravity of this new step as follows:

> The abandonment of a God 'out there' represents a much more radical break than the transition to this concept from that of a God 'up there'. For this earlier transposition was largely a matter of verbal notation, of a change in spatial metaphor, important as this undoubtedly was in liberating Christianity from a flat-earth cosmology. But to be asked to give up any idea of a Being 'out there' at all will appear to be an outright denial of God.[1]

In the development of his ideas, Robinson was clearly much influenced by the theology of Paul Tillich. Perhaps the most important part of Tillich's philosophy was that God should not be regarded as distinct from the actual process of being. God is the 'Ground of Being' he kept saying: not 'out there', outside what we know as existence, but the very basis of our existence. When asked why is it necessary to talk about a *ground* of being, Tillich said, 'It is not necessary, I would prefer to say "being itself". But I know this term is even more disliked. And so I speak of the ground of being.'[2] Robinson tells us at the beginning of *Honest to God* how profoundly he was affected – 'lit up' are the words he

---

[1] *Honest to God* (S.C.M. Press, London, 1963), p. 17.
[2] Quoted by P. Hamilton in *The Living God and the Modern World* (Hodder & Stoughton, London, 1967), p. 151.

used—by Tillich's sermon, 'The Depth of Existence', which he quotes and from which I take the following:

> The name of this infinite and inexhaustible depth and ground of all being is *God*. That depth is what the word *God* means. And if that word has not much meaning for you, translate it, and speak of the depths of your life, of the source of your being, of your ultimate concern, of what you take seriously without any reservation. Perhaps, in order to do so, you must forget everything traditional that you have learned about God, perhaps even that word itself. For if you know that God means depth, you know much about him. You cannot then call yourself an atheist or unbeliever ... He who knows about depth knows about God.[1]

Even more interesting from our point of view is Robinson's later book, *Exploration into God*. Here he sets out, using the analogy of the geographer, to 'chart' God's place in the modern intellectual world, and he speaks metaphorically of different 'projections' for mapping the relationship, just as one may speak geographically of Mercator's or other projections for representing the spherical earth on a flat sheet of paper. He says (on p. 37),

> ... the attachment of Christianity to the supranaturalist projection[2] is becoming less and less obvious. For many purposes we still find it virtually impossible to conceive of 'God' except as a separate, personified Being. And there is nothing 'wrong' with this projection, any more than there is with Mercator's. But I am convinced that to represent the spiritual reality (in its transcendent aspect) as a Being in another realm is to make it unreal and remote for vast numbers of people

[1] *The Shaking of the Foundations* (Penguin Books, Harmondsworth, 1962), p. 63.

[2] He explains earlier (p. 35) why he prefers the term 'supranatural' rather than 'supernatural': 'Of course both words mean the same. But "the supernatural" is used so loosely to mean the same as "the divine" (when it does not mean "the spooky"), that the more unfamiliar word may serve to pull us up and remind us that what is at issue here is not the reality of God as such but a particular way of representing or describing it.'

today. Not only do they take the projection for the reality and demand 'evidence' for the existence of such a Being (often as crudely as Khrushchev's astronauts), but, more importantly, it has the effect of rendering God marginal and peripheral.

He goes on to stress that whilst what we call God is both transcendent and immanent, the transcendent side of this divine element is not to be considered as occupying a realm 'above or behind the processes of nature and history', and breaking through into them by supranatural intervention, but is to be thought of as closely linked with the immanent. In a fine passage he says, 'This is a shot-silk universe, spirit and matter, inside and outside, divine and human, shimmering like aspects of one reality which cannot be separated or divided.' And he further says that 'we can say *nothing* of God apart from these relationships', implying that we can only speak in terms of our experience. And later he points out that the old dividing lines are not the real ones. 'In the past there was a clear division between theist and atheist ... Now there is a much more subtle line between those who believe and those who cannot.' And these differences are not confined to the Christian world:

> ... one of the notable features of our time ... has been a new openness to and humility before other world faiths. It has become evident that the supranaturalistic projection has bedevilled dialogue especially with the East. Because Buddhism is non-theistic it does not mean that it is atheistic in the Western sense, and its understanding of Reality must be viewed sympathetically alongside the more dynamic Christian view. Or again, because Hinduism has rejected the personification of God, that does not of itself close the possibility of discussion with Christianity: the question is whether it is finally incompatible with what Teilhard de Chardin calls a personalizing universe.
>
> So much for the common points, despite the diversity of expression and accent. What do they all add up to?[1]

[1] p. 82.

He now summarizes the position by taking a quotation from Aldous Huxley, one which he says 'he does not think is too wide of the mark'. The quotation is part of the first paragraph from *The Perennial Philosophy*, which I have already given at greater length in our consideration of the natural history of religion (p. 87). 'The metaphysic that recognises a divine Reality substantial to the world of things and lives and minds; the psychology that finds in the soul something similar to, or even identical with, divine Reality; the ethic that places man's final end in the knowledge of the immanent and transcendent Ground of all being.' Robinson goes on to ask, 'is there anything in this *projection* which is basically unchristian?'

Space will allow me only to make one further but very significant reference to this important book. Robinson has passed from the God of nature to the God of history.

> God has been pictured as a super-Self, deciding to act, intervene or send this, that or the other, including his own 'Son'. As anthropomorphic myth, this is easy on the human imagination and, of course, those who use this language are readily prepared to admit the 'as if'. But the projection it employs has the effect of locating the action of God as a Being outside, behind or between the processes of nature and history. It gives men today little help towards seeing him as the inside *of* these processes ... Somehow we must find a projection which enables us to represent the divine initiative as in the processes of nature rather than as acting on them from without, as exercised through the events of secular history rather than in some sacred super-history.[1]

Particularly note the expressions 'seeing him [God] as the inside *of* these processes', and as the 'divine initiative' within them. Now Tillich said something similar; in addition to saying that God was the ground of Being, he spoke of 'the truth that God is a living God' and that 'Life is the actuality of being or more exactly, it is the process in which potential being becomes actual being.' This

[1] p. 104.

concept of God being within the process of life, nature and history, emphasized by both Robinson and Tillich, brings us now to the new development I have just referred to. It is linked with what is now being called *process theology*, based upon the philosophy of Whitehead. How far Robinson would go with these ideas I am not at all sure, and Tillich at times was certainly critical of them. Being very much concerned with evolution and the process of becoming, they are particularly pertinent to the subject of our book.

Whitehead's writings are not always the easiest to follow for the layman unfamiliar with philosophical thought and expression; he wrote almost equally in the philosophy of science and religion. Although he was concerned with both, his ideas entered biology and theology independently; and they have now come together in a relatively new synthesis. One of the first biologists seriously to consider Whitehead's philosophy for the interpretation of the phenomena of life was W. E. Agar, Professor of Zoology at Melbourne; his book, *A Contribution to the theory of the Living Organism* (Melbourne University Press, Melbourne, 1943), made, however, little impression in the mechanistic biological atmosphere of the time. In America the philosopher Charles Hartshorne was bringing Whitehead's ideas further into theology.[1] Now we come to Charles Birch, Challis Professor of Biology in the University of Sydney, who is not only an eminent ecologist but a deeply religious man. He was one of Agar's pupils and it was Agar who advised him to read all he could of Whitehead and Hartshorne: hence the synthesis. Birch brings biological thought and the new process theology of Whitehead and Hartshorne together in his very readable paperback, *Nature and God* (1965), which he dedicates to Hartshorne; it is a highly significant work. He describes his thesis in these words:

The concept of God's operations in the universe as a series of fitful interventions from a supernatural sphere is quite

[1] *The Divine Relativity* (Yale University Press, Newhaven, Conn., 1948), see also C. Hartshorne and W. L. Rees, *Philosophers Speak of God* (Chicago University Press, Chicago, 1953).

unacceptable to science. No reconciliation is possible between religious fundamentalism and modern science. And yet there is hope. Within science and within theology and philosophy, some radical changes are taking place that are altering the whole traditional position. These changes are opening up a new and constructive way of looking at the natural world ... Because of them this generation could be within closer reach of an understanding of nature and God than any previous generation.[1]

This is why I find this development so important, not just because it is a new way, the process way, of looking at theology, but because it suggests a better synthesis of the idea of God and the biological system. In saying this, I do not wish to imply that I think this process approach is necessarily a true or final solution; as with all scientific theories it may well change in the future. Let us remind ourselves of this changing nature of science by recalling a quotation from the late Dr J. Bronowski:

There is today almost no scientific theory which was held when, say, the Industrial Revolution began about 1760. Most often today's theories flatly contradict those of 1760; many contradict those of 1900. In cosmology, in quantum mechanics, in genetics, in the social sciences, who now holds the beliefs that seemed firm sixty years ago? Yet the society of scientists has survived these changes without a revolution, and honours the men whose beliefs it no longer shares. No one has been shot or exiled or convicted of perjury; no one has recanted abjectly at a trial before his colleagues. The whole structure of science has been changed, and no one has been either disgraced or deposed. Through all the changes of science, the society of scientists is flexible and single-minded together, and evolves and rights itself. In the language of science, it is a stable society.[2]

[1] *Nature and God* (S.C.M. Press, London, 1965), p. 7.
[2] *Science and Human Values* (Penguin Books, Harmondsworth, 1964), p. 74.

It is such a progressive science that a future natural theology — the biology of God — should become. The present concepts of the new process theology may well change — must change — with greater knowledge, but nevertheless I believe they lead forward.

There are three aspects of this new synthesis that I find particularly attractive: those concerned with mind and consciousness, with the process of evolution and with the emphasis on experience. Regarding mind and consciousness the problem has always been to imagine just where or how in the process of evolution, or in the development of the individual organism, mind appears. For Whitehead, Hartshorne and Birch there must be an element of mind, not necessarily consciousness, but feeling, in everything including even the electron. Birch quotes Hartshorne as asking 'what scientist as such stands up to be counted on the question, where is the lower limit of feeling in the plant–animal series, or even is willing to say there is or can be a lower limit?' A number of eminent biologists have held a similar view. Sewall Wright, the distinguished American geneticist, writing of development, says, 'If the human mind is not to appear by magic, it must be a development from the mind of the egg and back of this, apparently, of the DNA molecules of the egg and sperm nuclei that constitute its heredity.[1] And a little later he expresses his belief that mind is universal, present not only in all organisms and in their cells, but in molecules, atoms and elementary particles. J. B. S. Haldane expresses the same idea in one of his essays in his *The Inequality of Man*, saying, 'We do not find obvious evidence of life and mind in so-called inert matter ... but if the scientific point of view is correct we shall ultimately find them, at least in rudimentary forms, all through the universe.' Haldane then, in the same essay, gives us a striking flight of imaginative thinking which, whilst not a part of the Whitehead–Hartshorne–Birch line of reasoning, presents a possibility that should not be overlooked. He writes thus:

[1] An essay in *Process and Divinity* (Open Court, La Salle, Ill., 1964), edited by W. L. Reese and E. Freeman, pp. 113–14.

Now if the co-operation of some thousands of millions of cells in our brain can produce our consciousness, the idea becomes vastly more plausible that the co-operation of humanity, or some sections of it, may determine what Comte called the Great Being. Just as, according to the teachings of physiology, the unity of the body is not due to a soul super-added to the life of the cells, so the superhuman, if it existed, would be nothing external to man, or even existing apart from human co-operation. But to my mind the teaching of science is very emphatic that such a Great Being may be a fact as real as the individual human consciousness, although, of course, there is no positive scientific evidence for the existence of such a being. And it seems to me that every-where ethical experience testifies to a super-individual reality of some kind. The good life, if not necessarily self-denial, is always self-transcendence. This idea is, of course, immanent in the highest religions, but the objects of religious worship retain the characteristics of nature-gods or deified human individuals.[1]

The new process theology sees God as intimately linked with organic evolution; this I am sure must be true. But how? That is the problem which is far from being solved. Are we to regard God himself as part of the evolving process? Whitehead himself was clearly influenced by Bergson's philosophy of change and his ideas of creative evolution. So was Teilhard de Chardin whose epic view of God in the evolutionary system, expounded in *The Phenomenon of Man* (trans. B. Wall, Collins, London, 1959), is held by some to make him a process theologian; his theoretical speculations, however, as to how God acts within the system, have not, as he had hoped, been accepted as a part of science.

Let us look for a moment at the remarkable appeal that Chardin's book, *The Phenomenon of Man*, has had, giving rise to many Teilhard de Chardin Societies and Discussion Groups in both Great Britain and America. So many people who had sup-pressed their religious feelings, because they thought that science

---

[1] *The Inequality of Man* (Chatto & Windus, London, 1932), p. 114.

had shown evolution to be an entirely materialistic process, now clutched at the book with such thankfulness and enthusiasm. Was not this, they thought, a truly scientific work demonstrating the Divine action within evolution itself? There can be no doubt that it is a book by a profoundly spiritual man who believes passionately that God must be linked with biological evolution. This indeed is an intuitive step in the right direction. In his preface, however, he says, 'If this book is to be properly understood it must be read not as a work of metaphysics still less as a sort of theological essay, but purely and simply as a scientific treatise.' This I am afraid it certainly is not. I like to regard it as an imaginative prose poem of the emergence of the spirit of man and his feeling after Divinity, but as science — no. In the development of his speculative scheme, he makes much play with the concept of energy having two forms which he proposes as a 'basis for all that is to emerge later'. In discussing 'the natural complexity of the stuff of the universe', he says that 'in each particular element this fundamental energy is divided into two distinct components: a *tangential energy* which links the element with others of the same order ... , and a *radial energy* which draws it towards ever greater complexity and centricity — in other words forwards'. These are not scientific concepts.[1] Teilhard was certainly a saint and a true mystic who will, I believe, have a secure place in history with his spiritual classic, *Le Milieu Divin*, rather than with scientific theory; nevertheless his conception of God within the evolutionary process is indeed in line with this latest theological development — process theology.

[1] In relation to this passage — on the same page (p. 64) — it is interesting to note that there was for nearly ten years an extraordinary mistake which went unnoticed in the English and American editions of his book, where he is made to say that 'we shall assume that, essentially, all energy is physical in nature'. To many this must have seemed that he was here linking his ideas to orthodox science, whereas in the original French the word rendered as physical was not 'physique' but '*psychique*'! It would appear that many of those who eagerly followed him quite misunderstood the real nature of his thesis. The error was not discovered until my book, *The Living Stream*, in which I had used this quotation from the English version, was being rendered into French; my translator was much shocked at this distortion of Chardin's views.

It will be clear from my earlier discussion in chapter 3 that I believe the Divine to be linked with the mental or psychic side of life and to be playing its part within the Darwinian system of selection. In this way I believe process theology may indeed link with the evolution process, but I would not be at all dogmatic. Linked it must be—and the question spurring us on to future effort towards solution is still that of 'How?'

At the end of my first volume of Gifford Lectures, *The Living Stream* (1965), I said,

> Our natural theology must be fearless. We must have the scientific approach and not shrink from what it may point to. At the *very least* I expect this power of which we speak may be some subconscious shared reservoir of spiritual 'know-how' which we call Divine ... ; I think, however, it is *far more likely* that above this there is something much more wonderful to which we give the name God. But even if it *should* be shown, and I don't believe it will, that this whole conception is a purely psychological one and, if, in some way, this mind factor *should* eventually be proved to be entirely of physico-chemical origin—it would not to my mind destroy the joy or help of *the experience we may call Divine* any more than it would destroy the glorious beauty felt in poetry or art.

Against the expression 'and I don't believe it will' was a footnote to explain why I thought this—it was 'because of the evidence from human experience'.

It is the emphasis on this experience that I feel makes process theology so important. Birch, in his *Nature and God*, brings this out so well:

> The most directly accessible clue we have to the nature of the universe is neither the electron, nor amoeba, but man. What is man? That is the relevant question to ask. It is man's self-awareness that leads him to ask this question. His answer determines his answer to the broader question that includes it,

what is the nature and purpose of the universe? Streeter once remarked, 'I have had experiences that materialism cannot explain.'[1] That is the point. What matters to me mostly is not mass, velocity and the like, but my own experience of value and purpose, all the qualities of friendship and love. It is precisely these qualities that the mechanistic theory of nature leaves out. Galileo called them the secondary qualities and because they could not be measured, he did not regard them as real. 'It seems an extremely unfortunate arrangement', said Whitehead, 'that we should perceive a lot of things that are not there. Yet that is what the theory of secondary qualities in fact comes to ... We may not pick and choose. For us the red glow of the sunset should be as much a part of nature as are the molecules and electric waves by which men of science would explain the phenomenon.'[2] Our difficulty is to exhibit the redness of the sunset on one system of thought with the electromagnetic waves and the agitation of molecules connected with it. That is one of our problems. Because this is difficult, are we to ignore it, or to be completely sceptical that there is anything but a mechanical side to nature? [3]

I agree with him. We are animals ourselves and so know animal life from the *inside*; whilst we must never attempt to interpret the lives of other animals and their behaviour in terms of our own particular feelings and activities, we have an experience of life in general that is fundamental to our philosophy.

We have seen that the ideas of Henri Bergson have played their part, through those of Whitehead and Hartshorne, in the shaping of the new process theology. Today his philosophy is in eclipse, but I believe it will in part come back. Perhaps one of the main reasons for it being out of favour at the present time is that his ideas on evolution have appeared to be incompatible with the

[1] *Reality: A New Correlation of Science and Religion*, ed. B. H. Streeter (Macmillan, London, 1929).

[2] A. N. Whitehead, *The Concept of Nature* (Cambridge University Press, Cambridge, 1920).

[3] Op. cit., p. 60.

accepted Darwinian position. His ideas were dismissed because he made little attempt to relate what he called the creative *élan vital* with Darwinism except for one suggestion that it might affect the direction of mutations (i.e. the changes in the genetical material) which the facts of modern biology cannot possibly support. This was an unfortunate mistake that had little relation to his main position. What he called the *élan vital* was really the creative *mental* side of life: the *en theos*, the god within, of which Louis Pasteur spoke with such feeling (p. 183). How do I think his biological philosophy might return? I think it likely that the ideas in chapter 3, about conscious behaviour playing a decisive role as a selective agent *within* the Darwinian system, may supply the connection which his creative *élan vital* can make with the physico-chemical basis of the organic world. It is the element effecting the course of evolution by Darwinian selection picking out, generation after generation, those chance bodily variations which give better and better means of carrying the developing mental side of life into action. I have always despised the facile gibe, 'you might as well talk of an engine having an *élan locomotive*', intended to ridicule the Bergsonian idea. It misses the point altogether. An engine is the product of a designer and has to be controlled by an operator; it is these of course who have the *élan vital*, the *en theos*, not the engine. Even if the locomotive is driven by a computer, as indeed today it might be, that computer has to be programmed by a conscious mind.

I must not go more deeply here into these philosophical considerations; I have dealt with them and allied issues at length in *The Living Stream* and *The Divine Flame*. Just as man's mind has invented and made tools and instruments which when used are really extensions added to his body (exosomatic organs as Medawar has called them) — telescopes to enable him to see further than he would otherwise be able to see, engines to take him faster and further than his legs could carry him and so on, so I believe the Divine spirit — the spirit of life — the *en theos* — the *élan vital*, call it what you will — brought about organic evolution through the action of Darwinian selection. The organs, the parts of the body—the limbs and feet, claws, teeth and beaks, tentacles, eyes and other organs of sense—are all tools or instruments carved out of the physical world by the mental element of the universe (to which consciousness and the Divine are related) by means of the behavioural selection I have discussed; the constantly varying DNA genetic code supplies the changing material for this selection to work upon.

All I want to stress in this chapter is that a new natural theology of the 'process' type can very well fit into the modern neo-Darwinian biological system so long as the biologists themselves are not dogmatic in dismissing consciousness as a mere epiphenomenon of the physico-chemical brain. Can such a system be grafted on to a more liberal interpretation of the Christian Gospel? This is for the theologians to decide. Can Christianity survive? Have we already, as many would assert, passed into the post-Christian era of history? Few, I believe, will deny that the Christian environment has meant so much for the development of all that Western civilization stands for, including intellectual freedom. Is there not a real danger of losing this if we lose the Christian spirit? The danger is increased if theology should remain dogmatic and static rather than scientific and progressive in its outlook.

For me it is the spirit of Christianity, not the hypothetical dogmas of theologians, that matters; and this spirit is indeed the essence of the new natural theology. The evidence of the working of a Divine Power that we may call God, the reality of religious experience, the sense of the sacred, and a belief in the way of life as taught in the Gospel of Jesus—these are vital; they form a far more substantial foundation for a theology than the blind acceptance of supposed events in the past—events which cannot satisfy the accepted rules of evidence used in other fields of historical research. In truth the dogmas of Christianity are in disarray, but fortunately not the spirit. Another recent article in *The Times* (11 May 1974) brings home to one the extent of the changes taking place in theological interpretation: the Rt Rev. R. P. C. Hanson, Professor of Theology at Manchester Univer-

sity, writes on 'The dangerous gulf between pulpit and pew'.
This is what he says:

> Revolutions do not always erupt like volcanoes. Sometimes
> they grow like trees. The revolution in examining the records
> of the past which we call the discipline of historical study
> has been active steadily for the last 200 years, and has had
> quite as far-reaching an effect on the study of the Bible as on
> any other part of historical study; ...
> But this revolution has had amazingly little effect upon the
> people in this country who use the Bible more than any-
> body else – the clergy and the faithful of all denominations.
> True, Adam and Noah are now usually relegated to legend.
> But most people still think of Abraham, Isaac, Jacob and
> Joseph as if they were historical characters about whom the
> Bible has woven a kind of Coronation Street family saga,
> even though historical scholarship gives no serious support
> to this view ...
> More serious still is the conventional treatment of St
> John's Gospel. This is a litmus-paper test for preachers and
> expositors. If you can convince yourself that Jesus really did
> go round Galilee and Jerusalem saying such things as 'I am
> the Resurrection and the Life', 'Which of you convinceth
> me of sin?' and 'I and the Father are one', then of course
> you can preserve a conventional view of Christianity. But
> if, following the current of modern scholarship, you come
> to the conclusion that this is incredible, what is to be said
> in the pulpit, what is to be taught to the faithful?
> The vast majority of preachers and teachers find it simpler
> not to face this question, not to question the conventional
> view. To commit oneself to the conclusion that the Fourth
> Gospel is not, generally speaking, a record of the words and
> deeds of Jesus of Nazareth, but a profound and invaluable
> interpretation of his significance written about the end of
> the first century A.D., is indeed to call for a drastic re-examin-
> ation of traditional Christian doctrine.

We are certainly living in days of theological revolution. There is a growing tendency today in academic circles to regard many of the statements in the Bible, creeds and other religious writings as *myths*, which in theological terms means that they are non-factual but nevertheless religiously significant. John Hick, Professor of Theology at Birmingham University, in his recent *God and the Universe of Faiths* (Macmillan, London, 1973), says that this admixture of mythological material with the factual (p. 23) was as evident to Origen in the third century as it is to Bultmann in the twentieth'. He goes on to say that few thoughtful Christians today would deny that in their discourse they include considerable mythological elements, and as an example he quotes Bishop James A. Pike:

> There are several phrases in the creed that I cannot affirm as literal prose sentences, but I can certainly sing them — as a kind of war song picturing major convictions in poetic terms ... Stated in plain prose, I certainly do not believe that Christ 'sitteth on the right hand of the Father' ... But I can sing this phrase with a real affirmation as to the place of Christ in the whole situation. I feel the same about 'ascended into Heaven'. And the same about 'conceived by the Holy Ghost, and born of the Virgin Mary'.[1]

Now let me give a very illuminating passage from Professor Hick himself:

> If, as I have argued, the idea of divine incarnation in Jesus of Nazareth has no literal meaning, the question has to be posed in a different form — whether, in spite of the mythic character of the idea of incarnation, salvation through Christ can be a reality and his God-Manhood an effective expression of that reality? However, we do not, as Christians, need to ask *whether* salvation through Christ can be a reality, for we start from the fact that it *is* a reality! Through their responses to the person of Jesus countless people have been

[1] *Christian Century*, 21 Dec. 1960, p. 1497.

opened to the divine presence; changed in the direction of their lives; reconciled to themselves, to their neighbours and to God; have become conscious of the reality of their loving heavenly Father who has forgiven and accepted them. This experience of salvation began in Jesus' own lifetime. Indeed the saving impact of his person and teaching must have been at its most intense in his personal historical presence. But we have noted that in all probability the historical Jesus, whose effect upon many people was their experience of salvation, neither thought of himself nor was thought of by his disciples as God incarnate. It was not he but his heavenly Father who saved. But Jesus was so fully God's agent, so completely conscious of living in God's presence and serving God's love, that the divine reality was mediated through him to others.[1]

Here indeed we see how we can now build a new interpretation of Christianity on to the old foundations; it is an admirable step forwards towards a progressive theology which, like science, is prepared to change its theories as new facts are revealed by scholarship. The older, more orthodox members of the Church will no doubt resist the change. They will say that even if the story of the empty tomb and the resurrection of Christ cannot be substantiated as recorded facts of history, there is the undoubtedly historical evidence of another kind, the clear demonstration of the almost miraculous growth and expansion of Christianity in the early days; this, they will say, could not have taken place without the absolute conviction of the risen Christ. Certainly that expansion was due to an almost superhuman enthusiasm, a brilliant burning of the Divine flame which was kindled and fanned by the spiritual force of the founder; we should also recognize that its remarkable and fanatical spread was part due to two other factors which came together to produce this zealous surge. One was certainly a belief in the stories of the resurrection; the other was the widespread view at the time,

[1] Op. cit., pp. 176–7.

said to have been expressed by Jesus himself, that the world was shortly coming to an end, and that this would herald the kingdom of God, with special places for those who were faithful followers of their risen Lord.

Let us take the second factor first, for this can certainly be shown to have been a popular but mistaken idea. We have the choice of believing that Jesus was wrong in his views or, as may be more likely, that he was misreported or that the alleged sayings were attributed to him, through the imagination of the authors of the gospels who believed the prophecy when writing so many years later. These are the reported sayings of Jesus: 'Verily I say unto you, this generation shall not pass away until these things be accomplished,' and again, 'Verily I say unto you, there be some here of them that stand by, which shall in no wise taste of death till they see the Kingdom of God come with power.' They could hardly be a more definite assertion of what was proved by history to be false; nevertheless, while the idea lasted, it clearly gave encouragement to the new faith.

The other factor driving the new faith forward was almost certainly the more important: the stories of the appearance of Jesus after his death. I think it likely that it was indeed these stories that gave the impetus to the new movement and accounted for the remarkable change which came over the disciples after they were first scattered in despondency following the crucifixion. Jesus in his life-time had made a tremendous impression on his disciples; in their state of dreadful psychological disturbance at his death, it may not seem so surprising to those who have knowledge of apparitions that they should have seen him. There are many examples in the literature of psychical research, but we need not go to such specialized sources to find a close parallel; there are today records of such experience just as vivid as that recorded in Luke xxiv 30–31. Let me give two examples.

For the first, I quote from the third volume of Harold Owen's autobiography, *Journey from Obscurity: Memoirs of the Owen Family*, published by the Oxford University Press (London, 1965; vol. iii,

p. 198). Harold's elder brother Wilfred, the poet, with whom he had a strong bond of affection and understanding, was killed just before the Armistice in 1918, one of the last casualties of the war. News of it reached his mother at noon on 11 November, as the bells rang out proclaiming peace. Harold, who was a young officer in the Merchant Service, only heard the news much later. I shall now quote his autobiography where he describes the Armistice celebrations at Cape Town where his ship had called:

> I could not get Wilfred out of my mind and wondering about him perhaps sharpened my sensitivity so that revulsion was all I could experience—revulsion for the mawkish patriotic songs, the drunkenness which was becoming more evident everywhere, ...
>
> Later on, when at last I got to the naval jetty, I looked upwards to the clean brightness of the night sky, while I was waiting for a launch to take me off: and once again my thoughts flew back to Mahim. What were they feeling and thinking now the fighting was ended? Was Wilfred all right, was Colin? I wished now I *had* sent that cable. I could not be happy about any of them at home. Something I knew was wrong. Monstrous depression clamped hold of me. I was glad to be back in my ship again.
>
> A few days later we sailed for Walfish Bay and the Cameroons.

He still had no news when they reached the Cameroons. I continue with a later quotation:

> We were lying off Victoria. I had gone down to my cabin thinking to write some letters. I drew aside the door curtain and stepped inside and to my amazement I saw Wilfred sitting in my chair. I felt shock run through me with appalling force and with it I could feel the blood draining away from my face. I did not rush towards him but walked jerkily into the cabin—all my limbs stiff and slow to respond.

I did not sit down but looking at him I spoke quietly: 'Wilfred, how did you get here?' He did not rise and I saw that he was involuntarily immobile, but his eyes which had never left mine were alive with the familiar look of trying to make me understand; when I spoke his whole face broke into his sweetest and most endearing dark smile. I felt no fear—I had not when I first drew my door curtain and saw him there; only exquisite mental pleasure at thus beholding him. All I was conscious of was a sensation of enormous shock and profound astonishment that he should be here in my cabin. I spoke again. 'Wilfred dear, how can you be here, it's just not possible ...' But still he did not speak but only smiled his most gentle smile ... I loved having him there: I could not, and did not want to try to understand how he had got there. I was content to accept him, that he was here with me was sufficient ... He was in uniform and I remember thinking how out of place the khaki looked amongst the cabin furnishing. With this thought I must have turned my eyes from him; when I looked back my cabin chair was empty.

Such first-hand accounts as this and many others recorded with such detail and sincerity cannot be ignored, whatever interpretation we put on them. We may note here that the appearance was sometime after the death of Wilfred which had occurred before the Armistice. One explanation might be that the impression of Wilfred's death had been communicated by telepathy to Harold by his family's shock and grief on hearing the news on Armistice Day, and that this impression had developed in the subconscious mind so that it finally produced the hallucination, at the point where he went into his cabin to write letters home. Those who feel convinced of the survival of human personality after death will be inclined to take a different view. According to either explanation, the people upon whom Jesus had made such a vivid impression of love and spirituality in his life might well be those to experience such a reappearance.

It is interesting to compare this account of the sudden disappearance of the figure of Wilfred Owen with the account of the appearance of Jesus on the road to Emmaus, especially Luke xxiv 31: 'And their eyes were opened and they knew him; and he vanished out of their sight.' It is clear from the account that it was not the *physical* resurrected body of Jesus that they saw; yet it was this appearance more than any other that convinced the disciples as we see from Luke xxiv, verses 33 and 34: 'And they rose up the same hour, and returned to Jerusalem, and found the eleven gathered together, and them that were with them, saying The Lord is risen indeed, and hath appeared to Simon.' Professor H. H. Price, Emeritus Professor of Logic at Oxford, in an Appendix to his *Essays in the Philosophy of Religion* (Clarendon Press, Oxford, 1972), says (p. 120):

Of all the post-Resurrection narratives, the one which is most easily credible, at least to a psychical researcher, is the Emmaus narrative in Luke 24: 13–35.[1] That is because the phenomena reported are purely visual and auditory. Nothing at all is said about tangibility. The only puzzling episode is the breaking of the bread. Was the bread physically broken? Or was this too a purely apparitional event? I suspect that it was.

My second example is from the book, *The Ring of Truth* (Hodder & Stoughton, London, 1967), by Canon J. B. Phillips, the eminent translator of the New Testament into English. Here he records (p. 89) the posthumous appearance of C. S. Lewis in the following terms:

Many of us who believe in what is technically known as the Communion of Saints, must have experienced the sense of nearness, for a fairly short time, of those whom we love soon after they have died. This has certainly happened to me several times. But the late C. S. Lewis, whom I did not know very well, and had only seen in the flesh once, but with whom

[1] There is also a brief reference to it in Mark xvi 12.

I had corresponded a fair amount, gave me an unusual experience. A few days after his death, while I was watching television, he 'appeared' sitting in a chair within a few feet of me, and spoke a few words which were particularly relevant to the difficult circumstances through which I was passing. He was ruddier in complexion than ever, grinning all over his face and, as the old-fashioned saying has it, positively glowing with health. The interesting thing to me was that I had not been thinking about him at all. I was neither alarmed nor surprised nor, to satisfy the Bishop of Woolwich, did I look up to see the hole in the ceiling that he might have made on arrival. He was just *there* — 'large as life and twice as natural'! A week later, this time when I was in bed reading before going to sleep, he appeared again, even more rosily radiant than before, and repeated to me the same message, which was very important to me at the time. I was a little puzzled by this, and I mentioned it to a certain saintly Bishop who was then living in retirement here in Dorset. His reply was, 'My dear J ... , this sort of thing is happening all the time.'[1]

These examples of apparitions, seen by responsible citizens of the present day, show us that we can accept the stories of the appearances of Jesus to those who had been close to him, and felt his love when he was alive, without any damage to our intellectual integrity. There can be little difference between these apparitions and those which may be produced under hypnotic suggestion (as briefly discussed on p. 125) and have been described in detail in the journals of medical hypnosis. It should be mentioned, alongside the present-day examples that I have given, that just as striking hallucinatory appearances have been recorded of persons who are actually living: relatives or close friends who, whilst some considerable distance away, sometimes hundreds of miles, have made their presence felt in apparition-form at a time

---

[1] A more detailed account is given in the *Journal of the Society for Psychical Research*, vol. 45 (1970), pp. 381–91, and vol. 46 (1971), pp. 203–5.

of acute psychological stress. The point I am trying to make is that the truth of Christianity is not dependent upon the concept of the physical resurrection of Christ which many of the old school cling to as being an imperative belief; it surely today depends upon the life of Jesus being the greatest demonstration of the working of the Divine love, and on the *experience* of God felt by those who make the approach to him as if he were a loving father.

In the West we have seen a new natural process theology being built upon our Christian foundations. The religion that has been deep in our culture, may indeed, I believe, be what is at the heart of this new conception. I should like to reprint here a paragraph from my earlier work, *The Living Stream*, which for the time being is out of print:

As one travels through the English countryside, taking the lesser by-ways rather than the great, one cannot, if one goes slowly and is prepared to stop, but be struck by the beauty of the old parish churches and be made to marvel that such glories could be built by such small groups of people, just as one marvels at the great mediaeval cathedrals in towns which, at the time of their building, must have had only moderate populations. If one goes inside such an old country church one cannot help feeling that here is something fashioned with real love and reverence; elements of superstition there may well be, but in spite of this, surely here is something created not just by an ignorant craving for magic, but by something of profound depth. A naturalist coming from another planet, if his space-ship had the ability to drift across the countryside like a balloon, could not but be struck by the prominence of these buildings in each small community. Amidst the little groups of houses their spires and towers stand up like the sporangia of some organism and he might well be excused for first thinking them to have the importance of some such reproductive process. Indeed they had an equal importance in the past when devotion to God was as real to the population as was that of sexuality. They hardly have the same significance today and some, alas, stand forsaken like fossil skeletons of the past; this, however, may only be a temporary phase due to the accelerated growth of a physical science, whose findings are difficult to reconcile with many of the old doctrinal dogmas. I say temporary because I believe the dogmas on both sides may be revised as theology becomes more natural and science's mechanistic interpretation of life is shown not to be the whole truth.

In the East the same new theology could be built upon the various old traditions. While he does not give the name, 'process theology', to his outlook, I cannot help feeling that Professor Hick in the book I have already quoted (*God and the Universe of Faiths*) is not far from it. In it he has a chapter on what he calls the Copernican revolution in theology. Just as in cosmology the ancient Ptolemaic idea of the earth being at the centre, with the sun and planets circling round it, has given way to the Copernican system of all the planets moving round the sun: so in a new theological revolution all the different faiths can be regarded as separate planets all held together by the same central God. In a subsequent chapter, he charts what he calls the new map of the universe of faiths. I must not here attempt to expound the details of his treatment, but direct my readers to his book. I can summarize his treatment, however, in his own words, and so bring my chapter to an end with a vision of this universal process:

Let me now try to draw the threads together and to project them into the future. I have been suggesting that Christianity is a way of salvation which, beginning some two thousand years ago, has become the principal way of salvation in three continents. The other great world faiths are likewise ways of salvation, providing the principal path to the divine reality for other large sections of humanity. I have also suggested that the idea that Jesus proclaimed himself as God incarnate, and as the sole point of saving contact between God and man, is without adequate historical foundation and represents a doctrine developed by the church. We should therefore not infer, from the christian experience of redemption through Christ, that salvation cannot be experienced in any other way. The alternative possibility is that the ultimate divine reality—in our christian terms, God—has always been pressing in upon the human spirit, but always in ways which leave men free to open or close themselves to the divine presence. Human life has developed along characteristically different lines in the main areas of civilisation, and these differences have naturally entered into the ways in which men have apprehended and responded to God. For the great religious figures through whose experience divine revelation has come have each been conditioned by a particular history and culture.

12. An experimental faith

This short concluding chapter is somewhat in the nature of an epilogue. A natural theology based on the experience of God as a force in the world, such as I have just outlined, could, I believe, lead to what I would call an experimental faith.

I may well be criticized for using such a term, in that by doing so I may mislead people into thinking that I mean a faith determined by a laboratory or at least a scientific experiment. Because the word 'experimental' has become commonly used in this more limited way in our scientific age I would have preferred not to use it; there are, however, reasons why, used in its original sense—i.e. based on experience, not on authority or conjecture—it conveys my meaning better than any other. Only later was the word *experiment*, originally meaning 'a test, trial, or procedure adopted on the chance of its succeeding',[1] taken over by science for the testing of hypotheses in the laboratory, a use which gave a new secondary meaning to the adjective. Indeed, 'experimental' was used in exactly the same way in which I am using it by none other than John Wesley; and it was similarly used by L. P. Jacks as we shall see. To explain why I find the word so particularly expressive of what I intend I must first make clear what is distinctive about the kind of faith I am discussing.

I hope that the evidence we are amassing at our research unit, when published, may induce many, who were sceptical on materialistic grounds, to try the experiment of approaching the power we call God in a particular way, not by prayer for the alteration of physical events or for personal safety or material ends, but for strength and guidance for a better way of life, or perhaps more specifically how best to deal with some difficulty or to achieve some worthwhile purpose. I believe if they make the experiment

[1] *Concise Oxford Dictionary.*

in the right way, they would find it works. 'Ask and ye shall receive.' Let me say at once that I do not believe in a God who, as a single mind, gives the solution to every particular problem that is put to him by the millions of people who may pray to him, and no doubt many doing so in the same instant of time. No — I think there is another psychological solution which I shall presently discuss, one which is nevertheless dependent upon *personal* prayer. Before I come to this, however, let me give two or three examples from our records of the kind of experience I am referring to. They are just brief quotations taken from the hundreds of such records in our collection, expressing how individuals are affected by this feeling of contact with a transcendental power appearing to be outside the self.

The experience of being filled with the Spirit is different for each person, but in all cases something happens to make you *know* it ... I now find I am enabled to help those who are sick in body, mind and spirit because I know the power of God working through me and my only desire is to be that sort of channel.

For some time now I have experienced myself in contact with what I may call some 'power' or guidance outside my ordinary day-to-day life ... By concentrated, voiceless prayer and, in a way, relaxation, I may feel my whole spirit filled with this power, and my whole being recharged. When this happens, then I know that anxiety, troubles and so forth will be solved; and indeed they are.

To learn this silent prayer is not easy at first, but even if nothing seems to happen, I found it was having a very definite effect on me ... I became conscious of being led or guided or even pushed against my will into courses of action I should never have thought of undertaking before.

It was then that I became aware of a new element in my relationship to God. I was conscious of a certain intimacy in my approaches to Him, that my prayers were now coming from a new depth ... which made it no longer an exercise of faith to pray to Him but a certainty that I was speaking to a personal God with whom I had such close personal relationship that I could now be dogmatic about it.

I have always felt myself sustained in my darkest hours by a loving and understanding power ... That abiding presence of a Father and a Friend has, thank God, become an increasing reality to me as the years have passed by, but it necessitates an effort at continual loyalty, such as any friendship demands.

Other evidence of this strength and power received has already been given in the quotations from Professor Sir Frederic Bartlett (p. 86), Baroness Mary Stocks and Beatrice Webb (p. 180) and from the records of the people of more primitive cultures given us by the social anthropologists (pp. 75–7).

Perhaps 'experiential' faith might be thought by some to be a better term; yet this does not express my intention. I mean a faith based not just on passive experience, but upon an active seeking. 'Seek and ye shall find.' It is an experiment in discovery that I believe the person who had hitherto been a sceptic might, from the evidence of others, be prepared to make; he should not just be making it to see what might happen with the attitude of 'I might by chance be lucky', but in a very different spirit—one of exploration. He should bring himself into a state of mind in which he can, *without destroying his intellectual integrity*, appeal in terms of devotion to what to him has hitherto been the Unknown God, asking, 'If you exist, help me to find You, and by finding You to feel Thy Presence and show me how to do Thy Will.' This is what I mean by an experimental faith. Now, however, I must make clear how I believe such an approach can be made without a man who has originally been a sceptic surrendering his intellectual integrity.

I do not, of course, as I have said before, believe in God as an old gentleman up there or out there, but I do believe, both from personal experience and from the recorded experiences of others which have the ring of truth, that there is a Power which *appears* to be transcendental, and outside the conscious self, and which we may call God, though it may also appear to be in part within us. Some, with Jung, may say that it lies in the collective unconscious, but I believe, and here I am expressing what William James would call my 'over-belief' that it is indeed something much greater, but which can only be approached as if it were a person, and this for the biological and psychological reasons discussed earlier in the book.

The power that enables the individual to have more courage, to overcome obstacles and to achieve the seemingly impossible is undoubtedly the greatest part of the response, but what of the solutions to particular individual problems; do they come in the same way? The answers do not usually come at once, and the solution that eventually comes may be one that is very different from the one that might have been expected, but nevertheless it is seen to be right. I have said that I find it difficult to suppose that *all* the different individual answers of *all* who pray are really coming from one transcendental source beyond the self. Would it not seem more in keeping with what we know of nature for each of us to have our own built-in solution-provider?—but one perhaps that is 'unlocked', as it were, by this transcendental or extra-sensory power. I have considered this problem in more detail in *The Divine Flame*; let me here summarize my argument, in part using the same words.

There are indeed psychological explanations for some very similar occurrences. There is what is sometimes called 'intelligent dreaming', where a person may see in a dream the solution to a problem which has been occupying his mind for some time. There are well-known examples of the solving of scientific puzzles in this way. The chemist, Friedrich von Kekulé, tells how in a dozing dream he saw snake-like rows of atoms twisting about, and then one seized its own tail; this, on waking, suggested to him the structure of the benzene ring. We must all know how, without such dreaming, we may go to sleep thinking of some difficult problem and awaken in the morning with a solution to it.

Our subconscious mind goes on working while we are asleep. Perhaps also the answers to our own particular difficulties which we seek in prayer are coming from a similar source? In part I think they may be, but there is more, I believe, to it than that; let us, however, first consider some allied psychological phenomena.

Freud has suggested that we may repress what seem to us to be irrational motives only to find that they may return unawares to affect our behaviour, making us perhaps miss a train or have a slight accident which prevents us keeping some appointments which we have previously thought may be disadvantageous to us. Claire and W. M. S. Russell in 'Raw Materials for a Definition of Mind', their contribution to the book *Theories of the Mind*,[1] say such incidents are by no means uncommon, and present us with the following striking illustration:

> Shakespeare, as usual, provides a splendid example. When Hamlet is about to leave for England with Rosencrantz and Guildenstern, he is in no doubt about their reliability and his own prospects. 'There's letters seal'd; and my two schoolfellows, Whom I will trust as I will adders fang'd,' etc. (act III, scene iv). In the same soliloquy he even outlines a strategy—that of hoisting the engineer with his own petard. By the time he is on ship-board, he has repressed all this, and goes to his cabin to sleep. But the repressed intelligent observation is still at work. In his heart (as he tells Horatio in act v) 'there was a kind of fighting that would not let me sleep ... our indiscretion sometimes serves us well, when our deep plots do pall; and that should learn us there's a divinity that shapes our ends, rough-hew them how we will.' Restless with insomnia, he has a vague impulse to look at the letter. He opens it, finds the order for his assassination, and proceeds to carry out the strategy he had formed in Denmark—without remembering this at all. To him it seems like a new and strange inspiration: 'ere I

[1] Edited by J. Scher (Free Press of Glencoe, New York, and Macmillan, New York and London, 1962).

could make a prologue to my brains, they had begun the play, – I sat me down, devised a new commission, wrote it fair' and so on. Anyone who has noticed him – or herself – having this sort of experience will recognize the perfect accuracy of the poet's description. The 'divinity' is, of course our own intelligence. This sort of behaviour is specially common in a particular class of the personality type we have called 'idealistic', to which Hamlet conforms in all other ways. The chief feature is a readiness to repress (either instantaneously or after first voicing them) accurate observations about the *hostile* intentions of others.

It may well be that the various separate solutions to our individual problems are always within us if only we could reach them, and that the act of prayer brings them to the surface. In saying this, I must again make clear that I am not implying that I believe this destroys our conception of the Divine. All the evidence of religious experience, I believe, shows us that man makes contact with this Power which appears partly transcendent, and felt as the numinous beyond the self, and partly immanent within him. I also think it likely, however, that it may well be this uplifting power which does in fact activate the subconscious solution-providing mechanism in a way which would not otherwise be possible. In a similar way it may be the same power which assists in the healing of a sick person.

Let me now return for a moment to the use of the word experimental. Dr L. P. Jacks, in discussing the commonly held view of God as the omnipotent legislator of the universe, says, 'In the religion of Jesus I am struck by the absence, by the total absence of all those pompous conceptions of the Divine Nature, which show such speaking signs of having originated under lawyers' wigs.' After describing this religion as a 'spirit of comradeship raised to its highest power, the spirit that perceives itself to be "not alone"', he goes on to say, 'In its essence the Gospel is a call to make the same experiment, the experiment of comradeship, the experiment of fellowship, the experiment of trusting the heart of things, throwing self-care to the winds, in the sure and certain faith that you will not be deserted, forsaken nor betrayed, and that your ultimate interests are perfectly secure in the hands of the Great Companion.'[1] I believe in fact that the word 'experiment' is here being used in very much the same way as Sir Cyril Hinshelwood used it in his Presidential Address to the Royal Society, to which I referred on p. 47. In discussing consciousness, he said, 'we are all the time trying experiments on our relations with other people'; he is not referring here to laboratory experiments but to our everyday contact with our fellow citizens. In just such a way, in our experimental faith, we are making contact with what we call the Divine which is in part within ourselves, in our subconscious, but in part beyond ourselves. How much is within and how much is beyond is a problem for which we cannot pretend to see an answer. We are only just beginning in a great new field of research. I delight in the remark made by Professor Cral Pansin, referring to the progress of scientific research in general: 'Very clever men are answering the relatively easy questions of the natural examination paper.'[2]

I have spoken of this experimental faith being based essentially upon an approach to the element we call God, made in an act of devotional prayer as to a person. Yes, but how would you do it, some may ask if they have not found the way. There must be many different ways which various people have found to work, and any particular person must feel reluctant to make any public statement upon a matter which is so personal, private and held by him or her to be sacred. Yet having talked so much about its importance I feel I must, at the risk of appearing ostentatiously to wear my heart on my sleeve, outline the method which I myself am quite sure will work if made in the right way. It is a very old one and you will recognize its origin at once; it is a formula for *generating religious experience*. It is *not*, however, or so I believe, a mere set of words to be repeated simply in the form in which they have come down to us. The sentences, or parts of

[1] *Religious Perplexities* (Hodder & Stoughton, London, 1923), p. 92.
[2] Quoted by Professor W. H. Thorpe in *The Times*, 25 Jan. 1969.

sentences, which comprise it, are, I like to think, headings for deep devotional thought; between each is the time to pause, for meditation, a time for opening the heart, yes, if one dare say so, a time for talking to God.

Make the approach as if you were a child speaking to a loved Father (or Mother) — 'Our Father which art in heaven' — knowing all the time that the form of this relationship is almost certainly a psychological one based upon one's own former filial affection. The personal form of it enables one to have the emotional sense of devotion that is a necessary part of the process, although again you know the reality must be something very different — a mystery we cannot fathom. The analogy, if you like, sets up the relationship with this element beyond the conscious self. Then comes the calling into being of the sense of the numinous — the sense of the Holy without which you may as well be talking to a brick wall — 'Hallowed be thy Name'; for the contact to work you must learn to open yourself to this feeling of the numinous — the *mysterium tremendum* — as in the cry of the *Te Deum Laudamus*: Holy, Holy, Holy. Having reached the state of feeling that you are now in the Divine Presence, ask to receive help and guidance in trying to bring about, in however a humble way, a better state of the world ('Thy kingdom come. Thy will be done ...'). Think in what ways one might oneself do something to this end, even in quite small ways. Improvements in the world are brought about through the actions of men and women and not by miraculous Divine interventions in the course of nature; yet again and again those who have altered the world for the better have declared that they have felt that they have received help from beyond themselves: 'it is God working through me', they have said. God works wonders in the world — but his hands are the hands of men.

Ask if one is doing one's best to keep oneself in good health to play one's part in the world, that, for example, one is not abusing one's body by taking more than one's proper share of 'our daily bread'; then one may here think of that other saying, 'Man does not live by bread alone', and ask to receive more of the Divine spirit into our lives that we may better do the will of God. We must open ourselves to the Spirit; here I may think of the motto of my school, 'God grant grace.' Ask that we may realize our faults and how best to mend them, and how we may *forgive them that trespass against us*. Ask that we may recognize, with thought, what are the real *temptations* and *evils* that are making our lives less worthy than they could be. If all this is done with real feeling, with devotion, I fully believe that those who do it will come to feel a new power in themselves; they will feel in touch with a *power* and a *glory* beyond themselves which can make the world a different place – a new kingdom.

These headings under which to pray were given to the world long ago with the injunction 'not to use vain repetitions as the heathen do'. It is not a prayer to be hurried through in a matter of seconds, as if it were a magic incantation. It is a spiritual exercise, a prayer to be used when one is alone: 'when thou prayest, enter into thy closet, and when thou hast shut the door, pray to thy Father who is in secret'. It must be used slowly and with thought. The exact words of the headings are surely not important, for they are merely guides to the different lines of approach.

Let me remind you of what I said at the very end of chapter 8 (p. 153). If we feel better able to pray on our knees, it should not be thought to be a childish act, but a part of human behaviour rooted deep in our animal past – an act of submission. Religion is not rational, it is essentially emotional. As I said in *The Divine Flame*, if it is to be real and to work, it must be as deep and sincere as human love. Without such sincerity, or emotion, faith if you like, it makes *no* response at all; with the right approach, however, lives can be transformed, seemingly impossible tasks achieved, and the drabness of the world turned to joy. Religion is at the heart of civilization.

'Ask and ye shall receive – Seek and ye shall find.' This I believe is the essence not only of the Christian Gospel but of other sacred writings; it is likewise the essence of what I am calling an 'experimental faith'.

The systematic study of the experience of God carried out in the spirit of the seeking naturalists, the pioneers working towards a more natural theology, can I believe prepare the ground for a religious faith in harmony with the true spirit of science: an experimental faith which can go forward and develop just as a science enlarges its horizons. And just as science is science in any country of the world, so in the future there may be a faith to bind all people together in a universal recognition that what they in their different ways have called God, Nirvana, Kwoth, and other names, is in truth a demonstrable part of the very nature of man — man the religious animal.

Index